The Conclusion of Luke–Acts

The Conclusion of Luke–Acts

The Significance of Acts 28:16–31

Charles B. Puskas

PICKWICK *Publications* • Eugene, Oregon

THE CONCLUSION OF LUKE-ACTS
The Significance of Acts 28:16–31

Pickwick Publications
A Division of Wipf and Stock Publishers
199 W. 8th Ave., Suite 3
Eugene, OR 97401

www.wipfandstock.com

ISBN 13: 978-1-55635-235-5

Cataloging-in-Publication data:

Puskas, Charles B.

The conclusion of Luke-Acts : the significance of Acts 28:16–31 / Charles B. Puskas.

viii + 198 p., 23 cm. Includes bibliographical references.

Eugene, Ore.: Pickwick Publications

ISBN 13: 978-1-55635-235-5

1. Bible. N.T. Luke—Criticism, narrative. 2. Bible. N.T. Acts—Criticism, narrative. 3. Bible. N.T. Luke—Criticism, interpretation, etc. 4. Bible. N.T. Acts—Criticism, interpretation, etc. 5. Bible. N.T. Gospels—Criticism, interpretation, etc. 6. Bible. N.T. Luke and Acts—Theology. 7. Narration in the Bible. I. Title.

BS2589 .P87 2009

Manufactured in the U.S.A.

Contents

Preface

ACTS 28, THE CONCLUSION OF LUKE–ACTS, IS REGARDED AS one of the most important chapters of Luke's twin-work. In this chapter are found several significant Lukan themes, all of which make some contribution to the purpose and aim of the author in writing Luke–Acts: the Gentile mission, the triumph of God's Word, the relationship of Christianity with Judaism and Rome. Acts 28 contains many historical problems that have been debated for centuries: The "we" statements, the figure of Paul in Acts 28, and the abrupt-ending. The conclusion of Acts is compared with other important chapters of Luke–Acts: the introduction of the Gospel, the conclusion of Acts, the "defense of Paul" chapters, as well as other passages. In this significant chapter of Acts 28 there are still fundamental problems of exegesis that need to be addressed: What is the literary function of Acts 28? What is Luke trying to tell his readers in the text?

This study was originally a doctoral dissertation presented to the graduate school faculty of Saint Louis University, 1980, under the direction of Robert F. O'Toole, S.J. A revision of this work was undertaken at the encouragement of both graduate students and published scholars who read the dissertation for their research. Composition criticism, the primary methodology of the dissertation, has now been supplemented with newer approaches of narrative, cultural, rhetorical, and socio-scientific criticisms. Many recent studies on this subject have also been examined and cited.

Special thanks to K. C. Hanson, for recommending this work for the Pickwick series, and, in my revision, encouraging me to "do whatever you can to make it the best you can." Thanks also to professors Mark Reasoner of Bethel University (St. Paul) and Robert Van Voorst of Western Theological Seminary (Holland, MI) for reading selected chapters. Finally, many thanks to Robert F. O'Toole, S.J., President of the Gregorian University Foundation, New York, my Doktorvater, who read through the entire manuscript *again*, proofreading it and providing me with helpful suggestions, although I, the author, assume full responsibility for the final contents of this book.

I dedicate this work with appreciation and gratitude to my loving and supportive wife, Susan, and my helpful and encouraging children, Rita and Bart. Soli Deo Gratia!

1

A Brief Survey of the History of Research on Acts 28:16–31

SINCE THE NINETEENTH CENTURY, SCHOLARLY RESEARCH on Acts 28 has been too preoccupied with speculative historical questions and not given sufficient attention to significant literary considerations.[1] Even with a majority of scholarly opinion that Luke and Acts should be studied as a two-volume literary work, no consensus has been reached on the question: What is the literary function and the theological significance of Acts 28 in Luke–Acts?[2]

1. This book is a revision of a dissertation originally written in 1980 when few studies had focused on the literary function and theological significance of Lukan texts, particularly Acts 28. Although no deficiency remains, there appears to be little agreement on the literary and theological concerns of Acts 28:16–31, various issues and problems have surfaced or re-surfaced that will also be noted in our survey of research that follows. Attention will also be given to some new methodical perspectives and approaches as they relate to an understanding of our text.

2. When we are talking about the literary function of Acts 28 we are concerned with the function and purpose of the literary forms, patterns, and motifs used in Acts 28. The literary function is also related to the theology of Acts 28 (as it will be shown in chapter 4) since Luke uses these forms, patterns and motifs as vehicles to communicate his theology. According to Paul Schubert: "Luke is a littérateur of considerable skill and technique. His literary methods serve his theology and his theology serves them," "The Structure and Significance of Luke 24," in *Neutestamentliche Studien* (Berlin, 1954) 185; see also: Luke T. Johnson, *The Literary Function of Possessions in Luke–Acts*, (Scholars Press, 1977) 9, 12–15, 22n. 1; Robert F. O'Toole, *The Unity of Luke's Theology: An Analysis of Luke–Acts* (Michael Glazier, 1984) 11–14 ("presuppositions"). Relevant also for our study of Acts is Werner Kelber's insight on each Gospel as "an intricately designed religious universe, with plot and character development, retrospective and prospective devices, linear and concentric patterning, and a continuous line of their cross-references and narrative interlockings," W. Kelber, "Redaction Criticism: On the Nature and Exposition of the Gospels," *PRSt* 6 (1979) 14. See also W. S. Kurz, *Reading Luke–Acts: Dynamics of Biblical Narrative* (Westminster John Knox, 1993).

To substantiate the above assertions and to understand the past and current problems related to this text, an investigation of Acts 28:16–31 in the history of *Actaforschung* will be undertaken in this chapter. Such a study will seek to detect some unfinished or unsettled tasks that need to be addressed or brought into dialogue. Also it is important to locate and identify one's position in the history of *Actaforschung* in order to define our methodology and area of investigation.[3] We focus on dominant trends here and relegate most definitions, supporting data, and divergent opinions to the footnotes.

The following five domains of study that we survey in this chapter are those of consequence for an understanding of the literary function of Acts 28 in the development of *Actaforschung*: first, significant themes (four major ones, each with varying interpretations by different scholars), second, historical problems (e.g., the portrait of Paul), third, the abrupt-ending question, fourth, Lukan parallels (six are noted), and fifth, positions taken on various verses (Acts 28:16, 17–20, 21–22, 23–28, 30–31). We will conclude the chapter with questions still to be answered.

3. Since 1980 (when this study was first undertaken) many new methods of interpreting Luke–Acts have surfaced. We will consult select studies in the areas of narrative criticism, rhetorical analysis, cultural, and social-scientific interpretation. See, e.g., Robert C. Tannehill, *The Narrative Unity of Luke–Acts*, 2 vols. (Fortress, 1986, 1990); Jerome H. Neyrey, ed., *The Social World of Luke–Acts* (Hendrickson, 1991); George A. Kennedy, *New Testament Interpretation through Rhetorical Criticism* (University of North Carolina Press, 1984); Loveday Alexander, ed., *Images of Empire* (Sheffield, 1991); Mikeal C. Parsons and Richard I. Pervo, *Rethinking the Unity of Luke and Acts* (Fortress, 1993) plus the articles by Michael F. Bird, Andrew Gregory, and C. Kavin Rowe in *JSNT* 29:4 (2007) 425–72; J. Verheyden, ed., *The Unity of Luke–Acts* (Leuven, 1999); Bruce W. Winter and Andrew D. Clarke, eds., *The Book of Acts in Its First Century Setting*, vol. 1: *Ancient Literary Setting* (Eerdmans, 1993). On narrative, see the influential: Robert Alter, *The Art of Biblical Narrative* (Basic Books,1981), Frank Kermode, *The Genesis of Secrecy* (Harvard, 1979); Meir Sternberg, The *Poetics of Biblical Narrative* (Indiana, 1987). Attention to diverse methodologies will not minimize the theological significance of Luke–Acts for our study: see Joseph A. Fitzmyer, *Luke the Theologian* (Paulist, 1989); Joel B. Green, *The Theology of St. Luke* (Cambridge, 1995); François Bovon, *Luke the Theologian (*1950–2005*)*, 2nd rev. ed. (Baylor, 2006).

Significant Themes of Acts 28

The Goal of the Progression of the Gospel (or Christianity) from Jerusalem to Rome

A majority who subscribe to this theme regard Acts 28 as crucial for an understanding of the purpose or plan of the book, particularly as a climactic conclusion to a historical or geographical scheme as stated in, e.g., Acts 1:8. "Paul at Rome, the apex of the gospel, the end of Acts . . . It began at Jerusalem; it finishes at Rome" (J. A. Bengel, 1742).[4] Most

4. The advance of the Gospel from Jerusalem to Rome: J. Albrecht Bengel, *Gnomon Novi Testamenti*, 8th ed. (Stuttgart, 1915) 511, 536; Bernard Weiss, *A Commentary on the New Testament* (ET, New York, 1906) 2:637; Johannes Weiss, *Earliest Christianity, A History of the Period A.D. 30–150* (ET, 1937) 1:384; Henry J. Cadbury sees Acts 28 as not only fulfilling the "scope of Jesus' commission (Acts 1:8)," but makes a "true, triumphant and effective conclusion" to the narrative in *The Making of Luke–Acts* (New York, 1927; repr., London, 1968) 323–24; Hans Conzelmann, *Die Apostelgeschichte* (Tübingen, 1972) and *Acts of the Apostles* (ET; Fortress, 1987). Martin Dibelius, *Studies in the Acts of the Apostles*, (ET; SCM, 1956) 3; Bruce, *Book of Acts*, 8, 11, 511; Ernst Haenchen cites this as a major theme of Acts but does not develop it in his exegesis of Acts 28 "The Book of Acts as Source Material for the History of Early Christianity" in *Studies in Luke–Acts*, eds. Keck and Martyn (Abingdon, 1966) 278 (edited book henceforth cited as *SLA*); D. Mealand, "Acts 28.30–31 and Its Hellenistic Greek Vocabulary," *NTS* 36 (1990) 595; J. A.. Fitzmyer, *Acts of the Apostles* (AB 31; Doubleday, 1998) 206–7, 793, 797. J. C. O'Neill sees this theme as the key to the book's structure and refutes Franz Overbeck's critique of it in his *The Theology of Acts in its Historical Setting* 2nd rev. ed. (SPCK, 1970) 73–76; W. G. Kümmel, *Introduction to the N.T.* rev. ed., trans. from 17th Ger. ed. by H. C. Kee (Abingdon, 1975) 164; Robert H. Smith, *Acts* (Concordia, 1970) 13–14; Jacob Jervell, *The Theology of Acts of the Apostles* (Cambridge, 1996) 97; "Bengel (489) ends his commentary with words that probably would have had Luke's approval," C. K. Barrett, *The Acts of the Apostles, XV–XXVIII* (ICC; T. & T. Clark, 1998) 2:1253. See also footnote 39 of this chapter.

The progress of Christianity from Jerusalem to Rome: Mayerhoff (1835) according to A. C. McGiffert in F. J. Foakes -Jackson and K. Lake, eds., *Beginnings of Christianity*, 5 vols. (Macmillan, 1920–33), here vol. 2: Proleg. II: Criticism, "Historical Criticism of Acts in Germany" by A. C. McGiffert, 2:366 (5 vol. work henceforth cited as *BC*); G. H. C. Macgregor, "The Acts of the Apostles" in *Interpreter's Bible*, 9, ed., Buttrick (Abingdon-Cokesbury, 1954) 352 (henceforth cited as Acts *IB* 9); Peter Lampe writes "Paul in Rome being the crowning conclusion of world mission (28:22ff, 30–31)" *From Paul to Valentinus* (ET from 2nd Ger. ed.; Fortress, 2003) 7 n. 1; "All roads led not only *to* Rome but *from* Rome, from the Golden Milestone in the forum, to the 'ends of the earth' and thus 'to all nations,'" Charles H. H. Scobie, "A Canonical Approach to Interpreting Luke" in *Reading Luke*, eds., Bartholomew et al. (Zondervan, 2005) 344. Loveday C. A. Alexander assesses the data and argumentation of various positions, favoring Rome "one of the most distant points on the circumference of a Jerusalem-centered compass" (e.g., Acts 2:9–11) in her "Reading Luke–Acts from Back to Front,"

assume that this (or a similar) theme is basically derived from 28:30–31.[5] It is a significant theme in the context of Luke–Acts but does not account for all of the content of Acts 28:16–31, especially the defense statements of Paul (vv. 17–20) and his pronouncement of hardening or spiritual dullness on the Jews (vv. 25–28).

The Concluding Account of the Mission to the Gentiles

Acts 28:25–28 (and its parallels, 13:46–47 and 18:6) are generally regarded as key verses of the above theme, but the interpretations of it are varied. One position views the mission to the Gentiles prompted by Jewish unbelief as a central concern in the account of Paul at Rome,[6]

Acts in Its Ancient Literary Context (Edinburgh, 2005) 212–14. David P. Moessner argues that "Rome is the symbolic center of the great pagan power at 'the end of the earth'" in his " 'Completed End(s)ings' of Historiographical Narrative," 220–21, in *Die Apostelgeschichte und die hellenistische Geschichtsschreibung* (Leiden, 2004) 220–21. See also our survey of Acts 1 and 28 in this chapter, footnote 39, and our detailed comparison of Acts 1 and 28 in our chapter 3.

5. A representative position of this sequential theme is that of C. H. Turner who posited a six-fold structure based on six summary statements dealing with the progress of Christianity from Jerusalem to Rome (Acts 6:7; 9:31; 12:24; 16:5; 19:20; 28:31), in "Chronology of the N.T." in *A Dictionary of the Bible*, ed. J. Hastings (Scribners, 1898) 1:421 (henceforth cited as *HDB*). See discussion in Henry J. Cadbury, "The Summaries in Acts," *Beginnings of Christianity (BC)*, edited by K. Lake and H. J. Cadbury, 5:392–402 (Macmillan, 1933); According to C. K. Barrett: "The summaries confirm his central theme of the triumph , the irresistible progress of the word of God," Barrett, *The Acts of the Apostles I-XIV* (ICC; T. & T. Clark, 1994) 1:160.

6. Eduard Zeller, *The Contents and Origins of the Acts of the Apostle* (ET, London, 1876) 2:86, 105–6; Adolf Harnack, *The Mission and Expansion of Christianity*, trans. and ed. J. Moffatt (London, 1908) 49 n. 1; J. Weiss, *Christianity*, 2:661; H. J. Holtzmann, *Die Apostelgeschichte* (Tübingen) 156–57; Dibelius, *Studies* 149–50, 199 n. 16; E. Haenchen, *The Acts of the Apostles*, ET of *Die Apostelgeschichte* 14th ed. (Westminster, 1971) 100–102, 728–30; J. T. Sanders, *The Jews in Luke–Acts* (Fortress, 1987) 261–62, 298; G. Wasserberg, *Aus Israels Mitte—Heil für die Welt* (de Gruyter, 1998) 71–115. One corollary to the above stated position is: a mission to the Gentiles continues because the mission to the Jews has proven unsuccessful due to Jewish unbelief. See Robert C. Tannehill "Israel in Luke–Acts: A Tragic Story," *JBL* 104 (1985) 69–85 and his impressive *Narrative Unity of Luke–Acts: A Literary Appreciation, Vol 2: The Acts of the Apostles* (Fortress, 1990) 344–57.

Regarding the names and labels used for group identities, see the following. Frederick W. Danker states: "Since the term 'Judaism' suggests a monolithic entity that fails to take account of the many varieties of social expression associated with such adherents, the calque or loan word, 'Judean' is used in this and other entries where Ἰουδαῖος is treated. See *A Greek-English Lexicon of the New Testament and Other Early Christian*

whereas another position places the emphasis on the Gentile mission in fulfillment of prophecy (e.g., Isa 40:5; 49:6).[7] A view that includes the two previous positions, regards Jewish rejection as the immediate cause and fulfillment of prophecy as the ultimate cause.[8] A distinctive view from the late twentieth century was postulated: The Gentile mission is mediated through a repentant Israel, a "mighty minority."[9] This latter

---

Literature, rev. and ed. by F. W. Danker, 3rd. edition (*BDAG*; University of Chicago Press, 2000) 478; also: Bruce Malina and Richard Rohrbaugh, *Social-Science Commentary on the Synoptic Gospels*, 2nd ed. (Fortress, 2003) 376–77; Bruce J. Malina and John Pilch, *Social-Science Commentary on the Book of Acts* (Fortress, 2008) 6–7, 177–80. Concern about the exclusive rendering of "Gentiles" for ἔθνη in James LaGrand, "Proliferation of the 'Gentile' in the NRSV," *BR* 41 (1996) 77–87. Herman Hauser, *Strukturen*, 105–7 on Lukan use of "the Gentiles." Paul Borgman prefers the "Way" ὁδός Acts 9:2; 16:17; 18:25–26; 19:9, 23; 24:14, 22) when speaking of Christianity or the church, *The Way according to Luke: Hearing the Whole Story* (Eerdmans, 2006) 3–4, 13–14, 261–63, 311–12; see W. C. Robinson, *Der Weg des Herrn* (Bergstedt, 1964) 8, 30–34, 43. Perhaps a greater sensitivity to group names and labels might overcome some of the current impasse faced when discussing the many issues about Jews, Gentiles, and Christians in Luke–Acts and the rest of the New Testament.

7. John Chrysostom, *The Homilies on the Acts of the Apostles*, 2:29–55 (ET, Oxford, 1852) 722, 724; Ammonii Alexandrii, *Fragments in Acta Apostolorum*, (MPG 85; Paris, 1864) 1603–5; Theophylakti, *Expositio in Acta Apostolorum*, (MPG 125; Paris, n.d.) 844–48; Paul Schubert, "Final Cycle of Speeches in Acts" *JBL* 87 (1968) 9 and "Luke 24," 177, 185; Paul Minear, *To Heal and To Reveal* (1976) 102–11; D. P. Moessner, "Paul and the Pattern of the Prophet Like Moses in Acts," *SBLSP* 22 (Scholars, 1983) 203–12, "Paul in Acts: Preacher of Eschatological Repentance to Israel," *NTS* 32 (1988) 96–104, and "The Ironic Fulfillment of Israel's Glory;" 35–30 in *Luke–Acts and the Jewish People*, ed., J. B. Tyson (Augsburg, 1988) 35–50; Mark Strauss, *The Davidic Messiah in Luke–Acts: The Promise and Its Fulfillment in Lukan Christology* (Sheffield Academic, 1995) 148–80.

8. S. G. Wilson, *The Gentiles and the Gentile Mission in Luke–Acts* (Cambridge University Press, 1973) 219–38; J. Dupont, "La Conclusion des Actes et son rapport a l'ensemble de l'ouvrage de Luc," in *Les Actes des Apôtres*, 359–404 (Leuven, 1979) 402–4, *Salvation* 13–19, 141, "Le salut des gentiles et la signification theologique du livre des Actes," *NTS* 6 (1959–60) 132–55; J. T. Squires, *The Plan of God in Luke–Acts* (Cambridge University Press, 1993) 34–36, 137–39, 187–88.

9. The Gentiles have a share in the promises of Israel only after Israel (the people of God) has been purged of unbelievers (Acts 13:46; 18:4–6; 28:25–28). With the conclusion of Acts the mission to the Gentiles commences and the Jewish mission concludes since Israel (the people of God) has already been gathered: Jacob Jervell, *Luke and the People of God* (Augsburg, 1972) 55–56, 61–64. See also by Jervell, "God's Faithfulness to the Faithless People: Trends in Interpretation of Luke–Acts," *Word and World* 12 (1992) 29–36; "The Mighty Minority" 26–51 in *The Unknown Paul: Essays in Luke–Acts and Early Christianity* (Augsburg, 1984); *The Theology of Acts of the Apostles* (Cambridge, 1996) 34–43, 84–5; *Die Apostelgeschichte* (Vandenhoeck & Ruprecht, 1998) 623–31 (especially 628).

theory is not without its shortcomings and difficulties, as, for example, C. K. Barrett asks, "What Minorities?"[10]

Although the theme of the Gentile mission certainly accounts for Acts 28:25–28, it does not adequately explain the specific inclusion of the remaining verses, especially vv. 17–20.

A Final Portrait of Christianity in Terms of Jewish Prophecies, Heritage, and Ideals

Positions on this theme vary: Christianity is heir to the promises of Israel,[11] the Christian community carries out Israel's mission as Servant of the Lord and to the world,[12] Christianity is a universal religion with

10. Mary Moscato, "A Critique of Jervell's *Luke and the People of God*," in *SBL Seminar Papers* II (Scholars, 1975) 161–68; Wilson, *Gentiles* 219–38; C. K. Barrett, "What Minorities?" *Mighty Minorities? Minorities in Early Christianity—Positions and Strategies*, eds. D. Hellholm, et al. (Oslo, 1995) 1–10; Joseph B. Tyson, *Luke, Judaism, and the Scholars* (Columbia, S.C., 1999), chap. 6 on Jervell, especially assessments 102–9, 166.

11. K. Lake and H. J. Cadbury, English Translation and Commentary (Macmillan, 1933) *BC* 4:348; Dupont, *Salvation*, 13, 33, 143 and "La Conclusion des Actes," 403; Maddox, *Purpose* 187.

Jervell's position here is distinctive: "What then is the church? It is nothing but Israel—not a new Israel, but the one and only people of God, Israel is in a new phase of history, namely that of Jesus." Jervell, "God's Faithfulness to the Faithless People," *Word and World* 12 (1992) 31.

12. F. W. Danker, *Luke* (Fortress, 1976) 89–90. The following statement of Danker finds some application in the whole text of Acts 28:16–31, "the Book of Acts presents Jesus as an imperial figure who associates the apostles and St. Paul with himself in the achievement of Israel's mission." Yet it is clear from the text that Paul, not Jesus, is the main character. Jesus does not associate himself with Paul in 28:17–20, Paul is identified by Luke as one like Jesus (see our chapter 2. Passion Recital Speech, 43–46). The apostles and Paul carry on the mission of Christ, the faithful Israelite, who has fulfilled the prophecies concerning Israel. Therefore both Christ and the church function as the faithful of Israel (see in chapter 4: "The Missionary Activity of Paul in Acts 28"); Robert F. O'Toole, "How Does Luke Portray Jesus as Servant of YHWH?" *Biblica* 81 (2000) 340–41, 343–46. We regard with keen interest, also, the concept of Christianity as the eschatological remnant of Israel, comprised of believing Jews and Gentiles, in D. P. Moessner, "Paul in Acts," *NTS* 34 (1988) 102.

its roots in Judaism.[13] The theme of Christianity, however, as the true faith of Israel finds strong support here.[14]

Although the theme of Christianity as the faithful of Israel might be gleaned from Paul's statements in 28:17–20, another significant (and perhaps related) theme is found in the text.

A Concluding Picture of Christianity's Fair Treatment Under Rome

This theme is often connected with the previous concept: Christianity is the true representative of Judaism, therefore it is entitled to the fair treatment extended to the Jews as a *religio licita* in the Roman empire.[15] Although the association of a Jewish polemic with a Roman apology is questioned by some (e.g., Hans Conzelmann), the relations of Christianity with Rome, for most scholars, are a plausible concern of Acts 28, especially in vv. 16, 18f and 30–31. Paul Walaskay views the theme as an apology for the church, *not* an interested Roman official (e.g., Theophilus, Luke 1:1). Richard Cassidy believes that Luke is more skeptical of Roman authority.[16] This theme of Christianity and Rome, of course, is only one of several that are to be found in Acts 28:16–31.

13. Bruno Bauer, *Die Apostelgeschichte* (Hempel, 1850) 110–14, according to W. Ward Gasque, *History of the Criticism of Acts* (Eerdmans, 1975) 76. Not sharing Bauer's historical presuppositions, Robert L. Brawley also focuses on Christian self-identity in his *Luke–Acts and the Jews*, 39, 71–72, 143–44, 159.

14. This last position sees Christianity portrayed as the true Israel, because it has fulfilled the promises of Israel (theme one) and its founding leaders are portrayed as loyal Jews (e.g. Paul, Acts 16:3, 4; 21:21–26; 26:4–7); Alfred Loisy, *Les Acts des Apôtres* (Paris, 1920) 934, 939; J. Weiss, *Christianity* 1:384; Holtzmann, *Apostelgeschichte*, 155, 157; Haenchen, *Acts* 630; some would add that this theme reflects the separation of church and synagogue during the time of Luke: Dibelius, *Studies*, 134, 173; Schubert "Final Cycle," 9; O'Neill, *Theology*, 75, 133.

15. J. Weiss, *Über die Absicht und den literarischen Charakter der Apostelgeschichte* (Göttingen, 1897) 177–80 as quoted by McGiffert "Criticism," *BC* 2:388; Cadbury, *Making*, 308–16; B. S. Easton, *Early Christianity: The Purpose of Acts and Other Papers*, ed. F. C. Grant (SPCK, 1955) 10, 33–118; Lake and Cadbury, "Commentary," *BC* 4:349; Bruce, *Book of Acts*, 8–13; Haenchen, *Acts*, 102–4, 726, 731–32; O'Neill, *Theology*, 176–81; E. Trocmé, *Le Livre des Actes et l'Historie* (Paris, 1957) 51–53.

16. Jervell, *Luke* 156–58; C. H. Talbert, *Luke and the Gnostics* (Abingdon, 1966) 80–81, 104; Van Unnik 'Book of Acts', 39–40; D. Wenham, "The Purpose of Luke–Acts," 79–103, *Reading Luke: Interpretation, Reflection, Formation*, eds. C. G. Bartholomew, et al (Zondervan, 2005) 94–98; Conzelmann in a review of Haenchen's Commentary (3rd ed.) *TLZ* 85 (1960) 244–45 considers the concept of *religio licita* to be non-existent,

The discussion of these four key themes in Acts 28 confronts us with a pressing series of questions: If all of the above themes find some grounds for expression in Acts 28:16–31, what are their relationships within the text? Are they to be read in tension with each other? If so, why? Or, perhaps these various themes should be read together as a meaningful unit? If so, for what reason? Futhermore, is there some underlying concept found in the narrative, that unites the different themes into a complete unit in order to present a less ambiguous message for the readers/auditors? What critical methodology would help us to answer these questions?

Historical Problems of Acts 28

The Existence of a Christian Community in Rome Before Paul's Arrival (28:14, 15)

Why before entering Rome does Paul only briefly greet the Roman Christians whom he had longed to see and be with (Rom 1:11–13), and upon entering Rome, immediately meet with prominent Jews who were not acquainted with him? Many regard the Lukan portrayal of Paul as

---

constructed on one occasion by Tertullian (*Apol.* 21:1). See also Conzelmann, *Theology of St. Luke* (Ger., *Die Mitte der Zeit*) 138, 144, Conzelmann argues that Christians in Acts never sought acquittal in Roman courts by appealing to religious toleration extended to the Jews; both statements above are derived from O'Neill, *Theology*, 180 n. 1; Conzelmann sees both a Roman apology and a Jewish polemic in Luke–Acts but they are two separate concerns, in his *Theology*, 141–42; Robert F. O'Toole "Why Did Luke Write Acts (Luke–Acts)?" *BTB* 7 (1977) 76 n. 31; Maddox, *Purpose*, 91–3. Joseph A. Fitzmyer retains the use of *religio licita* in Luke's apologetic, see *Luke* (1981) 1:10, 178. Jervell sees a more *ad hoc* treatment of foreign religions by the Romans, *Theology of Acts*, 102.

Paul W. Walaskay believes that a defense of Rome is made for the benefit of the church *not* for sympathetic Roman officials, *"And so we came to Rome": The Political Perspective of St. Luke* (Cambridge University Press, 1983) 18–22, 59–62.

Richard Cassidy argues against a Roman apology in Luke–Acts. His argument is based on (a) the radical prophecies (e.g., Luke 1:52–53), teachings (Luke 22:25–26, 35–38), contacts (Luke 6:15; Acts 1:13) and actions (Acts 4:20–21; 5:29) of both Jesus and the apostles related to, e.g., God's reign, and (b) the examples of corruption (Acts 24:26), cruelty (Luke 13:1–3; 21:12–15; 23) or indifference (Acts 24:27) regarding Rome's treatment of Jesus, Peter, and Paul, in *Jesus Politics and Society* (1978) 20–49, 50–76, 126–35; *Society and Politics in the Acts* (1987); and *Paul in Chains* (2001) 211–34 (Paul as a chained prisoner in Acts).

Loveday Alexander outlines five different apologies, in "Acts as an Apologetic Text," *Acts in It Ancient Literary Context*, 183–87 [183–206].

conflicting with the concerns of the historical Paul.[17] Others argue for the historical accuracy of the account on the basis of Paul's missionary priorities.[18] Some postulate the reference as a literary device of the author.[19] The last assertion may unlock some possibilities for understanding the literary function of Acts 28.

The Portrait of Paul in Acts 28

Most of the historical problems raised, concern the portrait of Paul as a faithful Jew or Israelite, especially in 28:17–20. One major position states that this picture of Paul in Acts conflicts with that of the Pauline Epistles and reflects the author's theological bias.[20]

17. Zeller, *Contents*, 86–88; H. Windisch, "The Case Against Tradition," *BC* 2:334–35; Haenchen, *Acts*, 718–20; Loisy thinks that Paul did speak with Christians in Rome first but a later redactor changed it, *Actes*, 932, 935; see also Overbeck, *Introduction*, 16. Barrett examines the historical issues and theories but refrains from "speculating why we do not have what is not there," in his *Acts*, 2:1235–36.

18. Paul has already won the Christians, he must now go to the Jews: B. Weiss, *Commentary*, 2:632–34; J. Weiss, *Christianity*, 1:381; Richard B. Rackham, *Acts of the Apostles* (1901; reprint ed., Baker, 1978) 499; Frank Stagg, *Book of Acts* (Broadman, 1955) 263; the very fact that he met these Roman believers is an answer to his prayer in Rom. 1:11–13, Bruce, *Book of Acts*, 502–4. Hemer states that there were Jews living in Puteoli/Dicearchia at this time (Josephus) and possibly even Christians residing in nearby Pompeii and Herculaneum before their destruction (Rotas-Sator square as Jewish-Christian symbol), according to Hemer, *Book of Acts*, 155–56; Peter Lampe adds that Christian presence in Puteoli and Rome correlates with Jews living there since Augustan times and earliest Christianity spreading along routes that Judaism followed. The Puteoli-Rome stretch was the main trade route between the East and Rome, Lampe, *From Paul to Valentinus*, 7–10.

19. The ecclesiastical situation is created which directly speaks to the reader: "Your service begins here," our trans. from Otto Bauernfeind, *Die Apostelgeschichte* (1939) 279; Haenchen thinks that the author hides the Roman congregation from view so that Paul can introduce Christianity to Rome, "Acts as Source Material," *SLA* 278; *Acts* 720; H. Conzelmann, *Acts of the Apostles* (Fortress, 1987) 224. O'Neill sees it as a literary habit of Luke to sometimes make reference to Christians *before* the arrival of the apostle Peter or Paul to a city (Lydda and Joppa, Acts 9:32, 36; Ephesus 18:19, 26; and Puteoli 28:13) *Theology*, 73; Wilson supplements O'Neill's statements *Gentiles*, 237. Peter Lampe thinks that Christians in Italy without apostolic mediation is inconceivable for Luke, *From Paul to Valentinus*, 7 n. 1; Tannehill writes "it is important to the narrator that Paul is recognized and welcomed by Christians in the cities he visits after the conclusion of his missionary work in the east," *Narrative Unity*, 2:342. Luke minimizes the mention of these ordinary, anonymous Christians for the dramatic arrival of Paul to the imperial capital, Maddox, *Purpose*, 77.

20. It reflects the attempt to appease the legalistic (Petrine) faction in the church

The traditional position regards Acts 28 as essentially an accurate account of the Apostle who once said: "To the Jews I became a Jew, in order to win Jews" (1 Cor 9:20).[21] Yet from both groups there is also a prevailing view that the portrait of Paul transcends the historical and is symbolical, especially as a figure of Christianity and/or a type of Christ.[22] There is now the need to bring out the implications and

---

with a portrait of Paul as a loyal Jew like Peter, Ferdinand Christian Baur, *Paul the Apostle of Jesus Christ* (2nd ed.; Williams & Norgate, 1875) 216–18; E. Zeller and M. Schneckenburger find general agreement with Baur here, according to Overbeck, *Introduction*, 17–22; see also interpretations of Zeller and Schneckenburger by McGiffert "Criticism," *BC*, 2:370, 375–76 and Gasque, *Criticism*, 32, 44.

This portrait of Paul in Acts 28 contradicts that of Paul in his Epistles: Baur, *Paul* 216–18; Zeller, *Contents*, 85–87; Overbeck, *Introduction*, 22, 26–31; Loisy within the text itself saw a contradiction in Paul's portrait: His "anathema" on the Jews (Acts 28:26–27) conflicts with the picture of him as a loyal Jew (vv. 17–20); *Actes* 936–37, 939; also see Dibelius, *Studies*, 174; Windisch, "Against Tradition," *BC*, 2:334–36; a classic study: Philipp Vielhauer, "On the 'Paulinism' in Acts," in *SLA*, 37–45; Haenchen, *Acts*, 112–16, 727–29.

21. The earliest to be grouped in this position saw Acts in general as a historical or biographical account of the Apostles and therefore assumed the account of Paul to be true: Chrysostom, *Homilies* 55:720–24; Didymus v. Alexandrien, *De Trinitate Liber Primus LIX*, J. P. Migne, MPG 39 (Paris, n.d.) 364–66, 657–59; Ammonii Alexandrii, *Acta* 1603–5; Oekumenius, *Commentaria in Acta Apostolorum*, J. P. Migne, MPG 118 (Paris, 1893) 301–8; Theophylakti, *Acta*, 841–45; M. Aurelii. Cassiodori, *Complexiones in Actus Apostolorum*, ed. J. Garetius, J. P. Migne MPL 70 (Paris, 1865) 1404–6; John Calvin, *Commentary on Acts* (Eerdmans, 1949) 2:420–32; Bengel, *Gnomon*, 535–36.

Advocates on the accuracy of the Lukan account of Paul from the nineteenth century to the present: M. Schneckenburger according to Gasque, *Criticism*, 35–39; and A. J. Mattill, "The Purpose of Acts: Schneckenburger Reconsidered," in *Apostolic History and the Gospel*, eds. Gasque and Martin (Eerdmans, 1970) 119–21; B. Weiss, *Commentary*, 2:635; J. Weiss with some qualification, *Christianity*, 1:381; Theodor B. Zahn, *Introduction to the New Testament*, trans. from 3rd German ed. by J. M. Trout et al., vol. 3, (T. & T. Clark, 1909; reprint ed. Kregel, 1953) 57–58, 150; William M. Ramsay, *St. Paul the Traveller and the Roman Citizen* (Baker, 1962) 345–62; Harnack, *The Date of and the Synoptic Gospels*, (Williams & Norgate, 1911) 93–99; Rackham, *Acts*, 500–507; E. Jacquier, *Les Actes des Apôtres* (Paris, 1926) 753–61; Bruce, *Book of Acts*, 503–11; Johannes Munck, *The Acts of the Apostles*, (Doubleday, 1967) 258–60; Colin Hemer, *The Book of Acts in the Setting of Hellenistic History* (Eisenbrauns, 1990) 383–410; Brian Rapske, *Paul in Roman Custody: Book of Acts*, 3:173–91, 227–42; Ben Witherington III, *The Acts of Apostles: A Socio-Rhetorical Commentary* (Eerdmans, 1998) 788–816; Stanley E. Porter, *The Paul of Acts: Literary Criticism, Rhetoric and Theology* (Mohr/Siebeck, 1999) 187–206.

22. That the portrait of Paul transcends the historical is presupposed by many since 1840 who regard Acts 28 as primarily conveying a key Lukan theme (see our earlier discussion in section "Significant Themes").

significance of this symbolic picture of Paul for an understanding of the narrative purpose in Acts 28.

Paul as symbolic of Christianity: J. Weiss, *Christianity*, 1:384; Rackham, *Acts*, 506; Haenchen, *Acts*, 628, 692–94 and "Acts as Source Material," 259, 276; R. H. Smith sees the significance of the figure of Paul for Luke and his readers as a bridge between them and the time of Jesus and the Twelve, "The Theology of Acts," *CTM* 42 (1971) 533–35; Dibelius, *Studies*, 213; Robert F. O'Toole, *The Christological Climax of Paul's Defense (Acts 22:1—26:32)* (Biblical Institute Press, 1978) 14, 147; O'Toole sees Paul as a symbol of Christinaity and of Christ since in Luke–Acts a real bond unites Christ with Paul and other Christians (159–60); Danker develops further this Christ/ Christian relationship: "Luke's theology can be summed up in a phrase: 'Christology is ecclesiology, and ecclesiology is Christology,'" *Luke*, 2. "The 'ecclesiastical' events are made understandable as Jesus's events . . . the depiction of Paul is christological" in Volker Stolle, *Der Zeuge als Angeklagter* (Kohlhammer, 1975) 283–84. Hauser, *Strukturen*, 158–68; Mikeal C. Parsons, *Luke: Storyteller, Interpreter, Evangelist* (Hendrickson, 2007); Tannehill, *Narrative Unity*, 2:344–57; "In this story the Christian faith and community come into their own as benefactor to the Roman Empire," in Richard I. Pervo, *Luke's Story of Paul* (Fortress, 1990) 93–96; Daniel Marguerat, "The Enigma of the Silent Closing of Acts (28:16–31)," *Jesus and the Heritage of Israel*, ed. D. Moessner (TPI, 1999) 284–304; and idem, *The First Christian Historian: Writing the "Acts of the Apostles,"* (ET; Cambridge University Press, 2002). Paul, the cosmopolitan Christian gentleman, who arrives in Rome, the center of power and prestige, inviting others to join the ever-growing community of Christians, J. C. Lentz, *Luke's Portrait of Paul* (Cambridge University Press, 1993) 4.

Paul presented explicitly as a type of Christ: Zeller, B. Bauer, H. H. Evans, and Windisch (concerning Jesus-Paul parallels in general) according to Mattill, "The Jesus-Paul Parallels and the Purpose of Luke–Acts: H. H. Evans Reconsidered" *NovT* 17 (1975) 18–20; O'Toole, *Christological Climax*, 3, 14, 22–25, 159–60 (dealing specifically with Acts 26); Acts 28 and Jesus-Paul parallels in general: Mattill "Jesus-Paul" 23–26, 28–31, 34, 42; the passion and resurrection of Jesus (Luke 20–24) parallel the "passion" and vindication of Paul (Acts 21–28): Rackham, *Acts* xlvii, 401, 404; M. D. Goulder, *Type and History in Acts* (SPCK, 1964) 34–51, 61, 67; Mattill "Jesus-Paul" 30–37 and "Schneckenburger Reconsidered," 114–22; Charles H. Talbert, *Literary Patterns, Theological Themes and the Genre of Luke–Acts*, 20 (Scholars, 1974) 16–18, 22, 24; Robert Morgenthaler, *Die Lukanische Geschichtsschreibung als Zeugnis* (Zwingli-Verlag, 1949) 1:180–94 (includes Jesus-Paul parallels throughout Luke–Acts); Walter Radl, *Paulus und Jesus im Lukanishchen Doppelwerk* (Lang, 1975) 42–43, (Luke 23, 24 and Acts 28) 248–65; Norman R. Peterson, *Literary Criticism for NT Critics* (Fortress, 1978) 31–92; For overview, questions, and suggestions, see Susan Marie Praeder, "Jesus-Paul, Peter-Paul, and Jesus-Peter Parallelisms," *SBL* 1984 *Seminar Papers* (Scholars) 23–39; Maddox, *Purpose*, 79–80, 89; see also O'Toole, "Parallels between Jesus and His Disciples in Luke–Acts," *BZ* 27 (1983) 195–212. D. P. Moessner, "Christ Must Suffer: New Light on the Jesus-Peter, Stephen, Paul Parallels," *NovT* 28 (1986) 220–56; although his focus is not on the Jesus-Paul parallels, Andrew C. Clark surveys the field and provides some internal and external controls relevant to our topic here, *Parallel Lives: The Relation of the Paul to the Apostles in the Lucan Perspective* (Paternoster, 2001) 55–114.

This discussion of Paul leads us to further questions: If the Lukan author is seeking to convey an unambiguous message in Acts 28 involving a variety of topics, and if this narrative is presenting us with a symbolic picture of Paul to convey its *message*, then could not a symbolic interpretation of Paul provide some *medium* for understanding the relationship of the various themes in Acts 28:16–31?

The Reply of the Jews in Rome (28:21, 22)

A great deal of time and energy has been expended on the historical problems of these verses. The ignorance of the Roman Jews concerning Paul's situation (v. 21) and their indirect acquaintance with Christianity (v. 22) have been criticized as contradictory and unhistorical[23] or defended as basically accurate.[24] It has been pointed out that these

23. The arguments against Luke's accuracy are: (1) The Jews of Rome received no letters from Judea regarding Paul's case and no reports on Paul from fellow Jews in Rome (v. 21). The reputation of Paul as an antagonist to Judaism is known everywhere by the Jews (Acts 21:21, 28; 24:5; Rom. 3:1, 8, 9) and Paul's Jewish antagonists in Judea missed a great opportunity to try and influence Paul's trial in Rome. (2) The vague and indirect acquaintance of the Roman Jews with Christianity as only a sect everywhere spoken against (v. 22). This uninformed attitude of the Roman Jews conflicts with the widespread knowledge about the Roman Church (Rom. 1:18; 16:19; Tacitus, *Annals* 15:44; Jewish rioting over alleged preaching of Christ "Chrestus" in Rome, Suetonius, *Lives of Caesars*: Claudius 25; Acts 18:2). Advocates of the above arguments: Zeller, *Contents*, 86–88; Loisy, *Actes*, 934–35; Windisch, "Against Tradition," *BC*, 2:335–36; Holtzmann, *Apostelgeschichte* 156; H. H. Wendt, *Die Apostelgeschichte* (9th ed.; Vandenhoeck & Ruprecht, 1913) 367; Haenchen, *Acts*, 726–28; C. K. Barrett approaches Acts 28 with similar questions *Acts*, 2:1235–37.

24. Various attempts at responding to the problems, in defense of Luke's accuracy are: (1) Regarding Paul's situation (v. 21), (a) the Jews actually knew of Paul's arrest and hearings in Judea but were trying to assume an "impartial attitude," Schneckenburger as cited by Zeller, *Contents*, 87 (Zeller felt that this attitude was as an unjustifiable falsehood on the part of the Jews) and Rackham, *Acts* 301; the Jews were being cautious and diplomatic, Bruce, *Book of Acts*, 505–6 and W. Neil, *Acts of the Apostles* (Attic, 1973) 257–53. (b) The Romans had severe laws against prosecutors who failed to make good their accusations (Sherwin-White), hence the anxiety of the Roman Jews to dissociate themselves from the case, Lake and Cadbury, *Commentary*, *BC*, 4:346; Stagg, *Acts*, 264; Neil, *Acts*, 257–58; Haenchen criticizes the argument by stating that such laws could not apply to these Roman Jews since they were not to be Paul's Judean persecutors, *Acts* 728; C. Hemer argues that such laws were "to compel prosecutors to prosecute not to provide release of the unaccused persons," *Book of Acts*, 391–92. (c) Paul must have arrived before his accusers or any letter from Jerusalem had arrived, H. A. W. Meyer as cited in Zeller, *Contents* 90; M. F. Sadler, *Acts of the Apostles* (Bell, 1906) 497; Munck, *Acts* 258; Bruce, *Acts of the Apostles*, Greek Text (3rd rev., enl. ed.; Eerdmans, 1990) 539

problematic verses may serve a literary function. It produces the missionary situation: ignorance of the Christian message, combined with the desire to learn about it.[25]

The Abrupt-Ending Question of Acts 28

The Abrupt-Ending Question Raised

Since the pre-critical period of research, the question was raised: why did the Lukan author not say more about Paul's situation?[26] In the nineteenth and early twentieth centuries, the question was pursued: Why is the mention of Paul's death or the outcome of his trial not given?[27] In the years following this period, exegetes have not ceased to be fascinated with this perplexing question.[28]

(henceforth cited as *Acts GT*). (2) Lack of acquaintance with Christianity (v. 22). (a) This attitude of the Jews reflects the strict separation of church and synagogue since the return of the Jews from Rome after their expulsion (Acts 18:2), Olshausen and Kling as cited in Zeller, *Contents*, 89; B. Weiss, *Commentary*, 2:635; Rackham, *Acts*, 501; Stagg, *Acts*, 264; Haenchen criticizes this view by pointing out that Paul's *Epistles to the Romans* indicates no such situation, *Acts* 728. (b) The Roman church was primarily a Gentile church and thus separated from Judaism, B. Weiss, *Commentary*, 2:635; Munck, *Acts*, 258. This point is a highly debatable assertion in view of the Jewish element in the church Paul often addressed (Rom 2:17–24; 3:1–9). For other harmonistic explanations and their critical assessment, see: Haenchen, *Acts*, 728.

25. Haenchen, *Acts*, 730.

26. Chrysostom in the fifth century asks: "But of his affairs after the two years, what say we? (the writer) leaves the hearer athirst for more . . ." *Homilies* 55:726 (parenthesis from the translator).

27. K. A. Credner (1836) noted the relative silence in Acts concerning the mention of Paul's death according to McGiffert "Criticism," *BC*, 2:366–67; Ramsay (1897) saw the end of Acts as incomplete and unfinished *St. Paul* 351–52; Zahn states the problem clearly: (1) nothing is told of Paul's preaching in Rome or of the outcome of his trial although the reader's attention has been fixed on these goals earlier in the narrative (Acts 19:21; 23:11; 25:10–11; 27:24); (2) Luke's reference to an exact period of time for Paul's imprisonment (28:30) indicates that a change has taken place at the time of writing; (3) in his prologue (Luke 1:1–4) the author has intended to write a history of Christianity up to his own day ("concerning the things accomplished among us") a plan not carried out if the story ends at Acts 28, Zahn, *Introduction*, 57–58; see also, B. Weiss, *Commentary*, 2:637; J. Weiss, *Christianity*, 1:382–83; Harnack, *Date*, 93–98; Rackham, *Acts*, li; see Darrell L. Bock's outline of these historical responses including a literary one, in his *Acts*, BECNT (Baker, 2007) 757–58.

28. Cadbury, *Making*, 314, 321–22; Lake and Cadbury, "Commentary," *BC*, 4:349–50; Bruce, *Acts*, GT 481; Macgregor, "Acts," *IB* 9:349–52; O'Neill, *Theology*, 59–60; Wilson, *Gentiles* 233–38; J. D. Quinn, "The Last Volume of Luke: The Relation of Luke–

Some Attempts at Answering the Abrupt-Ending Question

Favoring the position for an early date of composition, some have stated that the author wrote all that he knew, since he was writing before Paul's death, around A.D. 62.[29] A few have argued that Luke intended to write a third volume giving the results of Paul's trial and the remaining accounts of his life.[30] Others, generally favoring a late date of composition for Acts, regard the outcome of these fateful events as too well-known to the readers/auditors and were thus excluded, because the author had other priorities in what he wanted to tell.[31]

A majority of scholars regard the problem of an abrupt-ending as a rather superficial one since Acts 28 can be seen as a deliberate and/or complete conclusion from a variety of different literary, rhetorical, and theological standpoints (e.g., climactic, enigmatic, open-ended).[32]

Acts to the Pastorals" in *Perspectives on Luke–Acts*, ed. C. H. Talbert (Danville, Va., 1978) 62 (edited book henceforth cited as *PLA*). See discussion in Daniel Marguerat, "The Enigma of the Silent Closing of Acts (28:16–31)" *Jesus and the Heritage of Israel* (1999) 284–88 (Marguerat looks at "deferred expectation" in Luke–Acts); and Wm. F. Brosend II, "The Means of An Absent Ends," in *History, Literature and Society in the Book of Acts* (Cambridge, 1996) 348–58. Charles H. Talbert surveys various responses to a "suspended ending," in *Reading Acts* (Smyth & Helwys, 2005) 230–32; the "Gap of the End of Acts" in Kurz, *Reading Luke–Acts*, 34–36.

29. Harnack, *Date*, 93–98; Rackham, *Acts*, li; Munck, *Acts*, 260; Hemer, *Book of Acts*, 383–410; some would pursue this position further and argue that Acts was written specifically to influence the outcome of Paul's trial, see R. E. Cottle, *The Occasion and Purpose of the Final Drafting of Acts* (1967) 98–103, survey and critique by Wilson, *Gentiles* 233, (the above view is also held by Aberle, Plooij, and Duncan according to Gasque, *Criticism*, 262–63). See critique of early date position, Haenchen *Acts* 731–32; Wilson, *Gentiles*, 233; Richard I. Pervo, *Dating Acts: Between the Evangelists and the Apologists* (Polebridge, 2006) 334–40, 455–57.

30. Positions held by K. A. Credner, F. Spitta, and M. Goguel according to Haenchen, *Acts* 29, 38; for a more detailed argumentation of this theory see: Zahn, *Introduction* 57–61 and "Das dritte Buch des Lukas," *NKZ* 28 (1917) 373–95; Ramsay, St. Paul, 351–52; Quinn, "Third Volume," *PLA* 70, (see critiques of this theory by Haenchen, *Acts*, 137 n. 1, 724 n. 3; Wilson, *Gentiles*, 234; Trocmé, *Actes*, 34–36; Kümmel, *Introduction*, 159).

31. For example, Luke was more concerned about writing on the progress of the gospel/word rather than of the life (and fate) of Paul, see: Haenchen, *Acts* 731–32, and O'Neill, *Theology* 60–62; Lake and Cadbury, "Commentary," *BC*, 4:350; Wilson, *Gentiles*, 236; "It is a reasonable inference from 27:24 . . . that Luke knew, by the time he wrote, that Paul did in fact appear before Caesar" states Bruce also citing Bartlet on Luke's readers' knowing about Paul's condemnation and execution under Nero, *Acts*, GT, 542.

32. B. Weiss, *Commentary*, 2:637; J. Weiss saw the key problem of the abrupt ending theories to be found in their neglect of the literary character of Acts *Christianity*,

Lukan Parallels to Acts 28

Many parallels and similarities have been observed between Acts 28 and other Lukan passages, although the nature and extent of these relationships have not been fully developed, and their significance for an understanding of Acts 28 has not been fully articulated.

Acts 13:46; 18:6; 28:25–28

The account of Paul's mission at Rome recalls similar Pauline missionary practices followed elsewhere, particularly: the turning to the Gentiles after Jewish rejection, in Asia Minor (13:46–47), Greece (18:6) and Rome (28:25–28).[33] Yet if Acts 28 reflects a typical missionary

1:383; Chrysostom indicates that Luke included all that was sufficient for his readers within the book itself: "Why didst thou wish to learn what happened after these two years? Those too are such as these: bonds, tortures . . . imprisonments . . . false accusations, deaths, day by day," *Homilies* 55:727; Bengel, *Gnomon*, 536; Rackham, *Acts*, 502, 506–7; Bruce, *Book of Acts*, 509–11; Cadbury, *Making*, 323–25; Lake and Cadbury, "Commentary," *BC*, 4:350; see especially Schubert, "Luke 24," 185 and "Final Cycle," 9; Haenchen, *Acts*, 731–32; O'Neill, *Theology* 60–62; Smith, "Theology" 528–29; Wilson, *Gentiles* 236–38; F. Danker, *Jesus and the New Age* (Clayton, 1974) xix; Peterson, *Literary Criticism* 85, 87; Gaventa, *Acts* 363; M. A. Powell, *What Are They Saying About Acts?* (Paulist, 1991) 103–6; L. T. Johnson, *Acts of the Apostles* (Liturgical, 1992) 475; Matthew L. Skinner, *Locating Paul: Places of Custody as Narrative Settings in Acts* 21–28 (SBL, 2003) 168–70; F. Scott Spencer, *Journeying Through Acts* (Hendrickson, 2004) 247–51; Tannehill, *Narrative Unity*, 2:353–57. See especially Daniel Marguerat, "The Enigma of the Silent Closing of Acts," 288–304; Citing the works of Frank Kermode and Morna Hooker in support of Marguerat's interpretation with an analogy drawn from a popular television drama, see the whimsical SBL forum article by Micah Kiel of St. Ambrose University, "Did Paul Get Whacked? The Endings of the Sopranos and the Acts of the Apostles," (July 2007) http://sbl-site.org/Article.aspx?ArticleId=695; G. W. Trompf, "On Why Luke Declined to Recount the Death of Paul: Acts 27–28 and Beyond," *Luke-Acts: New Perspectives from the SBL Seminar* (Crossroads, 1984) 225–39; Wm. F. Brosend, II, "The Means of An Absent Ends," 348–62; Loveday Alexander, "Reading Luke-Acts from Back to Front," in her *Acts in Its Ancient Literary Context*, 207–29. "The 'plan for his narrative has reached its goal' . . . Acts 28 formally and 'finally' secures that grasp through a concluding event (τελευτή) 'from which . . . nothing of necessity must follow,'" in D. P. Moessner, "Diodorus Siculus and the End of Acts," *Die Apostelgeschichte*, 218–21.

It seems to us that the continued appearance of the abrupt ending question in contemporary commentaries is more a result of the self-imposed obligation of modern commentators to discuss the historical preoccupations of earlier commentators, than it is a result of the inherent importance of the question itself.

33. Calvin alludes to Paul's ministry among the Jews in Rome as characteristic of his work in Asia, Greece and Jerusalem, Acts 24:20–21; Asia, Greece, Italy: Bengel, *Gnomon* 535–36; Zeller, *Contents*, 105–6; Overbeck, *Introduction*, 76; B. Weiss, *Commentary*,

procedure, why is it restricted to only a few verses from Paul's work in the three locations noted above? Should not attention be given to other missionary settings in Ephesus (Acts 19) and elsewhere?

Luke 24 and Acts 28

It has been pointed out by many that Acts 28 and Luke 24 are parallel works in structure, form, and content,[34] but few scholars have adequately demonstrated this assertion as it relates to an understanding of Acts 28.

Acts 21–26 and 28

Regarding the parallels between Paul's defense (chaps. 21–26) and Acts 28, scholars have shown some intra-textual relations here, with some noteworthy observations, but no detailed comparison has been made.[35]

2:636; Holtzmann, *Apostelgeschichte*, 14–15, 156; Rackham, *Acts*, 508; Wendt, *Apostelgeschichte*, 368; Paul Wendland (1912) adds to this Ephesus (Acts 19:9) as cited in Haenchen, *Acts*, 33; Schubert follows Wendland in "Final Cycle" 9; Dibelius, *Studies*, 149–50; Haenchen, *Acts*, 729; Conzelmann, *Die Apostelgeschichte*, 2nd ed.. (Mohr/Siebeck, 1972) 159–60; and *Theology*, 190 n. 3; Joachim Gnilka, *Die Verstockung Israels Isaias* 6, 9–10 *in der Theologie der Synoptiker* (Kösel, 1961) 148; and Dupont on 13:46 and 28:25–28, *Salvation*, 18, 20; Peterson analyzes Acts 13 and 18 in terms of a "confrontation in the sanctuary scheme" which forces him to omit Acts 28 which does not occur in a sanctuary *Literary Criticism*, 86–91; Maddox, *Purpose*, 43–44; R. C. Tannehill, *The Shape of Luke's Story* (Cascade, 2005) 136–40, 145–65 (rejection by Jews and turning to Gentiles); David W. Pao, *Acts and the New Exodus* (Baker, 2000) chap. 3. Tannehill on Acts 19 states that Paul makes no announcement of a turning to the Gentiles although a shift from the synagogue to the school of Tyrannus takes place, 154. Although no explicit connection has yet been made here, see biblical type scenes in Robert Alter, *The Art of Biblical Narrative* (Basic Books, 1981) chap. 3; and in Luke–Acts, see Tannehill, *Narrative Unity*, 1:18–23, 93, 105, 170–71; 2:202–3; Spencer, *Journeying*, 169–71.

34. Schubert provides guidelines for such a comparison by noting a similar proof-from-prophecy theme, in "Luke 24," 185 and "Final Cycle," 9; Rackham sees the expounding of the Gospel to all nations and the concluding remarks as parallel features *Acts* 502 also Dupont, *Salvation*, 14–15; Talbert, *Literary Patterns*, 18, 22; Goulder, *Type*, 61; Mattill, "Jesus–Paul," 30–37; Peterson, following Goulder and others, sees Luke 24 and Acts 28 as the climax of the "passion" narratives: The reaffirmation of God's agents, *Literary Criticism* 83–86. The following noteworthy studies will be examined closer in the body of this work: Mikeal C. Parsons, *The Departure of Jesus in Luke–Acts: The Ascension Narratives in Context* (Sheffield, 1988) and Arie W. Zwiep, *The Ascension of the Messiah in Lukan Christology* (Brill, 1997).

35. Holtzmann, *Apostelgeschichte*, 155; Loisy, *Actes*, 932–34; Bruce, *Acts*, GT, 467–69; Haenchen, *Acts*, 722; Windisch, "Against Tradition," *BC*, 2:335; Schubert, describes

Luke 4 and Acts 28

Comparisons between the inaugural sermon of Jesus at Nazareth (Luke 4) and the concluding address(es) of Paul at Rome have been alluded to in the past, but only in recent decades has an attempt been made to view them as two parallel works.[36] Although any attempt to force two different Lukan passages into a detailed chiastic framework is questionable because of the author's variation of style and structure, such a study has at least established a noteworthy literary relationship between Acts 28 and Luke 4.

Luke 1–3 and Acts 28

The relationship observed between the introduction of Luke's gospel and the conclusion of Acts applies more specifically to the opening verses of the Gospel with Acts 28[37] and to the opening chapters of the

---

28:17–20 as the last of Paul's (post-) trial speeches summarizing Acts 22–26 in a new situation yet adding nothing of significance, "Final Cycle," 9–10; O'Toole distinguishes Paul's defense (22–26) from 28:17–20 because the latter is not in a trial setting and has no resemblance to a hearing *Christological Climax*, 15. Tannehill designates Acts 28:17–20 as a summary of the preceding trial narrative and imprisonment speeches of Acts 22–26, *Narrative Unity*, 2:344. Fitzmyer labels 28:17–20 a defense speech and vv. 25c-28, an indictment speech, *Acts*, 790. Is there a fictionalized trial setting here with Paul functioning as judge in a role reversal? See on this question Marguerat, "Enigma," 295–96; Trompf, "Death of Paul," 226–27; M. Skinner, *Locating Paul*, 166–67.

36. D. R. Miesner appears to be the first to point out such detailed similarities but his attempt to arrange both passages into a chiastic framework is less than successful, "Circumferential Speeches of Luke–Acts," *SBL Seminar Papers* (Scholars, 1978) 2:223–237; others have pointed out the theological singifiance of Luke 4 in Luke–Acts: Cadbury, *Making*, 61, 188–89; Smith, *Acts*, 78; Talbert, *Literary Patterns*, 19, 97–98; Goulder, *Type* 55, 74; David L. Tiede, *Prophecy and History in Luke-Acts* (Fortress, 1980) 19–63; for an excellent survey of discussion on Luke 4 and Acts 28, see Frans Neirynck, "Luke 4:16–30 and the Unity of Luke–Acts," *Unity of Luke-Acts*, ed., J. Verheyden (Leuven, 1999) 387–95. The relationship of Luke 4 to Acts 28 may provide further evidence for viewing Paul as a type of Christ.

37. Lake makes a case for comparing the preface (Luke 1:1–4) with the conclusion of Acts: "Prefaces then, as now, were probably written after the work was completed and hence would be likely to reflect the leading ideas of the last . . . part of the work. Conversely, a book would incline . . . to emphasize at its close the objects expressed in the preface," "Commentary," *BC*, 4:350; Schuyler Brown, "The Role of the Prologues in Determining the Purpose of Luke–Acts," *PLA* 110. See especially Loveday Alexander, *The Preface to Luke's Gospel* (Cambridge University Press, 1993) 1–22, 102–46, 187–216 and "Reading Luke-Acts from Back to Front," 218–23 in her *Acts in Its Ancient Literary Context* (T. & T. Clark, 2005) and also 21–42, 207–29. Alexander, however,

gospel with Acts 28.[38] No detailed comparison, to our satisfaction, has been done in the above areas.

Acts 1 and 28

A central focus has been the relationship of the words of Jesus' commission "to the ends of the earth" (1:8) and Paul's preaching at Rome (28:16-31).[39] Comparisons of the opening and concluding chapters of Acts have also been made. One study shows the significance of the ascended Christ in the account of Paul at Rome. It is of value for Acts 28, but the theme proposed seems to be implicit in the text and does not express a major theme of Acts 28:16–31, in our opinion. Other studies will be noted.[40]

---

regards it as dangerous to limit the author's point of view to that of pleasing one particular reader (i.e. "Theophilus") whether this reader is a real person, patron, or publisher, *Preface*, 200.

38. Dupont concludes that in Acts 28:28, Luke is alluding to the Isa 40:5 quote also in Luke 3:6, *Salvation*, 14–16, 57; also noted in Holtzmann, *Apostelgeschichte*, 156 and W. C. Robinson, *Der Weg des Herrn*, 39; P. Minear sees a link between the use of Isaiah in the prologue (Luke 1–2) and in the epilogue (Acts 28) "Luke's Use of the Birth Stories," *SLA* 116–18; David W. Pao sees a dramatic reversal taking between both Luke 3:6 (Isa 40:5, sight/salvation) and Acts 28:26–27 (Isa 6:9f blindness/judgment) in *Acts and the Isaianic New Exodus* (Baker, 2000) 108. See also: Kenneth Duncan Litwak, *Echoes of Scripture in Luke–Acts* (T. & T. Clark, 2005) 180–200. For Litwak's discussion on the "intertextuality" of Luke–Acts and Israel's Scriptures (replete in Luke 1–2), see 25–30.

39. Van Unnik does not see Acts 1:8 ἕως ἐσχάτου τῆς γῆς as referring to Rome but to the extreme limit of the world ("the Atlantic"), W. C. Van Unnik "The 'Book of Acts' the Confirmation of the Gospels," *NovT* 4 (1960) 39 and "Der Ansdruck *heōs eschatou tēs gēs* (Apg 1, 8)," *Studia biblica et semitica* (1966) 347–49; also E. Earle Ellis, "'The End of the Earth' (Acts 1:8)," *BBR* 1 (1991) 123–32 (Spain); T. C. G. Thornton, "To the End of the Earth: Acts 1:8," *ExpT* 89 (1977–78) 374–75 (Ethiopia, Acts 8:27). James M. Scott, "Luke's Geographical Horizon," *Graeco-Roman Setting:Book of Acts*, 2:541 (Spain). Jacques Dupont regards this theme as a religious rather than a geographical scheme, *Salvation of the Gentiles* (ET; Paulist, 1979) 12–13, 17–19; Robert L. Brawley also understands it to be ethnic (to the Gentiles) rather than geographical (Acts 1:8 with 13:46–48) in his *Luke–Acts and the Jews* (Scholars, 1987) 32–33. See footnote 4 of this chapter for a survey of Acts 1:8 "to the end of the earth" as referring or alluding to Paul's preaching in Rome (Acts 28) and our analysis of Acts 1 and 28 in chapter 3 of this study, 82–86.

40. R. H. Smith shows that Paul's Roman preaching balances or completes the account of Jesus' ascension. Combining this concept with that of Paul as a bridge between Luke's readers and the Twelve, he argues for Acts 28 as conveying the relevance of the enthroned Jesus for every passing generation of the church, "Theology," 531–32,

Positions Taken on Various Verses of Acts 28

As noted elsewhere, preoccupation with historical considerations become central here. Concern for literary function only emerges distinctly in the last two decades but stands in need of additional articulation and development.

Acts 28:16

The pericope of Paul in Rome begins for many commentators at 28:17.[41] Others regard its beginning at 28:16.[42]

However illuminating for historical speculation the longer reading of the Western Text may appear, commentators before the nineteenth century generally followed the longer reading,[43] while subsequent scholars follow the shorter Alexandrian reading with its superior textual support.[44]

---

535. See our analysis of Acts 1 and 28 in chapter 3, 82–86. See also: Mikeal Parsons, *Departure of Jesus* especially his discussion of Smith's work in 159, 206, 255, 257; and Arie Zwiep, *Ascension of the Messiah*, 30–31, 99, 172–74. David Moessner provides a good synopsis of the relationship of Acts 1 to 28 in his "Diodorus Siculus and the End of Acts," in *Die Apostelsgeschichte* (Brill, 2004) 221.

41. For example: Chrysostom, *Homilies*, 55:720–26; Oekumenius, *Acts*, 301–8; Theophylakti, *Acta*, 841; Overbeck, *Introduction*, 48; Lake and Cadbury, "Commentary," *BC*, 4:345; Loisy, *Actes* 932–34; Macgregor, Acts, *IB* 9:346–47; Haenchen, *Acts*, 721–23; L. T. Johnson, *Acts*, 467; Fitzmyer, *Acts*, 788.

42. Zeller, *Contents* 85; Rackham, *Acts*, 499–501; Jacquier, *Actes*, 753–55; Bauernfeind, *Apostelgeschichte*, 278; H. W. Beyer, *Die Apostelgeschichte* (Vandenhoeck & Ruprecht, 1949) 158–59; Hauser, *Strukturen* 13–18; Gaventa, *Acts* 363; Scott Spencer, *Journeying through Acts*, 247; Talbert, *Reading Acts*, 225; Ju Hur, *A Dynamic Reading of the Holy Spirit in Luke–Acts* (Sheffield, 2001) 267–70.

43. ὁ ἑκατόνταρχος παρέδωκε τοὺς δεσμίους τῷ στρατοπεδάρχῳ τῷ δὲ Παύλῳ ἐπετράπη ("the centurion delivered the prisoners to the captain of the guard; but Paul was allowed . . . ") is followed by Chrysostom, *Homilies* 55:720; Theophylakti, *Acta* 841; Calvin, Acts 2:420; Bengel, *Gnomon*, 535; see Ramsay's historical speculations in *St. Paul*, 347–49, 362.

44. For example: Wendt, *Apostelgeschichte*, 364; Jacquier, *Actes*, 754; J. H. Ropes, *The Text of Acts* (Macmillan, 1926) *BC* 3:253; Haenchen, *Acts*, 718; Bruce M. Metzger, *A Textual Commentary on the Greek New Testament* 2nd ed. (United Bible Societies, 1994) 443. Sympathy for the western text has been growing recently in France, but the discovery of the Bodmer Papyrus of Luke, the oldest witness for the Gospel, has secured the great age and value of the Egyptian text, in François Bovon, "Studies in Luke–Acts: Retrospect and Prospect," *HTR* 85:2 (1992) 182.

Acts 28:16 contains the last "we" statements of Acts.[45] Since the late second century it was believed that these statements indicated the presence of the author of Acts as an eyewitness in the accounts narrated.[46] Others saw in these statements part of an eyewitness source used by the author of Acts although dominated by his style.[47] An increasing number of scholars have come to appreciate the value of viewing the use of the "we" as a Lukan literary device.[48] The literary function of the "we" statement in 28:16–31 stands in need of further investigation.

45. The "we" sections are found in 16:10–17; 20:5–15; 21:1–18; 27:1—28:16, see Dupont's helpful survey on the subject in *The Sources of Acts* (ET; Herder & Herder, 1964) 75–93; see also Hemer's four headings of interpretation: eyewitness account, author's notes/diary, anonymous source, literary device," *Book of Acts*, 312–34; W. S. Campbell, "Who are We? The First-Person Plural Character in The Acts of the Apostles" (2000) 23–83; and *The "We" Passages in the Acts of the Apostles* (SBL, 2007) 1–13, 87–91; Susan M. Praeder, "The Problem of First Person Narrative in Acts," *NovT* 29 (1987) 193–218.

46. lrenaeus, *Adversus Haereses* 3 appears to be the earliest proponent as cited in Haenchen, *Acts*, 9; this is assumed in the works of Chrysostom, most of the other Patristic commentaries, and with Calvin, Grotius, and Bengel; in the conservative scholarship of the nineteenth and twentieth centuries: Ramsay *St. Paul* 200–201, 345; Zahn, *Introduction*, 95, 117–18, 127; Harnack, *Luke the Physician* (ET; Williams & Norgate, 1911) 26–120; Rackham, *Acts*, 278, 480; Bruce, *Book of Acts* 7, 308–9, 503; Hemer, *Book of Acts*, 321–34; Fitzmyer, *Luke the Theologian*, 3–11.

47. For example: J. Weiss, *Christianity*, 1:379; C. K. Barrett, *Luke the Historian in Recent Study*, new ed. (Fortress, 1970) 22; Kümmel, *Introduction*, 176–78, 184–85; after 28:16 the author of Acts completely abandons his source to produce 28:17–31, Overbeck, *Introduction*, 38–39, 48, 50 and Windisch, "Against Tradition," *BC* 2:330, 336; Loisy sees 28:16 and v. 30 as the only eyewitness sources here *The Origins of the New Testament* (ET; Allen & Unwin, 1950) 191; Jürgen Wehnert, *Die Wir-Pasagagen der Apostelgeschichte* (Vandenhoeck & Ruprecht, 1989); Stanley E. Porter, "Excursus: The 'We' Passages in Acts," *Book of Acts*, 2:545–74 and especially *Paul in Acts* (Hendrickson, 2001) 10–66.

48. As early as the mid-nineteenth century, Bruno Bauer saw them as purely the literary creation of the author, *Die Apostelgeschichte* (Hempel, 1850) 125–32; Cadbury sees it as a rhetorical device used by the author to identify more intimately with the events he is describing "The 'We' and 'I' Passages in Luke–Acts," *NTS* 3 (1957) 128–32; Dibelius, *Studies*, 205–6; Haenchen, *Acts*, 85–87, 489–91; Luke wanted to make them identify more personally with the events he is narrating, Haenchen, *Acts*, 491; Haenchen's view as summarized in Dupont, *Sources*, 128–30; Vernon K. Robbins sees the use of "we" as a characteristic style of ancient sea voyage genre, "The We-Passages in Acts and Ancient Sea Voyages," *BR* 20 (1975) 5–18; "By Land and by Sea: The We Passages and Ancient Sea Voyages," *PLA* (1978) 215–42. The shift between first and third person narration, however, is too frequent in sea voyage genre to account for any discernable literary function, on this criticism see Praeder, "First Person

Acts 28:17–20

Concerning the literary form of these verses there are still unsettled issues. Although many scholars regard vv. 17–20 as a Lukan speech,[49] some view it as a defense speech similar to those in Acts 22–26,[50] while others say it is not.[51]

The difficult historical problems of vv. 17–20, as elsewhere in Acts 28, have always kept scholarly attention well preoccupied. Many have pointed out here the conflicting statements of Paul regarding the conditions of his arrest.[52] Responses to these problems in support of Lukan accuracy have generally been in terms of harmonistic explanations.[53]

Narrative,"210–14 and Fitzmyer, *Luke The Theologian*, 16–22. W. S. Kurz explores the literary function but favors Fitzmyer's position (above) in Kurz, *Reading Luke-Acts* (1993) 111–24. William S. Campbell argues that "we" occurs as one of two characters in Acts (the other is Barnabas) who attest to the credibility of Paul and the divine purpose of his mission, "Who are We?" 133–93; and *"We" Passages*, 87–91.

49. For example: Cadbury, "The Speeches in Acts" Additional Notes to the Commentary *BC*, 5:403; Dibelius, *Studies*, 150 n. 30; Hauser, *Strukturen* 20–21; Fitzmyer, *Acts*, 790; Marion L. Soards, *The Speeches in Acts* (1994) 22, 130–33, Soards assumes that 28:17c-20 and 25b-28 are two parts of one speech; Barrett sees Paul's meetings with the Jews at Rome as two distinct events and not compressed into one, *Acts*, 2:1236–43.

50. Bruce, *Speeches in Acts* (1942) 5; Schubert, "Final Cycle," 9–10. Fitzmyer states that 28:17–20 is a defense speech, *Acts*, 790.

51. O'Toole, *Christological Climax*, 15; Radl, *Paulus-Jesus*, 252–65.

52. The arguments against Luke's accuracy are: (1) Contrary to 28:17, "I was delivered into the hands of Romans," Paul was rescued from a Jewish mob by the Romans (21:30–36), given the chance Paul willingly remained under Rome (25:9–11), Loisy, *Actes*, 933; Haenchen, *Acts*, 722; Conzelmann, *Apostelgeschichte*, 159. (2) Contrary to 28:18, "(the Romans) . . . wanted to release me," in 25:9–10, Festus the Roman wanted to give Paul over to the Jews, Loisy, *Actes*, 933; Holtzmann, *Apostelgeschichte*, 155; Haenchen, *Acts*, 722. (3) The statement of Paul in 28:17–20 is so brief that only Luke's readers (who are familiar with Acts 21–26) could understand what Paul is saying, Windisch, "Against Tradition" *BC* 2:335; Haenchen, *Acts*, 727; Barrett (following Conzelmann) states that Paul's arrest is described in terms drawn from Christ's own, *Acts*, 2:1239.

53. Attempts at defending Luke's accuracy are: (1) Paul is viewing his arrest as fulfillment of prophecy by Agabus (21:11) Bruce, *Book of Acts*, 505; (2) The Romans did want to release Paul after his appeal to Caesar (25:18, 25; 26:32), Munck, *Acts*, 258; Mattill "Paul," *PLA* 80; (3) Paul briefly introduces himself and explains his position to the Jews before he preaches to them (the latter being his chief motive) Rackham, *Acts*, 500; Neil, *Acts*, 257.

While attention has been diverted to these historical issues the nature and significance of the literary form of Acts 28:17–20 have not been sufficiently pursued. In the concluding scene of Paul at Rome are there two speeches presented (28:17–20 and 25–28) or only two statements of direct address given? Should Acts 28:17–20 be classed with Paul's defense speeches (Acts 22–26) or with Jesus' trial (Luke 23)?

Acts 28:23–28

Not a few commentators regard v. 23 and v. 31 as typical Lukan summaries of preaching.[54] Some view such preaching accounts as implying a continuity of witness from Jesus and the Twelve to Paul.[55] In comparison with other texts, scholars have pointed out the Lukan concern for the preaching of Christ as the fulfillment of Scripture (prophecy).[56]

While the majority of scholars note the obvious similarities between 28:23 and 30–31, many are reluctant to regard both as having the same form and similar functions in Acts 28.[57] What do both passages have in common and what makes them distinct?

In v. 24 a difference of opinion has arisen concerning the interpretation of ἐπείθοντο. One position explains that this verb implies that

54. Wendt (Acts 17:2–3; 18:5; 19:8) *Apostelgeschichte*, 367; Conzelmann, *Apostelgeschichte*, 195; and *Theology*, 218; Haenchen, *Acts*, 723; Talbert, *Luke and Gnostics*, 22.

55. Foakes-Jackson and Lake, "The Internal Evidence of Acts," *BC*, 2:181; W. C. Robinson Jr., "On Preaching the Word of God (Luke 8:4–21)," *SLA* 135–36; Talbert, *Luke and the Gnostics*, 17–18, 33–34. This observation is significant in showing that the same word proclaimed by Paul at Rome was proclaimed by Jesus, the Twelve, and others (e.g., Stephen, Philip, Barnabas), O'Toole, *Unity*, 75–94.

56. Schubert sees 28:23 as a climactic summary of Luke's proof-from-prophecy theology concerning Christ (Luke 24:27, 40–41; Acts 26:6–8, 22–23) "Final Cycle," 9; Dupont sees such accounts as an example of preaching that Christ is the fulfillment of Scripture (Luke 24:46–47; Acts 26:23) *Salvation*, 16–17, 29, 130–31; Smith, *Acts*, 384–85.Charles Talbert interprets this theme in its ancient Mediterranean milieu and cautions against regarding it as *the* major theme of Luke–Acts in his "Promise and Fulfillment in Lucan Theology," *Luke–Acts* (1984) 91–103; Darrell Bock, *Proclamation from Prophecy and Pattern* (Sheffield, 1987); Mark Strauss, *The Davidic Messiah in Luke–Acts* (Sheffield, 1995), especially 14–15, 288, 355.

57. For example, the following works regard 28:30–31 as a Lukan "summary statement" but not v. 23, which is in many ways similar, C. H. Turner, "Chronology of New Testament," *HDB*, 1:421; Cadbury, "The Summaries in Acts," *BC*, 5:396; Dibelius, *Studies*, 9–10, 127–28; Brian Rosner, "The Progress of the Word," 215–33 in *Witness to the Gospel* (Eerdmans, 1998).

some Jews were converted by Paul's preaching in Rome,[58] another position argues from the context, that ἐπείθοντο cannot imply conversion since the response of the entire group of Jews here is characterized by division and departure (vv. 24, 25a).[59]

The controversy continues when it is asked: To whom was the hardening statement of Isaiah directed (vv. 25–28/Isaiah 6: 9, 10)? Was it addressed only to the unbelieving Jews,[60] or to all the Jews as a group representing Judaism?[61]

58. Chrysostom, *Homilies* 55:722, 724–25; Calvin says "some did embrace those things that Paul spoke," *Acts*, 2:430; A. George, "Israel dans l'oeuvre de Luc," *RB* 75 (1968) 514–15; Jervell, *Luke* 63, 71–72; Robert J. Karris, *Invitation to Acts* (Image Books, 1978) 234–35; and "Missionary Communities: A New Paradigm for the Study of Luke–Acts," *CBQ* 41:1 (1979) 91, 94; "those persuaded and those refusing to believe" in Witherington, *Acts* 802. "Thus a portion of Roman Jews has been selected as believing and repentant," Jervell, *Die Apostelgeschichte* 17th ed. (Göttingen, 1998) 626; Strauss, *Davidic Messiah*, 176, 348. See the outline of views in Bock, *Acts* (Baker, 2007) 756–57.

59. Rackham says of vv. 24–25: "This was a sign of the fall of the kingdom of the old covenant; for a kingdom divided against itself cannot stand" *Acts* 504; Loisy, *Actes* 937; Haenchen, *Acts* 723–24; Conzelmann, *Apostelgeschichte* 159; all the Jews departed when (or as) Paul pronounced the hardening statement of Isaiah on them, Stagg, *Acts* 265; "whose discord Luke mentions explicitly" F. Bovon, "Studies in Luke–Acts" (1992) 189; and "'Schön hat der heilige Geist durch den Propheten Jesaja zu eruren Vätern gesprochenen' (Acts 28:25)," *ZNW* 75 (1984) 226–32; Hauser, *Strukturen*, 66.

60. Chrysostom, *Homilies* 55:722, 724–25; Calvin, *Acts*, 2:426– 430; Jervell, *Luke*, 63, 71–72; Karris, *Acts*, 234–35 and "Missionary Communities," 91, 94; "Isaiah's words were directed against those who steadfastly 'refused to believe,'" Cassidy, *Society and Politics*, 130; "To these unbelievers Paul declares . . . " (vv. 25–28) in Craig A. Evans, *To See and Not Perceive: Isaiah* 6:9–10 (Sheffield, 1989) 121,126; Evans and Sanders, *Luke and Scripture*, 208–11; Witherington, *Acts*, 802; K. D. Litwak discusses the scriptural echoes in 28:25–28 but fails to include Ezek 12:2 which is a close parallel to Isa 6:9–10 in his *Echoes of Scripture*, 183–97.

61. Rackham, *Acts*, 504; Loisy, *Actes*, 937; Haenchen, *Acts*, 102, 723–29; Conzelmann, *Apostelgeschichte*, 221; "He was seeking a communal decision, a recognition by the Jewish community as a whole," Tannehill, *Narrative Unity*, 2:347; "an expression of divine judgment on the Jews" G. Wasserberg, *Aus Israels Mitte—Heil für die Welt* (de Gruyter, 1998) 87–88. Jack T. Sanders even accuses Luke of being anti-Semitic in *The Jews in Luke–Acts* (Fortress, 1987) xvi–xvii, 47, 237, 310, 317. Sanders fails to interpret these Lukan statements in the context of intra-Jewish and sectarian controversy; for further criticisms of Sanders see Evans, *To See and Not Perceive*, 123–26; and Robert F. O'Toole, "Reflections on Luke's Treatment of Jews in Luke–Acts," *Biblica* 74 (1993) 529–55. Talbert suggests that a reversal of fortunes takes place in 28:28. According to G. F. Moore, it was a Jewish belief that God's revelation at Sinai was first offered to the nations who rejected it so that it went to Israel. Here, a new revelation is first offered to

The popular usage of Isaiah 6:9–10 in the New Testament has brought forth the hypothesis that such widely quoted passages were derived from a collection of Old Testament texts in a common testimonia book of the early church.[62] Yet scholarship has shown that the Isa. 6 quote in Acts occurs in a Lukan context, is introduced and concluded by Lukan statements, and is applied to a Lukan motif (Acts 13:46; 18:6).[63] While some commentators have argued that Isa. 6:9, 10 at least reflects the mind of Paul in Rom. 11:8, 10 (Isa. 6:9)[64] it has been shown to be a difficult case to prove, since the Isaiah 6 quote occurs in two different contexts reflecting two different views of Israel and salvation.[65]

The literary form of 28:25–28 is regarded by some as a short apologetic speech on the Gentile mission (with 13:46)[66] while others merely regard it as a form of direct address.[67] If Acts 28:25–28 and 13:46 func-

---

Israel who reject it and now it goes back to the nations who will now listen. We question, however, the antiquity and prevalence of this tradition in Luke's day, *Reading Acts*, 233.

62. J. R. Harris, *Testimonies* 2 vols. (Cambridge, 1920) 2:65, 74, 137; C. H. Dodd, *According to the Scriptures* (Nisbet, 1952) 36–38; Bruce, *Book of Acts*, 507–8; Witherington, *Acts* 805.

63. Dibelius, *Studies*, 149–50; Haenchen, *Acts*, 729; Gnilka, *Verstockung*, 148; Conzelmann, *Apostelgeschichte*, 159–60; see the critique of Dodd's testimonia theory in K. Stendahl, *The School of St. Matthew* (Fortress, 1968) 132; also B. Lindars, *The New Testament Apologetic* (Westminster, 1961) 164–67.

64. Note for example Raymond Brown's comment in *Gospel according to John* (Doubleday, 1966) 1:485; R. R. Williams, *Acts of the Apostles* (SCM, 1956) 169; Bruce, *Acts* GT, 479.

65. Overbeck in his *Kurze Erklärung der Apostelgeschichte* (ET) sees the view of Israel and salvation in Romans 9–11 as a direct contradiction to that of Acts, as cited in Mattill, "Luke as a Historian in Criticism since 1840," 423–24; Zeller, *Contents*, 106–7; Jervell contrasts Romans 9–11 and Luke–Acts in both his *Luke* 64 and *Apostelgeschichte*, 628.

66. Cadbury, "Speeches," *BC*, 5:403; apologetic speech, Bruce *Speeches* 26; aggressive speech, Kümmel, *Introduction*, 167; Craig Evans states, "He [Luke] is trying to show, on empirical and scriptural grounds, that the Gentile mission is legitimate, not that the Jewish mission will be terminated," in Craig Evans and James Sanders, *Luke and Scripture: The Function of Sacred Tradition in Luke–Acts* (Fortress, 1993) 209.

67. Dibelius probably did not class 28:25–28 as a speech since it lacked several of the characteristics of other Lukan speeches, *Studies*, 150 n. 30. E. Jane Via omits 28:25b–28 from her list of speeches yet includes 13:46–47, the latter being a very close parallel to the former in structure and content, Via, "Moses and Meaning in Luke–Acts: A Redaction-Critical Analysis of Acts 7:35" (PhD dissertation, Marquette University, 1976) 70–82. Fitzmyer states that "(vv 25c–28) is an indictment," similar to prophetic indictment speeches, *Acts*, 790. See our discussion of Acts 28:25–28 in chapter 2.

tion as a Lukan apology for the Gentile mission, there should be other Lukan texts to be classed with them. The form and function of this apology for the Gentile mission is still undefined. Concerning 28:29 from the Western Text (as with v. 16), commentators before the nineteenth century generally include the reading,[68] while modern commentators omit the verse, following the superior Alexandrian Text.[69]

Acts 28:30–31

A majority of scholars view vv. 30–31 as a Lukan summary statement forming a climactic conclusion to the book of Acts.[70]

Other scholars regard the concluding verses as an epilogue or confirming statement, perceiving a climax elsewhere in Acts 28.[71] A clarification of literary function is needed here.

68. καὶ ταῦτα αὐτοῦ εἰπόντος ἀπῆλθον οἱ Ἰουδαῖοι πολλὴν ἔχοντες ἐν ἑαυτοῖς συζήτησιν ("And when he had said these words, the Jews departed, and had great reasoning among themselves," KJV) is included in Chrysostom, *Homilies* 55:722; Theophylakti, *Acta*, 846–47; Calvin, *Acts*, 2:426, 430; Bengel, *Gnomon*, 536; In a recent study D. R. Miesner has included v. 29 in an attempt to make Acts 28:25–28 a complete chiasm. He forces the chiastic parallelism at several points (e.g. v. 26 with v. 28), and the strong textual evidence omitting v. 29, argues firmly against this attempt, "Circumferential Speeches," 230–35.

69. Wendt, *Apostelgeschichte*, 368 n. 1; Jacquier, *Actes*, 760; Ropes, "Text of Acts," *BC*, 3:255; Eldon J. Epp, *The Theological Tendency of Codex Bezae Cantabrigiensis in Acts* (Cambridge University Press, 1966) 114–15; Metzger, *Textual Commentary*, 444.

70. The conclusion of a series of notices on church growth, Rackham, *Acts* 502; C. H. Turner saw 28:30–31 as the conclusion of a series of six progress reports from which he outlined the book of Acts (6:7; 9:31; 12:24; 16:5; 19:20; 28:30–31), "Chronology," *HDB*, 1:421; Cadbury added several more reports to Turner's list (2:47b; 5:14; 11:21, 24), "Summaries," *BC*, 5:396–97, 400; and Cadbury, *Making*, 58–59.

On the climactic conclusion of Acts 28:30f, see Cadbury, *Making*, 323–24; Henry Chadwick, *History and Thought of the Early Church* (Variorum, 1982) 15–16; Dibelius, *Studies* 9–10, 127–28; O'Neill, *Theology*, 64–65; Kümmel, *Introduction*, 164; Barrett, *Acts*, 2:1253; Johnson, *Acts* 473; "Luke focuses on Paul's missionary activity with Paul in Rome being the crowning conclusion of world mission (28:22ff, 30–31)," P. Lampe, *From Paul to Valentinus*, 7 n. 1. "All roads led not only *to* Rome but *from* Rome, from the Golden Milestone in the forum, to the 'ends of the earth' and thus 'to all nations';" Charles Scobie, "Canonical Approach," *Reading Luke*, 344; Spencer, *Journeying through Acts*, 250–51; Irina Levinskaya, *Diaspora Setting: Book of Acts* 5 (1996) 195; Rosner, "Progress of the Word," 215–33 in *Witness to the Gospel*.

71. Harnack regards 28:30–31 as a postscript, vv. 25–28 being the real climactic conclusion in *Date*, 94; and Mattill, "Paul," *PLA* 85; Dupont follows Harnack in seeing

Concerning historical questions, some believe that "two full years" (διετίαν ὅλην) presupposes, at the time when Acts was written, a change of situation for Paul, either a favorable, or an unfavorable one.[72]

Concerning the theology of Acts 28:30–31, many have inferred from this concluding note (ἀπεδέχετο πάντας, v. 30), a continuation of Paul's mission to both Jews and Gentiles.[73] Others see in these verses

---

28:25–28 as the true conclusion of the chapter, *Salvation* 141; and "La Conclusion," 361; Schubert regards vv. 30–31 as a final confirmatory statement, v. 23 being the climactic feature, "Final Cycle," 9; Richard I. Pervo, *Luke's Story of Paul* (Fortress, 1990) 96. Litwak compares 4 Kingdoms 25 (2 Kings 25) with Acts 28, favoring "open-endedness," *Echoes of Scripture*, 198–99. Others have also made this comparison in Evans and Sanders, *Luke and Scripture*, 209 n. 158; P. R. Davies, "The Ending of Acts," *ExpT* 94 (1982–83) 334–35, and G. W. Trompf, "Acts 27–28," *Luke-Acts* (1984) 227. See "Open-Ended Finale" in Hur, *Dynamic Reading*, 267–70; Luke "wants us to continue the story for ourselves . . . There is no end, but addition." In Hooker, *Endings*, 66; "open-ended . . . opening out into the reader's world," Alexander, "Reading Luke–Acts from Back to Front," 229.

72. A favorable outcome for Paul since he was released shortly afterwards (early date advocates): Zahn, *Introduction*, 57–58; Ramsay, *St. Paul*, 349–50; Rackham, *Acts*, 507–9; see discussion in Bruce, *Acts* GT, 541–42; and *Book of Acts*, 511 n. 82 (although he states that "we cannot be certain" 511); Hemer reviews the discussion, favoring release by acquittal or default, *Book of Acts*, 390–92. Lake (and Cadbury to some degree) saw in διετίαν ὅλην a technical term designating a time fixed by Claudius for a case to be heard, if after two years the accusers did not appear, the accused was set free. Since this was to be the situation in Paul's day the "two full years" signified for Luke's readers the release of Paul, "Roman Law and the Trial of St. Paul," *BC* 5:326–38. Later critics have shown that much of the "evidence" cited by Lake and Cadbury is either misinterpreted, or misapplied to first century Rome, A. N. Sherwin-White, *Roman Society and Roman Law in the New Testament* (Oxford University Press, 1963) 108–19; Haenchen, *Acts*, 725 n. 4; Conzelmann, *Acts*, 228.

The outcome was not favorable, since Paul's death is presupposed in Acts (20:25,38, late date advocates): Haenchen, *Acts*, 731; O'Neill, *Theology*, 60–62. B. Weiss states that some change has occurred either execution or liberation, *Commentary*, 2:637.

73. Acts 28:30 . . . ἀπεδέχετο πάντας τοὺς εἰσπορευομένους πρὸς αὐτόν. In order to explain the word πάντας the Western reviser (12th century) added at the close of v. 30 the words Ἰουδαίους τε καὶ Ἕλληνας, see: Ropes, *Text of Acts*, *BC*, 3:255; Epp, *Theological Tendency*, 114–15; Metzger, *Textual Commentary* (1971) 502; see commentators: Calvin, *Acts*, 2:430–32; B. Weiss, *Commentary* 2:637; Bauernfeind, *Apostelgeschichte* 280; Loisy quotes from the Western Text in *Actes* 940–41; Floyd V. Filson, *Three Crucial Decades* (John Knox, 1963) 26; Karris, *Acts*, 236 and "Missionary Communities," 91; "his meaning (though not his text) is rightly given by the Western insertion, Barrett, *Acts*, 2: 1252; Spencer, *Journeying*, 250.

only a Gentile mission presupposed, since the Jewish mission is now over (vv. 25–28 being the final statement on the Jewish mission).[74]

The term ἀκωλύτως ("unhindered") is viewed by many as a climactic feature giving the book a deliberate and effective conclusion.[75] Interpretations of the Lukan meaning of ἀκωλύτως are numerous. The term reflects Christianity's external relations with Rome.[76] It signifies the internal struggles of the church with Jewish legalism.[77] Ἀκωλύτως conveys the triumph of the gospel over both external and internal obstacles.[78]

The discussion of the various verses of Acts 28:16–31 raises again the question: Does the author somehow draw together these diverse elements of the text into a meaningful unit of thought? Or are they kept in tension? Is there some underlying concept used by the author uniting these various elements into a complete unit to convey a concluding message for his readers/auditors? Or are these matters left open for the implied readers/auditors of Luke–Acts?

74. Paul received all who were once restricted: the Gentiles, Wendt, *Apostelgeschichte*, 369 and Haenchen, *Acts*, 726; for Luke it is now the time of the Gentile mission, Conzelmann, *Theology*, 188 n. 7, 190 and Danker on Luke 21:24 in *Jesus* 213; even Jervell states that Acts 28 ends the Jewish mission and begins the Gentile mission *Luke*, 64, 68; "But now the judgment is valid for the whole of unrepentant Judaism. All Jews throughout the world have heard the gospel. Now it is directed to Rome and the West and with that the fate of universal Judaism is sealed," our trans. of Jervell, *Apostelgeschichte*, 628.

75. W. F. Burnside, *The Acts of the Apostles in Greek* (Cambridge, 1916) 264; Cadbury, *Making*, 323–24; Bruce, *Acts*, GT 543; and *Book of Acts*, 535–36; Smith, "Theology," 530; G. Delling, "Das Letzt Wort der Apostelgeschichte" *NT* 15:3 (1973) 193–204; Spencer, *Acts*, 241; Skinner, *Locating Paul*, 168.

76. Haenchen, *Acts* 102, 726; Bruce, *Acts* GT, 25; and *Book of Acts*, 9; Lake and Cadbury, "Commentary," *BC*, 4:348; G. Delling, "Das letzte Wort der Apostelgeschichte" *NovT* 15 (1973) 193–204. Talbert, *Reading Acts*, 234

77. F. Stagg, "The Unhindered Gospel," *Rev Exp* 71 (1974) 461–62; and *Acts*, 12–17, 726; O'Neill: the gospel breaks free from Judaism, *Theology*, 76.

78. See especially Bengel, *Gnomon*, 511, 536; Rackham, *Acts*, 506; Kümmel, *Introduction*, 164; Smith, *Acts*, 387 and "Theology," 530; Eric Franklin, *Christ the Lord* (Westminster, 1975) 209 n. 3. Fitzmyer, *Acts*, 797; Spencer, *Journeying*, 250–52; Barrett, *Acts*, 2:1253. Cassidy challenges the other views by arguing for "the resoluteness with which Paul continues his teaching and preaching" in *Society and Politics*, 134.

Questions Still to Be Answered

An investigation of Acts 28:16–31 in the history of *Actaforschung* has indicated that there has been too much preoccupation with the more speculative historical questions but no consensus has been reached on the significant literary concerns.

Although study of the literary character and significance of Acts 28 has developed recently, the question of the literary function of Acts 28:16–31 still needs to be addressed. Related to this central concern are three problem areas of investigation: (1) The nature of the literary forms and the structure of Acts 28:16–31. (2) The nature and extent of the Lukan parallels of Acts 28:16–31. (3) The relationship and purpose (if they exist) of the various themes, patterns, and motifs of Acts 28:16–31 as the conclusion of Luke–Acts.

Even though our investigation will be concerned with the above three areas only in so far as they contribute to an understanding of the literary function and theological significance of Acts 28:16–31, there are several unsettled literary and thematic problems which must be addressed in the process.

1. Concerning the literary forms of Acts 28, several questions need to be answered. In 28:17–20 and 25–28 are we confronted with Lukan speeches or merely statements of direct address? Should 28:17–20 be then classed with Paul's defense speeches (chaps. 22–26) or with Jesus' trial scene (Luke 23)? If 28:25–28 with 13:46 and 18:6 are to be regarded as apologies for the Gentile mission are there any other significant texts in the narrative to be classed with them? What makes 28:30–31 a Lukan "summary statement" and v. 23, in many ways similar, not a summary statement according to the categories of Turner and Cadbury? Regarding the structure of our text, what constitutes 28:16–31 as a complete structural unit and not vv. 17–31?

In chapter 2, the above questions of literary form and structure will be pursued to provide the groundwork for the literary function of the text.

2. Concerning Lukan parallels to Acts 28 there is a need to define the nature and extent of these relationships. If Acts 28 reflects a typical missionary situation, why is a comparison restricted only to the accounts of Paul in Asia Minor (13:46), Greece (18:6), and Rome (28:25–28)? Attention should be given to other missionary settings in Ephesus (19)

and elsewhere. What is the relationship of Acts 28:16–31 with the account of Paul's defense (21–26)? Scholars have cross-referenced 28:17–20 with verses from Paul's defense but no extensive comparison has been made between Acts 21–26 with the complete text of 28:16–31.

Luke 24 and Acts 28 are regarded as parallel works in structure, form, and content, yet scholars have not adequately demonstrated this assertion nor have they investigated the significance of this comparison for an interpretation of Acts 28. The significance of the parallels between the beginning of Luke's Gospel (chaps. 1–4) and the introduction of Acts (chap. 1) with Acts 28 have not yet been fully developed for an understanding of the conclusion of Acts. In chapter 3, an investigation of these intratextual questions concerning Acts 28 and its Lukan parallels will be undertaken.

3. Commentators have identified several themes in Acts 28 that contribute to an understanding of its contents. Although most of the themes find some support in the text, which ones account for most if not all of the data in Acts 28:16–31? Can such a question be satisfactorily answered?

Many see in Paul's arrival and activity in Rome, the goal of the progression of the gospel (or Christianity) from Jerusalem to Rome. Although this important Lukan theme finds some support in 28:30–31 it does not explain why the author has Paul defend himself before the Jews (vv. 17–20) and why he afterwards has him pronounce a judgment of hardening upon them (vv. 25–28).

Others see Acts 28 as the final explanation for the mission to the Gentiles. This observation certainly accounts for vv. 25–28 but does not explain the inclusion of vv. 17–20. Advocates of other themes, including Christianity as the true faith of Israel or Rome's fair treatment of Christianity, regard these motifs as expressing the contents of Acts 28 without consideration of other elements in the text. Are these efforts not reductionistic? In chapter 4, these thematic concerns, along with significant patterns and motifs, will be examined for a broader understanding of the literary function and theological significance of Acts 28.

The elaboration of the above three problem areas must again raise a significant set of questions: Is there some common concept or image that the author is using to unite the various themes and elements in the text in order to formulate a clear and distinct message for his implied readers/auditors? Can this unifying factor be substantiated from the text itself and confirmed from the parallels and patterns of Luke–Acts?

In response to the above set of questions an hypothesis will be examined in the course of this study: that in Acts 28:16–31, the Lukan narrative is primarily concerned with defending Paul and his mission, by presenting him as one like Jesus who does the work of Jesus. With this image of Paul and his work, Acts 28:16–31 will be shown to be a meaningful and complete structural unit without excluding vv. 17–20[79] or any other verses in an exegesis of the text. This hypothesis will be confirmed by a comparison of Acts 28 with its parallels in Luke–Acts showing how the accounts of Paul and his mission are portrayed in terms of Jesus–Paul parallels.

With the picture of Paul at Rome as one like Christ engaged in Christ's mission, it will be argued that the author brings together a variety of themes and motifs which form a grand conclusion to his two-volume work. Is not Paul, like Christ, portrayed as a faithful Jew or Israelite who also was innocent before Rome? Did not Christ command Paul's mission to the Gentiles? In Paul's preaching of Christ at Rome is there not a historical continuity with Jesus and the Twelve and a geographical progression from Jerusalem to Rome?

For the author and his implied readers/auditors, the reaffirmation of Christ's representative and mission may serve as a legitimization of the Christianity of Luke's day and provide a model for a continued world mission. Through the image of Paul as one like Christ who completes Christ's mission, it will be shown that a close relationship between the Gospel to Acts is recognized and that the literary function of Acts 28 as the conclusion of Luke–Acts is effectively established.

There are several assumptions in methodology and understanding of Luke–Acts which should be noted. The primary method of approach will be that of composition criticism with insights gleaned from narrative criticism. We seek to discover why the author (whom we know from the narrative) composed Acts 28:16–31 and what he sought to tell his implied readers/auditors in and through the text.[80] It will be

79. This is the procedure of Schubert in his interpretation of Acts 28:17–31 in "Final Cycle," 10.

80. As stated earlier (footnote 2), this method follows the research of the following works: Dibelius, *Studies*, 1–25; Cadbury, *Making*, 299–350; Haenchen, *Acts* 90–110;

confirmed in the course of this study that Acts 28 is a deliberate and complete conclusion. The title "Luke" will be the hypothetical name used of the author implied in the narrative of Luke–Acts, whose historical identity outside the text is disputed in scholarship today.[81] A

and O'Toole, *Unity*, 11–14; Fitzmyer, *Acts*, 96–123; Barrett, *Acts*, 2:lxxiv–lxxxi. Other insights from narrative criticism, rhetorical analysis, and social-scientific interpretation will be noted as they relate to Acts 28. See, e.g., Tannehill, *The Narrative Unity*, 2 vols.; Kurz, *Reading Luke-Acts*; Kennedy, *New Testament Interpretation*; Neyrey, ed., *The Social World of Luke–Acts*; Loveday Alexander, ed., *Images of Empire;* Winter and Clarke, eds., *Book of Acts in Its First Century Setting*, 5 vols.; J. Lee Magness, *Marking the End: Sense and Absence in the Gospel of Mark* (1986; Wipf & Stock, 2002); Norman Peterson, "When is the End not the End? Literary Reflections on the Ending of Mark's Narrative," *Int* 34 (1980) 151–66; Mikeal Parsons, "Narrative Closure and Openness in the Plot of the Third Gospel," *SBL* 1986 *Seminar Papers* (SBL, 1986). On narrative, we consult also: Alter, *Art of Biblical Narrative;* Kermode, *Genesis of Secrecy*; Sternberg, *Poetics of Biblical Narrative*; Wayne C. Booth, *The Rhetoric of Fiction*, 2nd ed. (University of Chicago Press, 1983); *Narrative Ending* (special issue of *Nineteenth-Century Fiction*; Berkeley: University of California Press, 1979); Alan Friedman, *The Turn of the Novel* (Oxford University Press, 1966); Seymour Chatman, *Story and Discourse: Narrative Structure in Fiction and Film* (Cornell, 1981); Marianna Torgovnick, *Narrative Closure* (Princeton, 1981); David Richter, *Fable's End: Completeness and Closure in Rhetorical Fiction* (University of Chicago Press, 1974); Rimmon-Kenan, *Narrative Fiction: Contemporary Poetics* (Methuen, 1983). Attention to diverse methodologies will not minimize the theological significance of Luke–Acts in our study: see Fitzmyer, *Luke the Theologian*; Green, *Theology of St. Luke* (1995); Bovon, *Luke the Theologian (*1950–2005*)*.

81. Although for many centuries there has been a position favoring Luke the beloved physician (Col 4:14) as the author of Luke–Acts, the general consensus of modern scholarship is skeptical of this viewpoint. From Luke 1:1–4 (and Acts 2:39; 20:28–32) it appears that the author of Luke–Acts is probably a third generation Christian. The author's picture of Paul appears more idealistic and his understanding of Paul's theology is somewhat different (or distinct) from Paul's letters, reflecting a later viewpoint of someone distant from the time of the Apostle. See Cadbury "Tradition," *BC*, 2:209–64; C. W. Emmet, "The Case for the Tradition," *BC*, 2:265–97; Windisch, "Against Tradition," *BC*, 2:298–348; Haenchen, *Acts*, 112–16; Kümmel, *Introduction*, 147–50; Pervo, *Dating Acts*, 1–14, 359–68. It must also be noted that some scholars still make a fairly convincing case for the author's having traveled with Paul for a short period of time (i.e., in the "we" sections), Fitzmyer, *Luke the Theologian*, 3–11; Porter in *Book of Acts*, 2:545–74; and his *Paul in Acts* (2001) 10–66.

As stated, attention will also be paid to the author implied in the Lukan narrative and the readers/auditors implied in the Lukan text from reader-response criticism, see Wolfgang Iser, *The Implied Reader* (Johns Hopkins University Press, 1974); and his *The Act of Reading* (1978); see also James Resseguie, "Reader-Response Criticism and the Synoptic Gospels," *JAAR* 52 (1984) 307–24; John Darr, *On Character Building: The Reader and Rhetoric of Characterization in Luke–Acts* (Westminster John Knox, 1992); Kurz, *Reading Luke–Acts*, 9–16, 186–88.

date near the end of the first century (A.D. 80–90) is assumed for the composition of Luke–Acts.[82]

82. The account of Paul in Acts seems to presuppose his death around A.D. 64 (Acts 20:25, 38) and the Lukan redaction of the destruction of Jerusalem appears too vivid and detailed to predate the A.D. 70 disaster (Luke 13:34–35; 19:43–44; 21:20, 24). For discussion on the date of Luke–Acts, see: Kümmel, *Introduction*, 150–51, 185–87; Cadbury "Subsidiary Points," *BC*, 2:358–59; Windisch, "Against Tradition," *BC*, 2:308–11; Conzelmann, "Luke's Place," *SLA* 298–316; Buckwalter, *Character and Purpose*, 60–65. We regard Luke–Acts along with Mark, Matthew, and the later Pauline writings as responding to crises such as the fall of Jerusalem, delay of the parousia, conflicts with Judaism and Rome, threats of heresy, Puskas, *Introduction*, 212, 214–17. Despite the many insights gleaned from the careful argumentation, we remain unconvinced of an early second century date for Acts in Richard I. Pervo, *Dating Acts: Between the Evangelists and the Apologists* (Polebridge, 2006).

As a composite work Luke–Acts may have been written as one consecutive composition, with both volumes of this two-volume work written about the same general period, see: Cadbury, *Making*, 8–11. Even though they admit that Acts is a sequel to Luke and that both cohere theologically, Mikeal Parsons and Richard Pervo argue that each book is complete in itself and may even reflect distinct genres and narrative purposes, *Rethinking the Unity of Luke and Acts* (Fortress, 1993). See review in Michael F. Bird, "The Unity of Luke–Acts in Recent Discussion," *JSNT* 29 (2007) 425–48.

2

The Structure and Literary Forms of Acts 28:16–31

BEFORE THE LITERARY FUNCTION AND THEOLOGICAL SIGnificance of Acts 28:16–31 are determined, it is important to clarify several preliminary questions concerning the literary forms and structure of the text. What are the literary forms of Acts 28:16–31? What grounds are there for viewing vv. 16–31 as a structural unit instead of vv. 17–31? In what, ways is the text similar to, and different from, the rest of Luke–Acts in vocabulary, form and structure?

The pursuit of the above questions will serve as a response to several of the unsettled issues in the history of research of Acts 28 (chapter 1). Next, it will provide the groundwork for understanding the text in relation to its Lukan parallels (chapter 3). Finally, it will help us to determine the literary function and theological significance of the text (chapter 4).

Opening Panel: The Arrival of Paul in Rome, 28:16

The pericope begins with the announcement of Paul's arrival in Rome: "And when we entered Rome . . ." The term εἰσέρχομαι ("enter") and its root form ἔρχομαι ("come") are characteristic terms of the journey motif in Luke–Acts. In all four sections of the "we" passages (Acts 16:10–17; 20:5–15; 21:1–18; 27:1—28:16), the aorist form of ἔρχομαι in the first person plural (or a related verbal construction in the first person plural) is used to announce the arrival of Paul and others at a new location.[1] The

1. For each entry given in support of the above assertion, a scriptural reference will be provided, followed by the name of the location to which it refers, followed by a parenthetical explanation if the entry does not have the designated ἔρχομαι form.

last two sections of "we" passages in Acts are found in Paul's journey to Jerusalem (21:1–18) and Paul's journey to Rome (27:1—28:16). In both accounts, the "we" statements end after announcing the arrival of Paul at these particular destinations of Jerusalem (21:18) and Rome (28:16).[2]

It was discussed in chapter one, that an increasing number of scholars have come to regard the use of the "we" as a Lukan literary device.[3] One particular view, which will be substantiated in this study, is that the "we" statements are used by the Lukan author to identify his readers/auditors more intimately with the life and travels of Paul in the narrative.[4] Luke's readers/auditors would have easily "felt drawn into the fellowship of this missionary group and experienced its destiny as their own"[5] when they read the following "we" passage: "We sought to

---

Acts 16:10, Philippi ἐζητήσαμεν ἐξελθεῖν, the aorist infinitive of ἔρχομαι, with a third person plural aorist verb); Acts 20:6, Troas (aorist of προέρχομαι); 20:14, Mitylene; 21:8, Caesarea; 21:17 Jerusalem (the genitive absolute construction with the aorist participle γενομένων and the first person plural pronoun ἡμῶν; *BDAG*, 198: "change of location"); 27:8, Fair Havens, 28:13, Puteoli; 28:14, 16, Rome.

2. Although it is clear that the "we" statements are connected (in part) with sea travel (16:11; 20:5–6, 13–15; 21:1–3, 7; 27:1–44; 28:11–13), the assertion that the "we" statements usually *conclude after land is reached* does not account for those passages where the "we" statements are retained in accounts of land travel (21:4–18; 28:14–16) and narrated incidents occurring on land (16:12–17; 21:8b–14). The above critique would apply to Robbins, "By Land and By Sea" (1976), 382–87; "We-Passages in Acts," (1975) 5–18; "The We Passages," *Perspectives* (1978) 215–42. Also, the shift between first and third person narration is too frequent in sea voyage genre to account for any discernable literary function, see Susan M. Praeder, "The Problem of First Person Narrative," *NovT* 29 (1987) 210–14 and her "Narrative Voyage: Acts 27–28," (1980) 212–27; Fitzmyer, *Luke the Theologian*, 16–22. Regarding the examples cited by Robbins, Colin Hemer states that they are "not necessarily representative, nor are they always taken correctly in context, nor are they subject to any control, nor do they prove the conclusions he draws from them," 317 in his *Book of Acts* 317–19; see also his "First Person Narrative in Acts 27–28," *TynBull* 36 (1985) 79–109.

It does seem clear that the "we" statements end when the destinations of Paul's journeys to Jerusalem and Rome are reached (21:18; 28:16). Further discussion on this point is made in the pages that follow, in our chap. 2. Opening Panel, 36.

3. See our chap. 1. "Positions Taken on Various Verses, Acts 28:16," 20.

4. Haenchen, *Acts*, 490–91, and the discussion of Haenchen in Dupont, *Sources*, 128–30. Cadbury sees it as a rhetorical device used by the author to identify more intimately with the events he is describing "The 'We' and 'I' Passages in Luke–Acts," *NTS* 3 (1957) 128–32; Dibelius, *Studies*, 205–6. "The 'we' belong to a dialogue form with the reader," (our trans.) Hauser, *Strukturen*, 183.

5. Quotation from Haenchen, *Acts*, 491. Tannehill adds that "the anonymous we—a participant narrator—is a special opportunity for us and others to enter the narrative

go on to Macedonia, concluding that God had called us to preach the gospel to them" (Acts 16:10).

There are other similar "we" passages where Luke's readers/auditors would intimately identify with Paul and the early Christians (20:7, 8; 20:38—21:1, 12, 17; 27:2, 7, 14). Even in Luke 1:1–2, where the case for eye-witness reporting seems explicit, Loveday Alexander prefers the phrase "those who know the facts at hand" for αὐτόπται to avoid confusing it with its rare usage as forensic testimony.[6] The idea here seems to be one of intimacy with the events, rather than eye-witness reporting.

In view of the interpretation of the "we" passages conveying identity with the events narrated, Acts 28:16 could serve as a suitable way to bring Luke's readers/auditors in closer contact with the narrated events of the last scene of Acts. In the final "we" passages, Luke's readers/auditors may have identified with the triumph of Paul's long-awaited arrival in Rome, the city of his destination (19:21; 23:11; 27:24): "And so we came to Rome . . . And when we came to Rome . . ." (28:14, 16).[7]

---

as participants and to see ourselves as companions," 247 in *Narrative Unity*, 2:246–47, despite Praeder's misgivings about reader participation here, see also "First Person Narration," 199.

6. There are passages where Luke's readers might feel drawn into fellowship with Paul and the early Christians, Acts 20:7, 8; 21:17; where the readers could experience Christian hospitality extended to Paul and his associates, 27:2, 7, 14; and where Luke's readers could share in the agony of Paul's friends as Paul was about to face his "passion" and fate, 20:38–21:1; 21:12. In his prologue, Luke writes of the activities of Christ and the early church as "the things which were accomplished among us" although the implied author does not regard himself as an "eyewitness" of these events, Luke 1:1–2. Loveday Alexander, who prefers "those who know the facts at hand" for αὐτόπται, 120, also notes that only Polybius *Histories* 3.4.3 and Josephus *Against Apion* 1.55 (following Polybius) use the word to claim their actual presence at the events narrated, 38–39, both in her *Preface to Luke's Gospel* (1993).

7. Some view the "we" statements on Paul's coming to Rome as an etiology explaining the origin of the Church in Rome. V. K. Robbins, who regards the "we" style as characteristic of ancient sea voyage genre, explains the relevance of the "we" statements for Luke and his readers in the following manner: "as the author, a member of the church, pens his narrative sitting in Rome, the question is how 'we' got here when we started out in Jerusalem." Robbins, "By Land and By Sea: Acts 13–28," *SBL Seminar Papers* (1976), 394. This statement by Robbins is based on the questionable assumption that Luke is writing from Rome. F. Overbeck has argued that Luke could not be writing from Rome since he betrays no special knowledge of the city or church there (e.g., 28:21, 22). Because of the amount of detailed understanding of the locations along the Aegean sea region reflected in Acts, Overbeck and Conzelmann suggest the Aegean sea region as a likely place of writing, Overbeck, *Introduction*, 75–76; Conzelmann, "Luke's Place in the Development of Early Christianity," *SLA* 302. Robbins later avoids

The double reference of the coming of Paul to Rome (28:14, 16) appears to be a Lukan characteristic employed when an important figure approaches the destination of his travels: the coming of Paul to Jerusalem (21:15, 17), and the coming of Jesus to Jerusalem (Luke 19:28, 41, the last two references).[8]

The references of Paul's coming to Jerusalem and Rome are all "we" statements (21:15, 17; 28:14, 16) and have similar functions. The first set of references actually announce Paul's approaching the city and form the last stage of the journey (21:15; 28:14), while the second set of references announce Paul's arrival in the city as an introduction to the scene (21:17–26; 28:16–31).[9]

The two scenes of Paul at Jerusalem and Rome have several parallels which are noteworthy: (1) the double reference of Paul's coming with a "we" statement (21:15, 17; 28:14, 16); (2) the friendly reception of Paul by the church (21:17 arrival; 28:15 coming); (3) rumors about Paul are discussed (21:21 Jerusalem Jews know of them; 28:21 Roman

---

a specific geographical *Sitz im Leben* when he writes of the eastern Roman empire as the workplace of (Luke and) early Christianity, V. K. Robbins, "Luke–Acts: A Mixed Population Seeks a Home in the Roman Empire," in *Images of Empire*, ed. L. Alexander (Sheffield, 1991) 202–21.

8. Part of the difficulty of determining where in the Gospel Jesus' journey ends (Luke 19:27, 40, or 44?) is due to the numerous announcements of Jesus approaching the city (19:11, 28, 41). No clear statement of Jesus' arrival in Jerusalem is given, unlike Paul's arrival (Acts 21:17), although there is the statement that "Jesus entered the temple" (Luke 19:45). Hauser notes this last point also *Strukturen*, 16 n. 18. Filson states his view (Luke 19:27, 40, or 44?) in "The Journey Motif in Luke–Acts," *Apostolic History* 70–71. See also Green on Luke 19:45 in his *Luke*, 691–92.

9. Although Acts 21:15–16 is sometimes placed with the scene of Paul at Jerusalem (21:17–26) it is actually part of Paul's journey to Jerusalem since it describes the last stage in the journey from Caesarea to Jerusalem. It is at 21:17 where Paul actually arrives in the city and is greeted by James and the Jerusalem Church. This is a parallel argument for 28:11–15 as forming the last stage of Paul's journey to Rome and therefore distinct from the scene of Paul at Rome (vv. 16–31). Acts 28:14 announces Paul's approaching the city and v. 15 describes the brethren from Rome coming out to meet Paul at the Forum of Appius and Three Taverns as Paul was approaching Rome. Acts 28:16 describes Paul's actual arrival in the city and provides the setting for the scene. Hauser concludes here "Quite similarly 28:16 functions with Acts 21.17, a verse which marks the end of Paul's trip to Jerusalem trip as well as the beginning of Paul's stay there," (our trans.) *Strukturen*, 16.

We should not overlook here the apologetic function that the "we" statements establish for Paul and his mission. William S. Campbell argues that "we" occurs as one of two characters in Acts (the other is Barnabas) and both attest to the credibility of Paul and the divine purpose of his mission, "Who are We?" 133–93 and *"We" Passages*, 87–91.

Jews do not know of them); (4) Paul's innocence is reaffirmed (21:24; 28:17–20); (5) reference to the Gentile mission is made (21:19, 25; 28:28).The above parallels indicate that the scene of Paul at Rome is not unlike the account of Paul at Jerusalem at numerous points. This comparison also provides further grounds for viewing the double reference of Paul's coming and arrival to Jerusalem and Rome as an intended Lukan practice with the latter set of references forming the introduction to their respective scenes (21:17; 28:16).

Acts 28:16 explicitly mentions the location "Rome" which furnishes the geographical setting of the narrative, a characteristic of other Pauline missionary settings (13:14; 17:1; 18:14).[10] Without the mention of "Rome" in the opening verse (28:16) it would be difficult to recognize the location of the scene within the pericope itself.[11]

The phrase μένειν καθ' ἑαυτὸν ("to remain by himself") gives a preliminary sketch of Paul's living situation. A similar reference is found in the opening statements of Paul's second meeting with the Jews of Rome τὴν ξενίαν ("lodging") 28:23.[12] In the epilogue, a similar statement of Paul's living situation is mentioned: ἐνέμεινεν . . . ἐν ἰδίῳ μισθώματι ("he remained in his own rented quarters"), v. 30.[13]

10. See also the scene of Paul at Jerusalem (21:17) for another example of mentioning the location. For a more complete list of these location indicators in Acts 13–28, see Hemer, *Book of Acts*, 109–58.

11. It will be shown in chapter 3 that 28:23–28 is a typical Pauline missionary situation that could take place in Asia Minor or Greece. There is no mention of Rome in 28:17–31 and no indication within the pericope itself that the scene takes place in Rome, although it is clearly outside of Judea (v. 21). Haenchen, *Acts*, 726–32; Maddox, *Purpose*, 43, 62 n. 93.

12. In 28:16 καθ' ἑαυτὸν seems to be contradicted by "with the soldier that guarded him" but this phrase probably indicates that he resided apart from the other prisoners and guards. The use of "by himself" provides an appropriate occasion for Luke to end the "we" statements, see Cadbury, "'We' and 'I' Passages", 129; Paul lived alone in his own rented quarters under light custody with a soldier guarding him (Acts 28:16,30) according to Rapske, "Paul in Roman Custody," *Book of Acts*, 3:177–81. Because of 28:20, Rapske assumes that Paul is still chained to a soldier (181), Cassidy elaborates on this assumption, *Paul in Chains*, 232–33.

13. Hauser supports our observation above with word studies of μένειν and related terms, *Strukturen*, 156. Dupont also compares vv. 16 and 30–31 as the enclosures of our text on the basis of similar location indicators and terminology. Furthermore, Dupont compares the use of εἰσέρχομαι in v. 16 "when we came (εἰσήλθομεν) to Rome" and v. 30 "he (Paul) received all who came (εἰσπορευομένους) to him." Hauser concurs in *Strukturen*, 13–14; Dupont also compares v. 23 with vv. 30–31 on the

Acts 28:16 mentions that Paul was "permitted" (ἐπιτρέπω) to remain by himself. This term is used elsewhere of Paul's fair treatment under Rome.[14] The verb ἐπιτρέπω has a semantic connection to μηδὲν κωλύω. Both are used of the Romans extending certain privileges and liberties to Paul the prisoner (24:23; cf. 27:3). In this semantic context, the adverb ἀκωλύτως (28:31), a derivative of κωλύω, can also be regarded as implying Paul's fair treatment under Rome.[15]

The opening panel of the scene of Paul at Rome (28:16) functions as an introduction. It states the location of the scene and Paul's arrival there. Both the closing (vv. 30–31) and opening panels provide an account of Paul and his living conditions under Roman custody.

The First Meeting of Paul with the Jews in Rome 28:17–22

A Passion Recital Speech of Paul, vv. 17–20

A new paragraph within the text is introduced by the verb ἐγένετο with the temporal phrase μετὰ ἡμέρας τρεῖς. The above construction is used often by Lukan author to begin a new section or paragraph, and is frequently followed by an infinitive as in 28:17, συγκαλέσασθαι.[16]

---

same basis, adding to our comparison similar numerical indicators and prepositional phrases: v. 23 "they came to him (εἰς τὴν) in great numbers (πλείονες)" and v. 30 "he received all (πάντας) who came in to him (πρὸς αὐτόν)." See also Hauser, 16–17. On Dupont's interpretation, see his "La Conclusion," 362–63. On μίσθωμα as "rented lodging" see D. L. Mealand, "The Close of Acts and Its Hellenistic Vocabulary," *NTS* 36 (1990) 583–87.

14. The Roman soldier guarding Paul treated him kindly and "permitted" him to visit his friends at Sidon (27:3); a Roman tribune "allowed" Paul to defend himself in Jerusalem (21:39–40) Agrippa does the same in Caesarea (26:1) in all the above cases Paul is under Roman custody; ἐπιτρέπω in *BDAG*, 384–85.

15. Acts 28:30–31 may be interpreted as the closing account of Paul under Roman custody able to preach and teach quite openly and unhindered by Roman authority. This interpretation does not exclude other factors involved in the meaning of ἀκωλύτως and κωλύω, such as the overcoming of racial and religious obstacles (Luke 9:49–50; 11:52; 18:16; Acts 8:36; 10:47; 11:17); ἀκωλύτως in *BDAG*, 40; κωλύω, 580.

16. The verb ἐγένετο with a temporal phrase beginning a new section or paragraph: Luke 1:5; 2:1; 6:1, 6, 12; 7:11; 9:37, 51; 11:1; 20:1; 22:14, 66; Acts 4:5; 5:7; 8:16; 19:23; 27:39; where ἐγένετο with a temporal phrase provides the setting for a Lukan speech, see: Acts 4:5; 19:23. The verb ἐγένετο followed by a temporal phrase and an infinitive beginning a new section or paragraph: Luke 6:1, 6, 12; 9:51; Acts 4:5; ἐγένετο with the infinitive alone, beginning a new section or paragraph: Luke 3:21; Acts 9:3, 32; 16:16;

It should be mentioned that every paragraph in 28:17–31 begins with a temporal note providing a new temporal setting: v. 17 μετὰ ἡμέρας τρεῖς "after three days"; v. 23 ταξάμενοι . . . ἡμέραν "a set . . . day"; v. 30, διετίαν ὅλην "two whole years."[17]

In this chapter it will be argued that 28:17–20 and vv. 25b–28 are Lukan speeches. Much of the uncertainty regarding the literary forms of the above verses is partially due to the undefined or restrictive criteria employed in determining the identity of the speeches in Acts.[18]

An informative study on the speeches of Acts by E. Jane Via has addressed the above problem and has provided a confirmable criterion for determining what constitutes a Lukan speech.[19]

19:1; 21:1 plus Acts 9:37; 11:26; 14:1; 21:5; 22:6,17; 28:8, in Hauser, *Strukturen*, 12.

17. Dupont points out in his study the numerous temporal notes in Acts 28, for example: in v. 11 "after three months", v. 12 "three days", v. 13 "after one day," v. 14 "seven days", v. 17 "after three days". v. 23 "on an appointed day," v. 30 "two whole years." See also Hauser, *Strukturen*, 17. According to Dupont these temporal notes indicate the stages of the voyage up to the arrival in Rome, "La Conclusion," 362. It can be argued that Acts 28:11 ("after three months") begins a new paragraph in much the same manner as 28:17 ("after three days"). Dupont states that 28:11–15 form a transitional paragraph depicting the voyage from Malta to Rome. The narrative concerning Rome begins with v. 16, (Dupont, 362).

18. The following works provide their own lists of the speeches in Acts but do not define any criterion for identifying speeches: Dibelius, *Studies*, 150; Cadbury, "Speeches in Acts," *BC*, 5:402–27; Schubert, "Final Cycle," 1–16, and "The Place of the Areopagus Speech in the Composition of Acts," *Transitions in Biblical Scholarship* (Chicago, 1968) 235–61. The following studies provide some criteria for identifying speeches but these are too restrictive, e.g., based only on an analysis of the Jesus-kerygma speeches of the first half of Acts (Wilckens), or omitting the Areopagus Speech (17) and the Defense Speeches of Paul (22–26) from consideration: see E. Schweizer, "Concerning the Speeches in Acts," *SLA*, 208–16; Wilckens, *Die Missionsreden der Apostelgeschichte* (1961).

19. Elizabeth Jane Via, "Moses and Meaning in Luke–Acts: A Redaction-Critical Analysis" (1976) 46–92. Although Via's criterion for determining Lukan speeches has been confirmed in our study, her application of it is too restrictive and even contradictory. Via omits Acts 28:25b–28 from her list of speeches yet includes 13:46–47, the latter being a very close parallel to the former in structure and content. Also Cadbury's suggestion of Luke 4:16–30 as a Lukan speech is omitted from Via's discussion. Marion L. Soards states his criteria for identifying speeches (18–19) and identifies both Acts 28:17c-20 and 25b–28 as Paul's Speech to the Roman Jewish Leaders in his *Speeches in Acts* (Westminster John Knox, 1994) 18–22,130–33. Stanley E. Porter confines the speech to vv. 17–20, arguing that Paul's final words (vv. 25–28) "consists almost entirely of an extended quotation of Isa 6:9–10," and both words "were delivered on two separate occasions separated by days," *Paul in Acts* (Hendrickson, 2001) 162.

We agree with Fitzmyer that there are two speeches of Paul in Acts 28 with the first

By analyzing a representative group of speeches from the entire book of Acts unanimously regarded as Lukan speeches (Acts 2:14–36; 3:12–26; 7:2–53; 10:34–43; 17:22–31; 26:2–29) Via was able to deduce a six-fold structural pattern which can be detected to some degree in all the speeches of Acts:[20] (1) an occasion for the speech,[21] (2) an identification of the speaker,[22] (3) an audience for the speech is stated,[23] (4) an introductory statement which is generally a direct address to the stated audience,[24] (5) the body of the speech,[25] and (6) a conclusion usually giving the response of the audience to the speech.[26]

(vv. 17–20) he identifies as a defense and the second (28:25c-28) an indictment, *Acts*, 790. Cadbury saw two separate speeches in his "Speeches," *BC*, 5:403 so also Hauser, *Strukturen*, 49, 158, 233 and Barrett, *Acts*, 2:1236–43, Paul's meetings with the Jews at Rome are two distinct events and not compressed into one, ibid., 1236–37.

20. Within the limits of our study we will not attempt to show how the criterion applies to every speech in Acts (as Via has already adequately done) but will give key examples from major speeches including with them the short speeches in Acts 28 and others crucial to our study.

21. For example: a gathering of crowds out of curiosity (2:12–16; 3:11–12); assemblies of secular or religious authorities/leaders (e.g. Christian leaders, 15:6–7; Jewish leaders, 26:1–3; 28:17; secular officials, 19:35; 24:10); Christian or Jewish communities gathering for worship (13:14–16, 44–46; also Luke 4:16–19); crowds stirred up or called to meet (Acts 19:35; 22:1–2).

22. Usually the speaker is introduced by the narrator immediately before the speech (2:14; 3:12; 13:46; 28:25b) but sometimes the speaker is introduced earlier in the narrative (20:18; 28:17, also Luke 4:16).

23. Jews, Gentiles, Jewish or Gentile Christians (or any combination of these) often including official representatives of these groups (Acts 24:2; 26:2; 28:17).

24. The speeches usually begin with statements of direct address (e.g. Ἄνδρες ἀδελφοί, 1:16; 15:14; 28:17; other statements of address, 2:14; 4:8; 5:35; 7:2; 13:16; 26:2), but not in all cases (20:18; 24:10; 28:25b; also Luke 4:18–27). The introductory statement generally includes a verb signifying the action of speaking (2:14; 3:12; 28:25b).

25. It is difficult to detect common literary and thematic characteristics in the body of the speeches since their content varies in each group of speeches (e.g. the defense speeches of Paul, and speeches by non-Christians). Yet there are certain grammatical and stylistic preferences in the speeches: compound or complex sentences are generally favored (e.g. 13:46; 15:7; 24:10; 28:17b–20, 25b–28), participial phrases are employed often (e.g. 3:12; 5:32; 10:35; 28:17b–20, 25b–28) also the emphatic or demonstrative use of οὗτος is generally used (2:16; 4:10; 5:31; 7:19; 28:20, 28).

26. The response of the audience is often introduced by a participle or participial phrase (e.g. ἀκούσαντες, 2:37; ἀκούοντες, 7:54; 13:48; Luke 4:28; and other participles 4:13; 19:28; 20:36). It will also be argued in this chapter that 28:25a functions as a conclusion to Paul's speech although it is displaced at the beginning (see our study

Applying the above criterion to Acts 28:17–20 and vv. 25b–28, we note that in both speeches a gathering of the Jews at Rome provides the occasion for the speeches (28:17; although in v. 23 a larger group is indicated). Paul the speaker is identified in the first speech earlier in the narrative (v. 16), and immediately before the second address (v. 25b). The audience of the first speech is the prominent Jews of Rome (v. 17), in the second speech it is a great number of Jews (v. 23). The first speech begins with a statement of direct address Ἄνδρες ἀδελφοί (v. 17) while the second speech does not begin with one (v. 25b; see also: 20:18; 24:10). In the body of both speeches, there are compound sentences (vv. 17b–18; v. 28) and participial phrases (vv. 17b–18; vv. 25b–26) and the emphatic use of οὗτος (28:20, 28) is employed. The first speech contains a conclusion giving the response of the audience to the speech in the form of a dialogue, v. 21. Although Paul's second address has no apparent conclusion, one could be deduced from v. 25a immediately preceding the speech:

After Paul made one statement (v. 25b) to the divided Jewish audience (v. 24) the Jews were in disagreement and began leaving (v. 25a); this action of departing probably occurred after Paul's statement on the Gentile mission (28:28; as in Jerualem 22:21–22). It does not appear that the Jews began departing before or during Paul's speech; Luke would *not* have had Paul addressing no audience.[27]

This study on Lukan speeches has taken into consideration that the speech is only one form of direct address used in Luke–Acts: There are prayers, visions and dreams (Acts 1:24–25; 4:24b–30; 9:4–6; 10:3–6; 18:9–10), songs (Luke 1:46–55;1:67–79; 2:28–32), letters (Acts 15:23b–30; 23:26–30), dialogues between individuals (e.g. 1:6, 7; 16:30–31; 22:25–28) and other forms of direct address (e.g. 17:32; 18:6, 14–15; 26:31–32; 28:21–22) employed by the Lukan author.

Thus it has been shown that Acts 28:17–20 and vv. 25b–28 are more than mere forms of direct address but conform to the criteria of Lukan speeches, both occurring in frameworks similar to other speeches

---

of 28:25–28 later in the chapter). The response of the audience is also indicated in the form of a dialogue with the speaker (2:37; 17:32; 24:22; 26:31–32; 28:21).

27. For further elaboration of this argument see our discussion on 28:25 in this chapter.

and each containing similar structural patterns and characteristics of the speeches.[28]

It is in forms of direct address like speeches that the author conveys important themes to his readers/auditors.[29] The important theme of the Gentile mission, for example, is repeated often in Lukan speeches (Luke 4:24–27; Acts 2:21, 39; 3:25–26; 13:46–47; 15:13–19; 28:25–28). In chapter four of our study the significance of the speeches in Acts 28 will be investigated to discover how Luke defends Paul as one like Jesus (28:17–20) who does the work of Jesus (vv. 23–31).

Concerning the nature and identity of Paul's first address at Rome, it has been regarded as an apologetic speech[30] and a pre-trial (before Caesar) or post-trial (recalling Acts 22–26) speech to be classed with Paul's defense speeches in Acts.[31] The latter category seems to provide a more specific (personal) or nuanced (pre- or post-trial) explanation of the former category.

The formula of address in 28:17, Ἄνδρες ἀδελφοί, is used in the defense speeches (22:1; 23:1). The use of the first person singular ἐγω,

28. Our application of the criteria of Lukan speeches basically confirms the list of Cadbury in "Speeches," *BC*, 5:403, which includes Acts 28:17–20 and vv. 25–28 (and 13:46–47) as separate Lukan speeches. Acts 28:17–20 and 28:25–28 are distinguished by the temporal indicators ("after three days" v. 17; "when they had appointed a day" v. 23), each speech has its own audience (prominent Jews v. 17; great numbers of Jews v. 23) and each has a distinct function in the narrative (vv. 17–20 as a passion [instead of trial] recital speech; vv. 25–28 as an apology for the Gentile mission). Each speech meets the criteria of Lukan speech. Our investigation has also shown that Luke 4:16–30 is also a Lukan speech, in support of Cadbury's suggestion (417, 422).

29. For example, Schubert in his "Final Cycles," 2–4, divides up the speeches of Acts into three cycles in which he sees: (1) the main features of Lukan theology developed (Acts 1–5), (2) Lukan theology fully developed in all its aspects (Acts 6–20), and (3) Lukan theology rounded out skillfully and climactically (Acts 21–28).

30. F. F. Bruce, *Speeches in Acts* (London, 1942) 5. Bruce does not explain the category of apologetic speech but he probably associates it with Paul's defense speeches. See also by the same author, *Book of Acts*, 529–30. "Paul delivers an apologetical exposition in which the content of the preceding chapters in Acts is summed up and his innocence affirmed," (341) in H. Van de Sandt, "Acts 28:28: No Salvation for the People of Israel?" *ETL* 70 (1994) 341–58.

31. Schubert, "Final Cycle," 9–10; vv. 17–20, a defense speech of Paul, Fitzmyer, *Acts*, 790; the apologetic speech here is "a more personal defense in view of his approaching trial," Frans Neirynck, "Luke 4:16–30 and the Unity of Luke–Acts," *Unity of Luke–Acts*, ed., J. Verheyden (Leuven, 1999) 389–90.

με, μου is a characteristic "I" style of the defense speeches.[32] The content has parallels to Chaps. 22–26. Paul's plea of being a law-abiding Jew (28:17d, 19b) has some similarities to his defense before the Jerusalem crowd (22:3), Felix (24:12–17), and Festus (25:8–10). The mention of Paul's appeal to Caesar (28:19a) recalls his short speech before Festus (25:10–11; see also 25:25; 26:32). Paul's statement on the hope of Israel (28:20b) is an element in the defense speeches regarding the hope of the resurrection (23:6; 24:15; 26:6–8). The mention of "this chain" recalls Paul's reference to "chains" in his speech before Agrippa (26:29c).

In opposition to the above view, it has been pointed out that in Acts 28:17–20 we have nothing characteristic of a trial setting as in chaps. 22–26. In the defense speeches of Paul, he is brought before the officials as any other prisoner, while in chap. 28 Paul summons the Jews.[33] Also there are no charges stated to which Paul responds (21:38; 24:5–9; 25:16–22). The speech does not identify itself as an apology as in Acts 22:1; 24:10; 25:8; 26:1–2, 24. There is no opening *captatio benevolentiae* as in the defense speeches (24:10; 26:2–3). There is no verdict revealed (24:22; 25:12; 26:30–32).

There are allusions in Acts 28:17–20 which conflict with the data of Acts 21–26. Regarding Paul's arrest, 28:17 states that "I was delivered into the hands of the Romans," yet 21:30–36 indicates that Paul was rescued from a Jewish mob by the Romans, and given a choice Paul willingly remained under Rome, 25:9–11. Concerning Rome, 28:17, 18 states: "The Romans . . . wanted to release me" yet Festus, the Roman, wanted to give Paul to the Jews (25:9). Although the allusions in 28:17–18 conflict with Paul's arrest and trial, they closely conform to the passion of Jesus (Luke 23).

Acts 28:17–20 makes several allusions to the passion of Jesus in Luke's Gospel.[34] The arrests of Jesus and Paul are viewed as being

32. ἐγω, (22:19; 23:1, 6; 24:21; 26:9, 10); με (22:7–21; 23:3; 24:12, 18; 25:10–11); μου (22:1, 24:13, 17, 20; 25:11; 26:3–4); ἐγω εἰμι (22:8; 25:10; 26:15); see Schubert, "Final Cycle," 4; Haenchen, *Acts*, 722.

33. O'Toole, *Christological Climax*, 15. Daniel Marguerat sees Paul (not the Jewish leadership) functioning as a judge in a trial scene where the roles are reversed (28:17–28) "Enigma of the Silent Closing of Acts," *Jesus and the Heritage of Israel*, 295; M. Skinner expands on Marguerat's fictive courtroom reversal here, *Locating Paul*, 166–67.

34. Allusions in Acts 28 to the passion of Jesus have also been pointed out in Walter Radl, *Paulus and Jesus*, 258–65. Also, "the passion of the servant of Christ is described in terms drawn from Christ's own," Barrett, *Acts*, 2:1239. See also Hauser, *Struckturen*,

"delivered into the hands of" Gentiles (Acts 28:17c; Luke 24:7; aorist passive of παραδίδωμι with εἰς τὰς χεῖρας).[35] The Romans "who examined" Jesus and Paul (Acts 28:18; Luke 23:14; aorist participle of αονακρίνω)[36] declared that there was "no cause for death" in them (Acts 28:18b; 13:28; Luke 23:22, αἰτίαν θανάτου; αἴτιον θανάτου).[37]

Luke says of Paul and Jesus that the Romans wanted "to release" them (Acts 28:18a; Luke 23:20; also Acts 3:14, ἀπολύω).[38] In the case of Paul and Jesus, it was because of the opposition of the Jews that each encounter their fate: for Paul, the opposition of the Jews compels him to appeal to Caesar, before whom he meets his fate (Acts 25:6–12; 28:19),[39] for Jesus it was because of the opposition of the Jews that He meets His fate of crucifixion (Luke 23:18–25). As Paul's passion recital includes the hope of the resurrection (Acts 28:20; cf. 23:6; 24:15; 26:6–8) so also does the passion of Jesus (Luke 23:42–43, life after death; 24:6–7, 46–47, passion predictions fulfilled).

To draw a conclusion from the above study, it should be noted that Acts 28:17–20 has some linguistic and formal similarities to Paul's defense speeches without the typical trial setting.

Most of the allusions which conflict with Paul's arrest, however, find close parallels in Jesus' trial and passion. Therefore it would not

161–62; "In the Pauline Passion Narrative," Jack T. Sanders, "The Jewish People in Luke–Acts," *SBL* 1986 *Seminar Papers*, 127 (referring to Paul's arrest, trial, and imprisonment in Jerusalem and Caesarea, although also relevant here, we believe).

35. This motif is repeated again in Luke 9:44; the prediction concerning Paul's fate by Agabus is recited again in the terms of Jesus' passion (Acts 21:11). The use of the παραδίδωμι motif in this manner is probably derived from the Suffering Servant imagery in Isa 53:6, 12 (Septuagint).

36. This activity is also described in the defense chapters of Paul (αονακρίνω 24:8; 25:26).

37. In the trial of Paul a similar phrase: he has done "nothing deserving death" (23:29; 25:11, 25) recalls the trial of Jesus (Luke 23:14, 15). Hauser argues for an ABCDC'B'A' pattern of introverted parallelism (or chiasm) in Paul's words of Acts 28:17–20 with "no cause for death" as D, the central point, also in Talbert, *Reading Acts*, 222. See David R. Bauer, "Chiasm," *NIDB*, 1:587–88; Lund, *Chiasmus in the New Testament* (1942; repr. 1992).

38. Like Pilate (Luke 23:15, 20; Acts 3:14), Agrippa (and Festus) reflects a desire to release Paul (ἀπολύω, 26:32).

39. The idea of Paul's appearance before Caesar as a fateful or divinely-ordained encounter seems especially clear in the theophany of Acts 27:24 "You must stand before Caesar."

contradict the evidence to suggest that Acts 28:17–20 is a passion recital speech defending Paul as one innocent like Jesus.[40] The final words of Stephen function in a similar manner: "I see the heavens opened and the Son of Man [τὸν υἱὸν τοῦ ἀνθρώπου] standing at the right hand [ἐκ δεξιῶν] of God [τοῦ θεοῦ]" (7:56; Luke 22:69 "the Son of Man [ὁ υἱὸς τοῦ ἀνθρώπου] will be seated at the right hand [ἐκ δεξιῶν] of the power of God [τοῦ θεοῦ]"); "Lord Jesus receive my spirit [δέξαι τὸ πνεῦμά μου]" (Acts 7:59; Luke 23:46 "Father, into your hands I commend [παρατίθεμαι] my spirit [τὸ πνεῦμά μου]").[41]

40. In his *Christological Climax*, 22–25, R. F. O'Toole, has established a close parallel relationship between Acts 25–26 and Luke 23:1–25, arguing that the hearing of Jesus before Pilate and Herod Antipas is the model for the hearing of Paul before Festus and Agrippa II (22). In his research he has shown that a real link exists between Paul and Christ. Paul has similar experiences as Christ and carries on the task of Christ (25). This observation will find some confirmation in our study of Acts 28 where we will argue that Luke defends Paul and his ministry at Rome as one like Jesus who does the work of Jesus (see especially our ch. 4, 109–10, 115–20). O'Toole has also demonstrated in his study (156–60) the unifying and climactic significance of the Christology in the account of Paul's defense before Agrippa II (Acts 26). With this insightful study, O'Toole has established a precedent for further research in the Jesus-Paul parallels in Acts. If Luke has used Christological elements in Acts 26 to unify the text and speak climactically to his readers, could not Christological features be found in Acts 28 with similar purposes? See also his "Disciples Continue the Work of Jesus" chap. 3 in *Unity*, 62–94; "Luke's Notion of 'Be Imitators of Me as I am of Christ' in Acts 25–26," *BTB* 8 (1978) 155–61; and his "Parallels between Jesus and His Disciples in Luke–Acts," *BZ* 27 (1983) 195–212; and further studies: Radl, *Paulus und Jesus* (1975); Mattill, "Jesus-Paul," (1975) 15–46; Praeder, "Jesus-Paul" (1984) 23–39 (noting both similarities and differences, 37); D. P. Moessner, "Christ Must Suffer: New Light on the Jesus-Peter, Stephen, Paul Parallels," *NovT* 28 (1986) 220–56. Hauser mentions the Jesus-Paul parallels in Acts 28 but does not explore their significance, *Strukturen*, 138, 161–62, 164–65, 233–34. For the above reasons, we argue that Acts 28:17–20 is a passion recital speech, rather than a trial recital speech, to distinguish it from the forensic speeches. Even the parallels with Acts 21–26 can also be regarded as parallels to a Pauline passion account (J. T. Sanders, "Jewish People," 127).

41. It is hard to deny the numerous parallels between Jesus and Stephen, see: Cadbury, *Making*, 231; O'Toole, "Parallels in Luke–Acts," 195–99, 203–9; Trompf, "Luke and the Death of Paul," 231–32; Moessner, "Jesus-Peter, Stephen, Paul in Luke–Acts," 227–34. We contend that the similar function of these passion statements of both Stephen and Paul (both innocent like Jesus) lend additional support to a passion recital form that we have advocated for Acts 28:17–20. Even the entrusting prayer of Jesus and Stephen (Luke 23:46/Ps 31:5 (Ps 30:5 LXX); Acts 7:59) in light of Jesus' passion, death, and resurrection predictions (Luke 9:22; 18:31–33; 24:6–7) echo faith in God who raises from the dead (Acts 2:27–28, 31; cf. 23:6; 24:15; 26:6–8; 28:20), Green, *Luke*, 826. For noteworthy parallels to the passion of Stephen (and Paul) with the literature of

There are adequate allusions to Acts 22–26 to make 28:17–20 have a similar function as a speech defending Paul and his cause, yet there are sufficient reasons for classing this speech separately from chapters 22–26 (with its forensic setting), as we have stated earlier in this section.

The Reply of the Jews in Rome, vv. 21–22

The response of the Jews following Paul's first speech is in the form of direct discourse, Luke sometimes uses it to conclude a speech, presenting the response of the audience as a dialogue with the speaker.[42] This form serves as a reply to the speech and continues the movement of the narrative.[43]

The function of Acts 28:21, 22 as a reply to Paul's "defense" speech (vv. 17–20) can be argued as follows:

1. In reply to Paul's assertion of being "delivered a prisoner from Jerusalem" the Jews respond, "we have received no letters from Judea about you."
2. Statements on his innocence regarding Judaism, are made by Paul: "though I had done nothing against the people . . . I had no charge to bring against my nation." The Jews confirm these statements to some degree: "none of the brothers coming here has reported or spoken anything evil about you."[44]
3. In response to Paul's declaration, "for this reason therefore I have asked you to see and speak with you" the Jews answer, "we would like to hear from you what you think . . ."
4. The statement of the Jews about this (Christian) sect "that everywhere it is spoken against (ἀντιλέγω)" may be a reply to Paul's remarks about "when the Jews opposed (ἀντιλέγω)" him.[45]

martyrs and martyrdom in Mediterranean antiquity, see Talbert, *Reading Acts* (2005) 60–68, including the martyr's hope of salvation, 65.

42. As an earnest request, 2:37; an inquisitive reply, 17:32; 28:21–22; or an official statement, 24:22; 26:31–32 (not in dialogue with Paul the speaker).

43. For direct replies to speeches, see 2:37 ("what shall we do?"), 24:22 ("I will make my decision . . .").

44. The statement by the prominent Jews about "none having spoken evil of Paul" (paraphrase) may also be a reply to Paul's statement on those Jews who opposed him (v. 19).

45. What is investigated above is not an attempt to solve the difficult historical

There is also some evidence for regarding 28:21–22 as having a preparatory function for Paul's second meeting with the Jews, vv. 23–28. In the text it is noted that the interest of the Jews concerning Paul's views results in their coming to hear him on a set day:

The Jews reply: "We desire to hear from you what your views are . . . concerning this sect" and this is followed by the next scene where "they came to him at his lodging in large numbers" to hear Paul preach.

Luke presents the interest of the Jews to hear Paul (v. 22) as in some way connected with their ignorance about Paul ("we have received no letters from Judea about you" v. 21) and from their lack of direct acquaintance with Christianity ("for concerning this sect we know that everywhere it is spoken against" v. 22). It is the ignorance of the Jews regarding Paul and Christianity as well as their interest in hearing Paul's teaching that provides the occasion for Paul's preaching activity.[46]

A similar pattern can be detected in Acts 17. Before Paul begins his sermon at Athens, the Greeks display ignorance regarding Paul and Christianity (17:18, 20a) and reveal an interest in hearing his teaching (v. 20b) both of which provide the occasion for Paul's sermon. This inquisitive attitude (which is evident in 28:20–21) occurs in other narratives preceding a speech.[47]

Therefore on the basis of other Lukan parallels and from within the text itself, the direct discourse in 28:21–22 can be seen to have a dual function: as an audience response to Paul's first address and as an occasion for Paul's second address.[48]

---

problems of the reply of the Jews here (vv. 21–22) but merely an attempt to show how these Lukan statements might function as an audience response to a Lukan speech (vv. 17–20). In the course of his two-volume work, Luke may be criticized at points for historical or literary inexactitude, yet it will be argued within this pericope that he has composed a thoughtful literary work where all parts function together for a purpose.

46. See Haenchen's statement on the function of Acts 28:21–22 to produce the missionary situation in vv. 23–28, *Acts*, 730. Talbert supports our point here with an ABA' pattern: "A—v. 21 Roman Jews have received neither letters nor oral reports form Judea with negative comments about Paul personally. B—v. 22a The Jewish leaders would like to hear Paul present his views. A'—v. 22b Roman Jews know the Messianist sect of Judaism is denounced everywhere." Talbert, *Reading Acts*, 222, the central member (B) indicates the main point.

47. Acts 2:12; 4:7; 13:42; 25:22; also an inquisitive attitude before a narrated sermon like 28:23, e.g. 8:34–35, Philip and the eunuch.

48. Dupont in his article in Acts 28, regards vv. 17–20 and vv. 21–22 as two parallel panels of a larger diptych comprised of 28:17–22 and vv. 23–25a. Dupont, "La

The Second Meeting of Paul with the Jews in Rome, 28:23–28

A Summary Statement on Paul's Preaching, 28:23[49]

A new paragraph in the text begins with a different temporal setting: Ταξάμενοι . . . ἡμέραν, parallel to the temporal notes in v. 17 μετὰ

Conclusion," 367–68. Dupont attempts to establish a symmetry between vv. 17–20 and vv. 21–22 on the basis of common constructions: (1) a negative with a principle verb, (2) a principle verb accompanied by an indicator of origin, (3) expressions with similar denotations. In point one (1), Dupont breaks up the grammatical syntax in attempting to compare a compound sentence with a simple sentence. For example, in v. 17 the principle verb παραδίδωμι ("I was delivered into the hands of the Romans") is combined with the negative οὐδὲν ("I have done nothing against the people") to form a parallel with the simple sentence in v. 21 "we have received (ἐδεξάμεθα) no (οὔτε) letters concerning you." Such constructions are not easily recognized by many as symmetrical. In point two (2) Dupont makes a noteworthy comparison of v. 17 "I was delivered from Jerusalem" with v. 21 "we received from Judea." We have used this comparison to show vv. 21–22 function as a reply to what was said in vv. 17–20. In point three (3) Dupont's wants to show that "hope of Israel" v. 20 and "this sect" are both designations for Christianity. It is clear that the "hope of Israel" (28:20) is connected with the messianic hope of the resurrection for Paul (23:6; 24:15; 26:6–8), and "this sect" in 28:22 is the derogatory label given it by the Roman Jews. As a result, the symmetry in Dupont's construction is noteworthy, although an explanation for its function in the text is lacking. We also wish that some analogous constructions of symmetry would have been shown in other passages of Luke–Acts. Hauser provides a comparison chart of vv. 17–20 and vv. 21–22 following Dupont, with little additional explanation concerning its relevance or significance, *Struckturen*, 25–29. We have argued in this section, that vv. 21–22 have a dual function as a reply to Paul's "defense" speech (vv. 17–20), perhaps the symmetry helps here to establish a preparatory function for Paul's missionary situation in 28:23–28 (its primary function). These two roles have been established on the basis of internal evidence within the text and on the basis of parallel constructions in Acts (2:12; 4:7; 13:42; 17:13–20; 25:22). The above argument concerning the dual role of vv. 21–22 with regard to the speeches in Acts 28, is an example of the importance of first defining the literary forms in the text before determining their literary function.

49. There are various types of summaries in Luke–Acts such as summaries on church growth and stability, the progress of the word, and the growth and development of John and Jesus. In this chapter we will argue that preaching summaries are a distinct type of summary statements (which include several of the passages in C. Turner's arbitrary "progress of the word" summaries). It will be shown that these preaching summaries are characterized by such witnessing terminology as: preaching, teaching, bearing witness, persuading. The common message conveyed by this terminology is that in the divinely-willed events of Christ's life, suffering, death, and resurrection, God's kingdom has dawned for the salvation of all nations. See Hauser, *Struckturen*, 112–18. On the preaching and message of both Jesus and his followers (which include our summaries), see also O'Toole, *Unity*, 75–79.

ἡμέρας τρεῖς and v. 30 διετίαν ὅλην, and a reference to Paul's living situation: τὴν ξενίαν parallel to the notes on Paul's habitation in v. 16 μένειν καθ' ἑαυτὸν and v. 30 Ἐνέμεινεν . . . ἐν ἰδίῳ μισθώματι. The account of Paul witnessing to the Jews at Rome (28:23b) constitutes a preaching summary used often in Luke–Acts with a variety of witnessing terminology.[50]

These narrated statements characterized by such phrases as preaching and teaching about Jesus, proving from Scripture that he is the Christ, and proclaiming the gospel, generally presuppose the contents of the Jesus-kerygma speeches in Acts (2:14–36; 3:11–26; 4:8–12; 10:34–43; 13:16–41).[51] It is in these speeches that we learn what Luke means by preaching Jesus, proving from Scripture that Jesus is the Christ, and proclaiming the gospel.

In the Pauline mission, it is from Paul's sermon in the synagogue of Pisidan Antioch (13:16–41) that Luke's readers/auditors could understand the summary statements of Paul preaching in the synagogues (17:1–3; 18:4–5; 19:8).[52] In the third gospel, it is from the sermon of

50. When we are talking about "witnessing terminology" we are not restricting our study to the technical usage of μαρτύρομαι (and equivalents) as the apostolic witness to the risen Christ, see O'Toole, *Christological Climax*, 100–104. This technical usage of apostolic witness to Christ should be qualified by the following data: (1) The usage of "bearing witness" is not restricted to testifying of Jesus Christ (Acts 8:25; 20:24; 28:23). (2) The function of "bearing witness" is not restricted to the apostles and Paul. Stephen is called Christ's witness (μάρτυρός, Acts 22:20). The statement in the persecution pericope of Luke 21:12–19, "this will be a time for you to bear testimony" (μαρτύριον, v. 13) does not seem to apply only to the apostles. A broader audience is indicated in the pericope, Luke 20:45; 21:5, 37–38; see in O'Toole, *Christological Climax*, 14, where Luke 12:11–12 is applied to Christians in general.

51. For the preaching summaries in Luke's gospel, it will be shown that they generally presuppose the contents of Jesus' sermon at Nazareth (Luke 4:16–30), which is the only complete speech of Jesus in the Third Gospel.

52. There is no reason for assuming that Paul's speech to the Greeks in Athens (17:22–31) is presupposed in his preaching summaries to Gentiles throughout his mission. Acts 17:22–31 (and the related speech in 14:15–17) are primarily connected with Paul's confrontation with true "pagans" and idol worship. The Gentiles in Paul's mission are generally connected with the synagogues as proselytes or God-fearers. This assertion may explain why there is no apparent distinction in the witnessing terminology to Jews and Gentiles: both hear the word of God/the Lord (18:6–11; 19:8–10), both hear Christ and the kingdom proclaimed and taught (28:23, 30–31). See Wilson *Gentiles* 215–18; and Irina Levinskaya, "Diaspora Setting," *Book of Acts*, 5:19–49 proselytes, 51–126 God-fearers; see also M. C. de Boer, "God-Fearers in Luke–Acts" in *Luke's Literary Achievement* (Sheffield, 1995) 50–71.

Jesus at Nazareth that Luke's readers/auditors could understand the summary statements of Jesus' teaching and preaching in the synagogue (4:15, 31–32, 44; 13:10).

In order to better understand the function and significance of the preaching summaries in Luke–Acts, it is now appropriate to examine in both Acts 28:23b and v. 31, the witnessing terminology (πείθω, διαμαρτύρομαι, κηρύσσω, and διδάσκω), the objects of witness (τὴν βασιλείαν τοῦ θεοῦ, and Ἰησοῦ Χριστοῦ) and the witnessing procedure (e.g., appealing to "the law of Moses and the prophets"). The term πείθω (28:23) is used several times in preaching summaries. Paul persuades (or attempts to persuade) others: concerning the kingdom of God (19:8), concerning Jesus (28:23), to remain in the grace of God (13:43), or to become Christians (26:28, cf. 18:4).

In Acts there is not only persuading (πείθω) about Jesus (28:23), but testifying of him (διαμαρτύρομαι, 10:42; 18:5; 20:21; 23:11; μαρτύριον 4:33). There is also teaching (διδάσκω 5:42; 18:25; 28:31), speaking boldly (παρρησιάζομαι, 9:27–28; 18:26)[53] preaching (κηρύσσω 8:5; 9:20; cf. Luke 8:39), and proclaiming the good news of Jesus Christ (εὐαγγελίζομαι, Acts 5:42; 8:12, 35; 10:36; 11:20) in Luke's two-volume work.

The witnessing term of "testifying" (διαμαρτύρομαι 28:23) is employed by Luke to testify of: Jesus Christ (Acts 4:33; 1.1. μαρτύριον, 10:42; 18:5; 20:21; 23:11), the word of the Lord (8:25), the gospel of the grace of God (20:24), and the kingdom of God (28:23).

Concerning the concept of the kingdom of God (28:23), Christ and his followers testify to it (28:23), preach it (κηρύσσω) Luke 8:1; 9:2; Acts 20:25; 28:31), proclaim the gospel of it (εὐαγγελίζομαι, Luke 4:43; 8:1; 16:16; Acts 8:12), announce it (διαγγέλλω Luke 9:60), speak concerning it (λαλέω Luke 9:11; Acts 1:3), and try to persuade others about the kingdom of God (πείθω Acts 19:8).

Luke appeals to Moses and the prophets with regard to Jesus Christ (Acts 28:23; also: 26:22, 23; Luke 24:27, 44–46) in support of Christianity (Acts 24:14; cf. Luke 16:29–31 repentance), and as confir-

53. The terms παρρησιάζομαι and παρρησία (28:31) function as a boldness motif, speaking boldly: (1) about Jesus Acts 2:29; 4:13; 26:26 (12–23); 28:31; (2) in the name of Jesus 9:27, 29; (3) the word of God 4:29, 31; (4) with regard to proclaiming the Kingdom of God, 28:31; (5) of the Gentile mission 13:46; 26:26 with vv. 12–23. See also discussion in Hauser, *Struckuren*, 142–44.

mation of world missions (Luke 24:44–49; Acts 26:22–23). He refers to the prophets as fulfilled, in regard to the passion, death, and resurrection of Jesus (Luke 18:31–33; 24:26–27, 44–49; Acts 3:18; 10:43; 13:27; 26:22–23), and concerning the Gentile mission (Luke 2:32; Acts 13:47; 26:22–23; 28:25–28). Luke also refers to the fulfillment of "Scripture" concerning Jesus Christ (Luke 22:37; 24:27, 44–49; Acts 8:35; 17:2, 3; 18:28) and the universal mission (Luke 24:45–47).

It can be seen that the preaching summaries of Luke–Acts take on a variety of terms and themes, yet from an analysis of the above data a common message is conveyed: that in the divinely-willed events of Christ's life, suffering, death, and resurrection-exaltation, God's reign has dawned for the salvation of Jew and Gentile, and that this message is to be taught and proclaimed to all nations.

Preaching summaries (*Predigtsummarien*) function as reports of preaching activity/speeches (*Redeberichte*) in summarized form. They give the narrative of Luke–Acts a continuity and a general line of development. There is a progression of proclamation and a continuity of witness beginning with Jesus (Luke 4:43–44; 8:1; 9:11; 20:1), continued by his disciples (Luke 9:6; 10:8–11; cf. 8:39), carried on by the early church (Acts 5:42; 8:12) and brought to a culmination by Paul (9:27–29; 15:35; 17:2–3; 18:5; 19:8; 28:23, 30–31). The message of God's reign in the deeds of Jesus is taught and proclaimed in Galilee and Judea (Luke 4:31, 44), Jerusalem (Luke 19:47–20:1; Acts 5:42; 9:26, 29), Samaria (Acts 8:4–5, 25), the coastal regions (8:40), Antioch (15:35), Asia Minor (13:49; 14:1; 19:8, 10), Greece (17:2–3; 18:5, 11) and Rome (28:23, 30–31).

While all preaching summaries make some contributions to the movement of the narrative, not all preaching summaries function as introductions or conclusions, dividing or connecting scenes, and summarizing the contents of adjacent narratives.

This latter group of summaries (also called "stops" or "progress reports") has been investigated by C. H. Turner, H. J. Cadbury, M. Dibelius, P. Benoit, J. Fitzmyer, and B. Rosner.[54] These summary statements per-

54. Turner, "Chronology," *HDB*, 1:421; Cadbury, "Summaries," *BC*, 5:392–402; and *Making* 58–59; Dibelius, *Studies*, 9–10, 127–28; Benoit, "Some Notes on the 'Summaries' in Acts 2, 4, 5," in *Jesus and the Gospel* (1973) 1:95–103; Fitzmyer catalogues as "minor summaries" Acts 1:14 (upper room communion?); 6:7; 9:31; 12:24; 16:5; 19:20; 28:30–31 but does not include here the summaries of Luke's Gospel (4:14–15; 4:31–32,40–41; 6:17–19; 8:1–3; 19:47–49; 21:27–38), although they also serve as signals to the reader of the progress of God's word in the narrative, his "major summaries" all occur in Acts

tain to a variety of topics: church growth and stability, the progress of the word, and the growth and development of John and Jesus.

The above literary form includes our category of preaching summaries (progress of the word) but is concerned only with those summaries which function either as introductions or conclusions, dividing or connecting scenes, and summarizing their contents.[55] This distinction between preaching summaries that introduce or conclude a scene (as a generalization of it) and those that do not, characterizes the difference between Acts 28:30–31 and v. 23. Both passages report the witnessing terminology and contribute to the development of the narrative, yet only vv. 30–31 concludes the scene with a general summary of Paul's activities in Rome. For more further explanations, see our discussion of vv. 30–31 later in this chapter.

The Mixed Response of the Jews, 28:24

The response to the narrated summary of Paul's preaching is that of belief/unbelief: "And some were persuaded ἐπείθοντο by that which was said (referring to Paul's preaching in v. 23) while others disbelieved ἠπίστουν." The reaction of belief/unbelief has close affinities with the responses of other summary preaching accounts and speeches.[56] Luke generally includes a reaction from his designated audience following a speech or a preaching summary, to show the effects of the proclaimed word on its hearers.

Although v. 24 serves as a response to the preaching summary of Paul (v. 23b) it also provides the occasion for Paul's second address (along with v. 23a):[57] there is a gathering of Jewish leaders who are di-

---

2–5, are longer, and thematically related to one another (2:42–47; 4:32–35; 5:12–16) *Acts*, 97–8; Brian Rosner (correctly) omits 1:14 from Fitzmyer's list of minor summaries, and includes in a note Acts 2:47; 4:4; 5:16; 11:24; 18:11 as possible summaries "Progress of the Word," in *Witness to the Gospel* (Eerdmans, 1998) 221–2 (216–33, entire chap). Although it is not included in his list of "minor summaries," Fitzmyer regards 28:23 as "a Lucan summary of Paul's testimony in Rome," *Acts*, 794.

55. Luke 4:14–15, 31–32, 44; 8:1; 9:6; 13:10, 22; 19:47; 20:1; 21:37–38; 24:27; Acts 4:33 (32–37); 5:42; 8:4–5, 25, 40; 9:22; 11:19–26; 12:24; 14:1; 15:35; 18:4, 11; 19:8–10, 20; 28:30–31.

56. Responses to preaching summaries: belief, Acts 8:12–13; belief/unbelief, 14:1, 2, 4; 17:4–5; 18:6, 8; 19:9–10; responses to speeches: unbelief 7:54, 57; belief/unbelief, 13:42–43, and 48, 50; 17:32, 34.

57. The occasion for the speech is the first of our six-fold structural pattern of Lukan

vided over Paul's teaching. There are similar occasions in other speeches. The occasion for Peter's speech at the Jerusalem Council (15:7–11) is a gathering of Christian leaders who are divided over an issue (vv. 5–7). In Pisidian Antioch, the occasion for Paul's first apologetic speech on the Gentile mission (13:46–47) is a gathering of Jews who are opposing the teaching of Paul and Barnabas (v. 45).[58] Before Felix, the occasion for Paul's defense speech (24:10–21) is in a secular assembly where the Jews have brought charges against him (vv. 5–9).

In all of the above cases the occasion for the speech occurs in a setting where there is division or opposition. This observation is not unlike the occasion for Paul's second apologetic speech on the Gentile mission (28:25b–28), where there is a gathering of divided Jews: some who "were persuaded by what he said, while others disbelieved" (v. 24). As in Pisidian Antioch, this situation provides an occasion for Paul to address the unbelief of the Jews and make his defense for the Gentile mission (13:46–47; 28:25b–28).

In the scene at Rome it was the division of belief/unbelief among the Jews (v. 24) that prompted Paul's pronouncement of hardening upon them (vv. 26–27), the disagreement and departure of the Jews (v. 25a) only confirmed Paul's statements.[59] Despite the accounts of large numbers of Jewish believers in Jerusalem (2:41, 47; 4:4; 6:7; 15:5; 21:20) Paul generally encountered division and opposition in his work among

---

speeches, for e.g. assemblies of Christian leaders, 15:6, 7; assemblies of secular authorities, 24:10; Christian communities gathered for worship, 13:44–45; crowds stirred to action, 19:35. In Acts 28:17–24, Robert Brawley sees polarities in the narrative between Paul with his message who stands alongside the believing Jews (principle axis) over against the unbelieving Jews who reject Paul's message (polemical axis), *Centering on God* (1990) 101–2.

58. The above parallel is especially significant since it will be shown that Acts 13:46–47 and 28:25b–28 are similar in form, structure, and content as apologetic speeches for the Gentile mission.

59. As indicated by the terms: ἀπιστέω, ἀσύμφωμνος, ἀπολύω, (vv. 24–25a) the emphasis is on unbelief (or at least indifference) of the Jews at Rome (especially in view of 28:26–27/Isa 6:9–10). It may even be argued from the above data that those who "were persuaded" did not continue in that attitude, Haenchen, *Acts* 723–24. Barrett, however, sees πείθεσθαι as the opposite of ἀπιστεῖν, "that is, it means *to believe* . . . Luke is at pains not to represent all Jews as unbelieving. He refers first to those who were persuaded by Paul's message," *Acts*, 2:1244; so also Bock, *Acts* 754; David Ravens, *Luke and the Restoration of Israel* (Sheffield, 1995) 239.

the Jews of the diaspora (13:45, 50; 14:2, 4, 19; 17:5, 13; 18:5–6, 12; 19:8–9).

An Apologetic Speech for the Gentile Mission, 28:25–28

Even though Paul's speech has no apparent conclusion it has been argued that v. 25a functions like one: "and since they were in disagreement with one another, they left."[60] The aorist participle in the phrase εἰπόντος τοῦ Παύλου ῥῆμα ἓν functions as a circumstantial participle of time and probably indicates action which precedes the activity of the main verb ἀπελύοντο ("they began leaving"): "and because they were in disagreement (over Paul's "one statement") they began leaving, after Paul made this one statement . . ." (AT). It does not appears that the Jews departed before or during Paul's speech since Luke never has Paul addressing no audience.[61] Parallels in Acts can be provided (AT) showing the action of the participle preceding the action of the main verb as argued in v. 25 (ἀπελύοντο, εἰπόντος).

- And after they carried her out (ἐξενέγκαντες aorist participle) they buried her (ἔθαψαν aorist) Acts 5:10. The action of carrying Sapphire out necessarily preceded her burial.

60. The participial phrase ἀσύμφωμνοι δὲ ὄντες is in the historical present (cf. Acts 8:36; 10:11,27) ὄντες functions as a circumstantial participle of cause: "because or since they were . . ." The verb ἀπελύοντο is an ingressive imperfect with accent on the beginning of the action: "because they were in disagreement . . . they began leaving." The participial phrase explains why they began leaving: "because they were in disagreement." The question of why they were in disagreement is not because of Paul's preaching (v. 23) for we are already given the concluding audience's response to that account, (see our discussion on v. 24) it is rather a result of Paul's statement of hardening: "after Paul made this one statement . . . (quoting Isa 6:9 and announcing the mission to the Gentiles). Frank Stagg makes a similar argument for the above position, *Acts* 265 and "Unhindered Gospel," 462. See also in support of above, M. Culy and M. Parson, *Acts* (2003) 545, contra Barrett, *Acts*, 2:1244.

61. Luke in almost all cases has a conclusion to his speeches with a response from a given audience: Acts 2:37; 4:13; 7:54; 10:44; 13:42, 48; 17:32; 19:28, 41; 20:36; 21:20; 26:30–32; 28:21.

The western reviser was apparently aware of this literary custom of Luke and therefore added his own conclusion to the speech καὶ ταῦτα αὐτοῦ εἰπόντος ἀπῆλθον οἱ Ἰουδαῖοι, πολλὴν ἔχοντες ἐν ἑαυτοῖς συζήτησιν ("and when he had said these words, the Jews departed and had great reasoning among themselves"). See Metzger, *Textual Commentary*, 444; Epp, *Theological Tendency*, 114–15.

- And after they shook off (ἐκτιναξάμενοι aorist participle) the dust from their feet against them (in Pisidian Antioch) they came (ἦλθον aorist) to Iconium 13:51. Luke would not have Paul and Barnabas doing both actions simultaneously, their action against the Antiochenes had to precede their arrival in Iconium.

- After he received (λαβὼν aorist participle) this order, he put (ἔβαλεν aorist) them into the inner prison, 16:24. The jailor put Paul and Silas in prison only after he received the order to do so.

On the basis of syntax and parallel constructions in Acts, it would not be inconsistent with Luke's thinking to render ἀπελύοντο, εἰπόντος (28:25): "they began leaving, after (Paul) said . . ." (AT). This translation would therefore give 28:25a the typical function of a conclusion to a Lukan speech (although occurring before rather than afterward).

To have 28:25a follow v. 28 (salvation to the Gentiles) is in keeping with the fierce reaction of the Jews of Jerusalem to Paul's statements on the Gentile mission (22:21, 22) and even the strong reaction of the Jews at Nazareth to Jesus' announcement of God's favor upon certain Gentiles (Luke 4:25–29). Luke has probably displaced v. 25a for dramatic effect, to let Paul have the last word on the matter:[62]

It has already been argued that Acts 28:25b–28 meets our criterion of a Lukan speech.[63] It is yet to be shown that vv. 25b–28 function as an apologetic speech on the Gentile mission. To establish this assertion we will compare the text with Acts 13:46–47, a parallel speech on the mission to the Gentiles.[64]

62. Concerning v. 25, Dupont in his study on Acts 28, "La Conclusion," appears to contradict himself. He first regards the Jews as already departed ("ant deja quitté la scene," 364) arguing that this is Luke's way of envisioning a larger audience (addressing the Lukan readers/auditors). Later Dupont states that vv. 23–27 are to be understood as a developing preparation for the decisive response that Paul makes to the Jews in v. 28 ("que Paul fait aux Juifs dans le v. 28," 369 see also: 372 top line). How could this latter assertion be possible if the Jews have already left the scene as Dupont has earlier stated? The message, of course, is for both the Jewish audience at Rome and the Lukan readers/auditors.

63. It should be pointed out here that several terms in vv. 25b, 28 are employed in Lukan speeches: for example, ἀκούω, Acts 2:22; 3:22; 7:2; 15:13; 22:1; γνωστός, 2:14; 4:10; 13:38; and πνεῦμα with λέγω or μαρτυρέω, 1:16; 4:8; 5:32; 11:12; 20:23.

64. In chapter 3 other similar missionary encounters will be investigated along with

In a comparison of Acts 13:46–47 and 28:25b–28 it is noted that both are short speeches which occur in a designated geographical location with a temporal setting: Antioch of Pisidia on the sabbath (13:14, 44); Rome on a set day (28:16, 23). Both begin in a missionary situation where Paul has already preached the Jews first (13:43–44; 28:23). In the speeches both are introduced by verbs of speaking in the aorist participle form (παρρησιάσμενοί 13:46; εἰπόντος 28:25b). Both speeches are prompted by an unfavorable response by unbelieving Jews (13:45–46; 28:24b). Both contain Paul's statement on turning to the Gentiles (13:46 with Barnabas; 28:28). Both speeches include a quotation from the book of Isaiah, Acts 13:47/Isa. 49:6; Acts 28:26–27/Isa. 6:9–10 in support of the mission to the Gentiles.[65] The context of both speeches

Acts 13 and 28 (14:1–7; 17:2–5; 18:4–11; 19:8–10). We are restricting our comparison here to Acts 13 and Acts 28 because only these share the same form as Lukan speeches. Both Acts 13:46–47 and 28:25b–28 fulfill our criterion as Lukan speeches: an occasion (13:44–46; 28:17, 23), identification of the speaker (13:46; 28:25), a stated audience (13:44–46; 28:17) use of compound and complex sentences in the body of the speeches (13:46; 28:25b, 28), an audience response at the conclusion (13:48; 28:25a).

65. The Isaianic quote as used in Acts 13 speaks explicitly of a Gentile mission: "I have set you to be a light to the Gentiles" (Acts 13:47/Isa 49:6). The quote from Isa 6 used in Acts 28, functions as the occasion for the Gentile mission: "You (unreceptive Jews) shall indeed hear (ἀκούω) but never understand . . ." (28:26–27/ Isa 6:9–10, AT), "therefore (οὖν) let it be known to you that (ὅτι) this salvation has been sent to the Gentiles, they will hear" (ἀκούω) Acts 28:28/Isa 40:5). "The emphasis . . . is on hearing," Ravens, *Restoration* 241; an important criterion for inclusion in God's people (Acts 3:22–24; Johnson, *Acts*, 70, 74). "Paul concludes using the particle οὖν 'therefore' as he ends his words to those who have come to him. It connects what follows in the object clause (introduced by ὅτι) to his quotation of Isaiah," Fitzmyer, *Acts*, 795–96. "Jewish unbelief fulfills Scripture . . . and justifies the Gentile mission," Evans, *To See and Not Perceive*, 126; Evans states "He [Luke] is trying to show, on empirical and scriptural grounds, that the Gentile mission is legitimate, not that the Jewish mission will be terminated," Craig Evans and James Sanders, *Luke and Scripture*, 209; "from the middle of chapter 21 to through the middle of 28 . . . Paul is a prisoner mainly engaged in self-defense. At Acts 28:23 he resumes his missionary career, which is still going at full force when the book concludes," Pervo, *Dating Acts*, 401 n. 283.

On external inverted parallelism in Isa 6:10, also called chiasm (highlighting spiritual blindness), see Norman Gottwald, "Poetry, Hebrew," in *IDB*, 3:833 and David Bauer, "Chiasm," in *NIDB*, 1:587–88; John Breck, *Shape of Biblical Language* (St. Vladimir's Seminary, 1994) 30–31; Hauser, *Strukturen*, 38. In Acts 28:25b–28, however, Luke places greater emphasis on "hearing" (ἀκούω, ἀκοή vv 26–28; cf., 2:22; 3:22; 7:2; 15:13; 22:1) although allusions in 28:28 to Isa 40:5 "all flesh shall see"(Luke 3:6 ὁράω) are there (see discussion above). On the use of the Septuagintal text of Isa 6:9–10 in Acts 28, see Haenchen, *Acts*, 724; Conzelmann, *Acts*, 227; Pao, *Acts*, 102–3.

indicate the success of the mission to the Gentiles with a summary statement, (Acts 13:49; 28:30–31).[66]

The pattern most characteristic in these speeches as apologies for the Gentile mission is that of the (1) unbelief of the Jews and (2) the turning to the Gentiles:

1. "since you thrust it (the word of God) from you and judge yourselves unworthy of eternal life,
2. behold (ἰδοὺ) we turn to the Gentiles" (13:46).

1. "You shall indeed hear but never understand . . . for this people's heart has grown dull . . . (28:26–27)
2. Let it be known (γνωστὸν) then that this salvation of God has been sent to the Gentiles . . ." (28:28).[67]

Both speeches are situated at crucial points of Paul's missionary encounters: at the beginning of his missionary journeys (13:46–47) and at the end (28:25–28). The former speech sets the tone of Paul's missionary encounters with the Jews, the latter speech (it will be shown) seems to provide a climactic conclusion to the encounters in Acts.

From the above comparisons we note that both Acts 13:46–47 and 28:25b–28 have similar formal, structural, and thematic features. Both

66. It should be noted that only 28:30–31 is a concluding summary of a narrative. In Acts 13 although a mission to the Gentiles is a success, v. 49, more trouble follows with the Jews there, v. 50, yet the whole scene at Antioch of Pisidia ends on a positive note. See Acts 13:52 which parallels Luke 24:52–53 and contributes to our understanding of Acts 28:30–31. These parallels will be investigated in chapter 3 of this study.

67. Acts 28:25b–28 is an apologetic speech for the mission to the Gentiles with v. 28 (salvation to the Gentiles) as the concluding exhortation of the pronouncement upon the unreceptive Jews (vv. 26–27 chiastic focus on spiritual blindness) with v. 25b as the opening panel. Because of the spiritual blindness and deafness of these Jews (vv. 26–27), salvation has been sent to the Gentiles ("all flesh will see" Isa 40:5; Luke 3:6) who will listen (v. 28). On five functions of Scripture detected in Luke–Acts (e.g., christological, apologetic) see Evans and Sanders, *Luke and Scripture*, 209–11.

Near the end of Jesus' speech at Nazareth (Luke 4) the germinal thoughts of (2) God's favor upon the Gentiles are found (God's benefits extended to the widow of Sidon v. 26 and Naaman the Syrian v. 27). (1) The unbelief of the Jews there is at least implied in the speech ("no prophet is acceptable in his own country" v. 24) and certainly demonstrated in the fierce audience reaction at the conclusion (vv. 28–29). The relationship of Luke 4:16–30 and Acts 28 will be further investigated in chapter 3 of this study, 91–96.

speeches occur in similar contexts and have a common concern: to justify the a mission to the Gentiles.[68]

Closing Panel: A Final Summary on Paul and His Preaching Activity, 28:30–31

A new paragraph begins with a new temporal notation: ἐνέμεινεν δὲ διετίαν ὅλην v. 30 (parallel to the temporal notes in vv. 17 and 23) and a reference to Paul's living condition: ἐν ἰδίῳ μισθώματι, v. 30 (parallel to vv. 16 and 23). The closing verses about Paul's witnessing in Rome "to all who came to him" (vv. 30–31) contain a Lukan preaching summary having close parallels with the account in v. 23b:

> Διαμαρτυρόμενος τὴν βασιλείας τοῦ θεοῦ
> πείθων τε αὐτοὺς περὶ τοῦ Ἰησοῦ . . . (v. 23)
>
> κηρύσσων τὴν βασιλείαν τοῦ θεοῦ καὶ
> διδάσκων τὰ περὶ τοῦ κυρίου Ἰησοοῦ Χριστοῦ . . . (v. 31)

Both passages are concerned with the message of the "kingdom of God" and "Jesus" and indicate a variety of witnessing terminology (persuading, testifying, preaching, and teaching) to convey the message. As discussed in the study of 28:23, both passages contain preaching summaries, reflecting a common message, presupposing the contents of the Jesus-kerygma speeches, and providing the narrative of Acts with a continuity and progression. Although both Acts 28:23 and 30–31

68. First, we regard this defense of Paul's mission to the Gentiles as a way to legitimize the inclusion of Gentiles in the people of God, the faithful remnant of Israel, and thus provide a sense of Gentile self-identity with Israel's Scriptures. Luke's intertextual use of Scripture is not limited to an apologetic purpose and concerns inclusion ("all" Acts 28:30) not exclusion. God is taking from among the Gentiles a "people for his name" who call upon God (15:14–18) and hear (ἀκούω) the prophet like Moses (Jesus) whom God has raised up (3:22–24; 7:37), Johnson, *Acts*, 70, 74,129–30, 136–38, 264, 272. See also the intertextual focus on eschatological fulfillment rather than concern for the transition from Jews to Gentiles, in Denova, *Things Accomplished among Us*, 16–21, 38–40. Second, in describing Acts 13:46–47 and 28:25b–28 as apologetic speeches for a mission to the Gentiles we also do not wish to have them classed with the defense speeches of Paul which are identified in Acts as "apologies" (22:1 ἀπολογία; 24:10; ἀπολογέομαι; 25:8; 26:1–2, 24). Acts 13:46–47 and 28:25b–28 are speeches which function specifically to defend or justify the mission to the Gentiles, a mission prompted by rejection from unreceptive Jews and regarded as a fulfillment of scriptural prophecy, Evans, *To See and Not Perceive*, 126, 214 n. 31.

function as preaching summaries, only vv. 30–31 serve as a concluding summary of Paul's activities at Rome.

To understand the form and function of such concluding summaries as 28:30–31, the well-known "progress reports" of C. H. Turner[69] will be analyzed (Acts 6:7; 9:31; 12:24; 16:5; 19:20; 28:31) including with them additional texts generally regarded as summaries by scholars (Luke 1:80; 2:40; 2:52; Acts 2:41–47; 4:32–37; 5:12–16; 11:19–26).[70] The content of these summaries is varied: church growth and stability (Acts 2:41–47; 4:32–37; 5:12–16; 9:31; 11:19–26; 16:5), the progress of the word (6:7; 11:19–26; 12:24; 19:20; 28:31), the growth and development of John and Jesus (Luke 1:80; 2:40; 2:52). Yet from an analysis of the above summaries the following characteristics of form and function can be detected.[71]

1. These statements serve as links between two scenes, either as a connective (Luke 1:80; 2:52; Acts 2:41–47; 4:32–37; 6:7; 11:19–26; 12:24; 15:12–16) or as a divider of two similar scenes (19:20; also 4:4; 8:25).[72]
2. They are generalized descriptions of some specific adjacent material, either as a conclusion summarizing some definite activity (Luke 1:80; 2:52; Acts 5:12–16; 16:5; 19:20; 28:30–31),[73] or as a summarized introduction preparing for a specific scene (Acts 2:43–47 and 4:32–37 with regard to the scene in 5:1–11; also Luke 2:40 with regard to vv. 41–51).
3. They provide continuity or a general line of development in the narrative (Luke 1:80; 2:40, 52; Acts 2:47; 5:14; 6:7; 11:19–26;

69. Turner, "Chronology," in *HDB*, 1:421.

70. Cadbury, "Summaries," *BC*, 5:392–402; Benoit, "Notes on 'Summaries,'" *Jesus*, 1:95–103; Rosner, "Progress of the Word," 216–33. See in this chapter our discussion of The Second Meeting, 28:23–28. Summary Statement on Paul's Preaching, *v.* 23.

71. Some of the above characteristics are a confirmation of Cadbury's investigation, "Summaries," *BC*, 5:392–402. It should be observed from the variety of summaries above, how difficult it would be to restrict the summaries of Acts to six progress reports providing a six-panel structure of Acts, as done by C. H. Turner, "Chronology," in *HDB*, 1:421.

72. This is why the above summary statements are often referred to as "stops" in the narrative, see Benoit, "Notes on 'Summaries,'" *Jesus*, 1:95.

73. This characteristic explains the designation of 28:30–31 as a "concluding summary."

12:24; 16:5; 19:20; include also: 4:4; 8:4, 25; 9:31; 13:49; 15:30–35, 41; 18:4, 11; 19:8–10).[74]

Following the above criterion, many more statements can be regarded as summaries in Luke–Acts, including numerous preaching summaries.[75]

It is now appropriate to apply the criterion for identifying narrative summaries to our investigation of Acts 28:30–31. As a conclusion to the narrative (28:16–28), vv. 30–31 summarizes the activity of Paul at Rome for "two whole years" as typical of what Paul had done upon his arrival there: he continues to receive fair treatment under Rome (vv. 16, 23 with vv. 30–31),[76] people continue to come to him (v. 17 συνέρχομαι; v.23 ἔρχομαι; v. 30 εἰσέρχομαι), and Paul continues to proclaim the kingdom of God and Jesus (vv. 23 and 31). There is a continuity between (1) Paul's situation and activity among the Jews upon his arrival in Rome vv. 16–28 and (2) Paul's situation and activity among Gentiles (and Jews) for "two whole years" after his arrival, vv. 30–31[77] Central to this last concept of continuity is that the same message is proclaimed to Jews (v. 23) and Gentiles (vv. 30–31 with v. 28).[78] Hence it can be seen

74. This feature explains the description of summaries as "progress reports."

75. Luke 4:14–15,31–32, 44; 8:1; 9:6; 13:10,22; 19:47; 20:1; 21:37–38; 24:27; Acts 4:31; 5:42; 8:4–5,25,40; 9:22; 12:24; 14:1; 15:35; 18:4,11; 19:8–10,20; 28:30–31.

76. That Paul stayed at "his own hired dwelling" v. 30 reflects the privilege Paul received to live as a private resident "by himself" v. 16 (implied in v. 23). The term ἀκωλύτως v. 31 may reflect a similar concept as ἐπετράπη v. 16 with regard to fair treatment under Rome (see also: Acts 24:23; 27:43, κωλύω; 21:39–40; 26:1; 27:3 ἐπιτρέπω).

77. For a discussion of διετίαν ὅλην and its alleged legal connotation see our chapter 1, "Acts 28:30–31," pp. 25–26. Hemer reviews the discussion, favoring release by acquittal or default, *Book of Acts*, 390–92. Lake (and Cadbury to some degree) saw in διετίαν ὅλην a technical term designating a time fixed by Claudius for a case to be heard, if after two years the accusers did not appear, the accused was set free. Since this was to be the situation in Paul's day the "two full years" signified for Luke's readers the release of Paul, "Roman Law and the Trial of St. Paul," *BC*, 5:326–38. Later critics have shown that much of the "evidence" cited by Lake and Cadbury is either misinterpreted, or misapplied to first century Rome, Sherwin-White, *Roman Society and Roman Law*, 108–19; Conzelmann, *Acts*, 228. "Luke did not emphasize the release but rather the unrestricted freedom which Paul enjoyed in the two preceding years, Haenchen, *Acts*, 725 n. 4.

78. In the epilogue at Rome, Paul proclaims the same message as in v. 23 to "all who came to him" (v. 30), see also: Acts 18:6–11; 19:8–10. Hauser notes, however, certain differences. In 28:23, Paul is "setting forth ἐξετίθετο (11:4; 18:26), testifying of the kingdom of God" and "persuading" πείθων the Jews "concerning Jesus both from

that the closing panel of 28:30–31 serves adequately as an epilogue to the pericope.

Acts 28:30–31 plays a significant part with other preaching summaries in the progression of Luke–Acts. It shows that the same message preached by Jesus, and his disciples in Judea and Galilee, was proclaimed by the early church and Paul in Judea, Syria, Asia Minor, Greece, and finally Rome, to both Jew and Gentile.[79] Thus vv. 30–31 also summarizes Paul's activity at Rome as typical of what Paul and others had done elsewhere in Luke–Acts.

The inclusion of ἀκωλύτως (v. 31) brings a climactic element to the idea of continuity and progression in Luke–Acts, implying the final triumph of Christianity over various religious, racial, and political obstacles.[80] The use of ἀκωλύτως and the function of Acts 28:30–31 as

---

the law and the prophets," whereas in v. 31, Paul is "preaching" κηρύσσων about the kingdom of God and "teaching διδάσκων about the Lord τοῦ κυρίου Jesus Christ with all boldness παρρησία and unhindered" ἀκωλύτως to "all who came to him," *Strukturen* 125–58. These are differences in form, not the substance of the preaching, enable Paul to say, according to Luke, what was appropriate for each situation and audience, whether in speeches or summaries of speeches (*Redeberichte*, ibid., 172). See Thucydides, *Historiae* I.22.

79. Other preaching summaries may be added here that do not introduce or conclude a narrative yet assist in the continuity and progression of Luke–Acts. Luke 9:11; Acts 8:12, 35; 9:28, 29; 17:2–3; 28:23. For both 28:23 and 31 as preaching summaries (*Predigtsummarien*), see Hauser, *Strukturen*, 16, 45–46, 113–14, 157.

80. Although ἀκωλύτως is a hapax legomenon, a semantic context can be found for it in κωλύω, a related term. The latter word occurs in a context of various human restrictions and obstacles to God's salvation: religious and racial (Luke 9:49–50; 11:52; 18:16; Acts 8:36; 10:47; 11:17), as well as political (Acts 24:23; 27:43). The term κωλύω in the above passages conveys the idea of the triumph of Christ or Christianity over various obstacles. Another term providing a linguistic context for interpreting ἀκωλύτως is ἐπιτρέπω which further indicates the breaking down of (Rome's) political obstacles (Acts 21:39–40; 26:1; 27:3; 28:16). Hauser notes that ἀκωλύτως also occurs in Josephus *Antiquities* 16.41,166,169; 19.290 permitting the Jews to pursue their religious duties "without hindrance," *Strukturen*, 144–45.

The triumph of Christianity over various religious, racial, and political obstacles is achieved through a number of means. It is accomplished through the actions of Christ (Luke 9:49–50; 11:52; 18:16), and the church (Acts 8:36; 10:47; 11:17), as well as through the tolerant actions of Rome (Acts 21:39–40; 24:23; 27:3, 43; 28:16). Yet the end result is the same: the human restrictions and obstacles to God's work (e.g. sectarian rivalry, imprisonment) have been overcome. "Here the author of Acts directs the attention of his readers to the proclamation of God's reign and teaching about Jesus as something which is unchecked, unstopped, unhindered," (596). In Mealand, "The Close of Acts," 589–97.

the conclusion to the long progression of preaching summaries provide some basis for regarding these final verses as climactic.

It has been shown that verses 30–31 function as an epilogue to the pericope. It is a final note summarizing Paul's activities in Rome, and provides a closing panel of Paul's situation in Rome, as v. 16 provided the opening panel.

As the final preaching summary of Luke–Acts, 28:30–31 brings the continuity of witness and progression of proclamation to a climactic conclusion.

Conclusion

In this chapter, certain reasons for regarding Acts 28:16–31 as a structural unit have been articulated. Verses 16 and 30–31 form the opening and closing panels providing the setting and tone of the pericope. Verse 16 as a "we" statement characteristically introduces the readers/auditors to a scene and drops out of the narrative.

The identity and function of the literary forms have been established. Both vv. 17–20 and 25b–28, and their immediate framework, fulfill the criterion of Lukan speeches. The former address functions as a passion recital (defense) speech, and the latter address as an apologetic speech for the Gentile mission. Acts 28:23 and 30–31 are both preaching summaries having similar contents and function showing continuity and progress. Acts 28:30–31 has the additional function of concluding the narrative and summarizing its contents in a typical and generalized manner. These are the forms and their function in the narrative.[81]

81. Hauser, *Strukturen*, 198–202, includes an outline of *three* narrative situations (virtual, actual, resultant) with *four* corresponding points of activity: 1. Virtual Situation (*histoire*?): calling together and gathering with prominent Roman Jews, Acts 28:17a, agreement to meet with large numbers of Roman Jews, vv. 22a, 23a, mixed response, disagreement, vv. 24–25a, receiving visitors at residence, v. 30; 2. Actual Situation (*récit*?): Paul's introductory speech, vv. 17b–20, Paul's proclamation from morning to evening, v. 23b, Paul's speech on salvation to Gentiles, vv. 25b–28, Paul's unhindered proclamation to all who came to him, v. 31; 3. Resulting Situation (*narration*?): Response of Roman Jews to Paul's introductory speech, vv. 21–22, disagreement and departing, vv. 24–25a, the way opened up to Gentiles, v. 28b., open-ended conclusion (AT). All components of each situation are to correspond to one another, although the actions in vv. 24–25a (disagreement and departure) are in both the Virtual and Resultant Situations. It is an interesting (and possibly correct) adaptation of Gérard Genette, *Figures III* (Paris, 1972; ET, *Narrative Discourse* 1980). See discussion of Genette's *histoire, récit,* and *narration* as "story, text, and narration," 3–4 and narrative levels, 91–92 in Rimmon-Kenan,

The investigation of the structure and forms has aided in the clarification of those elements in the text which are important for an understanding of the literary function and theological significance of Acts 28:16–31. The study has sought to answer unsettled questions concerning the structure and literary forms of Acts 28 in the history of *Actaforschung* (chapter 1). The results of this analysis will provide adequate groundwork for understanding the text in the context of its Lukan parallels (chapter 3) and both its literary function and theological significance (chapter 4).

Narrative Fiction: Contemporary Poetics (Routledge, 1983), who describes Genette's book as a "theoretical and descriptive poetics, analyzing both the system governing all narrative and its operation . . . new is the section on temporal frequency and the distinction between focalization and narration," 151. Mark Powell refers to Genette's *Narrative Discourse* in his discussion of story time (in story world of implied author) and discourse time (for the reader by the narrator) in his *What is Narrative Criticism?* (Fortress, 1990) 36–38, 115, and 79, 119. Genette's three main elements of "Narratology" (plot, story, narration: adapted by Hauser?) are also explained in W. Randolph Tate, *Interpreting the Bible* (Hendrickson, 2006) 235. There are significant differences of interpretation and application regarding Genette's narrative and story levels. See also Gérard Genette, *Nouveau discours du récit* (Paris, 1983; ET, *Narrative Discourse Revisited*, Cornell, 1988), which the author describes as a "postscript" to his earlier work, 7.

3

The Lukan Parallels and Patterns of Acts 28:16–31

IN CHAPTER ONE IT HAS BEEN SHOWN THAT MANY PARALlels and similarities have been observed between Acts 28 and relevant Lukan passages.[1] Yet several questions remain: What is the nature and extent of these parallels in relation to Acts 28? What contributions do these parallels make toward an understanding of the function and significance of Acts 28? How do they function as narrative strategies for the conclusion of Luke–Acts? It is with the above questions in view that the investigation of the Lukan parallels and patterns of Acts 28:16–31 is undertaken.

This chapter will seek to understand the relationship of the conclusion of Acts to the rest of Luke–Acts as a whole, particularly the beginning and middle. This understanding will be attained by comparing Acts 28 with key texts in Luke–Acts that share common features. By

1. See our chapter 1, "Lukan Parallels to Acts 28," 15–18. Meir Sternberg also explores patterns of similarity and repetition in biblical texts, all based on the principle of analogy (two characters, events, strands of action, etc.) in *The Poetics of Biblical Narrative: Ideological Literature and the Drama of Reading* (Indiana University Press, 1985) 365–440.

It is noteworthy that a narrative study of closure in modern novels mentions the framing techniques of circularity and parallelism with the latter device (parallelism) illustrated by the literary depiction of different characters or groups of characters undergoing similar experiences or portrayed in similar ways, see Torgovnick, *Closure*, 13, 15, 40–41, 51–53, 62–63, 80–81, 108, 147–48, 189–91, 199–200; see on this last point, Parsons, *Departure of Jesus*, 69–70, 159–60, and especially Tannehill, *Narrative Unity*, 2:354, where he states: "Through circularity and parallelism, 28:17–31 serves as conclusion through these expanding stretches of narrative: (1) the arrest at Jerusalem and defense scenes, (2) the mission of Paul, (3) the whole of Acts, (4) the whole of Luke–Acts."

doing these comparisons we will gather significant data to address the question of the literary function and theological significance of the text in Luke–Acts (chapter 4).

In the comparative analysis of this chapter we will deal with three intratextual concerns: (1) typical patterns and motifs, (2) linear-historical relationships and (3) the contribution of the comparisons to an understanding of Acts 28 as the conclusion of Luke–Acts.

In chapter 1, "Historical Problems of Acts 28," 8–12, it has been shown that the author does not seem to be merely interested in a historical account of events in a simple linear scheme. Luke is also concerned with patterns and types, as indicated by the Jesus–Paul parallels. This latter feature in the author's writing gives the narrative a reciprocal aspect, where events are symbolic and personages are typical.[2] Acts 28 will be compared with parallel texts in Luke–Acts to discover the typical patterns conveyed in them, and to understand the relationship of the conclusion to the beginning and middle within Luke's narrative scheme.[3] The value of such a comparison for an understanding of Acts 28 as a concluding narrative will then be articulated.

2. See Goulder, *Type and History* (1964); Talbert, *Literary Patterns* (1974); Radl, *Paulus und Jesus* (1975); Mattill, "Jesus–Paul," (1975) 15–46; R. F. O'Toole, S.J., "Luke's Notion of 'Be Imitators of Me as I am of Christ,'" *BTB* 8 (1978) 155–61; "Parallels between Jesus and His Disciples," *BZ* 27 (1983) 195–212; and his "Disciples Continue the Work of Jesus," chap. 3 in *Unity*, 62–94. Hauser mentions but does not explore the significance of the Jesus–Paul parallels in Acts 28 *Strukturen*, 138, 161–62, 164–65, 233–34; Praeder, "Jesus–Paul," 23–39 (both similarities and differences); David P. Moessner, "Christ Must Suffer: New Light on the Jesus–Peter, Stephen, Paul Parallels," *NovT* 28 (1986) 220–56. On Scripture, typology, and parallel patterns in Luke–Acts, e.g., Peter as a type of Elisha, see Denova, *Things Accomplished among Us* (Sheffield, 1997) 26, 92, 112–16, 210.

3. In the fourth century, BCE, Aristotle stated that an artistic whole "is what has a beginning, middle, and end," *The Poetics* 7.3 (LCL; Cambridge, 1965) 30–31. In her study of the narrative strategies of closure, Torgovnick mentions that the conclusion has a relationship to the middle and beginning of the work, *Closure*, 5–8, 13, 15, 80–81, 93–95, 109–10, 115–18, 122, 125, 129, 147, 158–59, 162, 180, 199.

In his article on Acts 28, J. Dupont has shown the relationship of this text to many of its Lukan parallels but did not explicate the significance of the many patterns and types found, see "La Conclusion," 380–402.

Acts 28:16–31 and the Arrest and Defense of Paul (Acts 21:17—26:32)

Acts 21–26 is not only part of the immediate context of Acts 28, but also has several formal, linguistic and thematic parallels with the last chapter of Acts.[4] Although in past studies, allusions have been made to phrases and concepts common to both passages, no extensive comparison has been made between Acts 28:16–31 and Acts 21–26.[5]

The purpose of this analysis will be to investigate the common features shared by Acts 28 and 21–26, to define further their relationship and to understand better the literary function of Acts 28:16–31.

It has been noted in chapter 2 that although Acts 28:17–20 has several distinctive features,[6] there are some formal and thematic similarities with Acts 21–26. In both contexts Paul makes his defense before the Jews (21:40–22:21; 23:6–10, the "prominent Jews" of the Council). Acts 28:17 begins with the formula of address ἄνδρες ἀδελφοί and makes extensive use of the first person singular, both of which are characteristics of Paul's defense speeches.[7]

The following phrases in Acts 28 occur also in the defense speeches: "appeal to Caesar" (25:10–11, 21, 25; 26:32; 28:19) and the "hope" of Israel/the resurrection (23:6; 24:15, 21; 25:19; 26:6–8; 28:20).

In a comparison of Acts 28:16–31 with chaps. 21–26, the following structural, linguistic, and thematic commonalities can be noted.

4. Even though Acts 21–26 and 28 are not exact parallel accounts they do have a special relationship by the common elements they share. Acts 28 "summarized the context of chapters 21–26 quite nicely," Schubert, "Final Cycle," 10. Although we will be comparing here a pericope having one setting and designated audience (28) with a group of pericopes containing numerous settings and audiences (21–26), the latter group of passages do have a common concern with the arrest, trial, and defense of Paul, subjects to which Acts 28 alludes or creates a fictive setting. On the fictive setting of Acts 28, see Marguerat, "Enigma," 295–96; Skinner, *Locating Paul*, 166–67.

5. For a survey of research on this comparison, see: chapter 1, "Acts 21–26 and Acts 28," 16. Dupont in his recent study has also made a comparison of Acts 21–26 with 28:17–20, but, like other scholars, he has omitted the entire text of Acts 28:16–31, "La Conclusion," 380–83.

6. See our discussion of the differences between 28:17–20 and chaps. 21–26 in our chapter 2, 42–45. See also: O'Toole, *Christological Climax*, 15.

7. Address Ἄνδρες ἀδελφοὶ (22:1; 23:1; 28:17); use of the first person singular ἐγω (22:19; 23:1, 6; 24:21; 26:9–10; 28:17) με (22:7–21; 23:3; 24:12, 18; 25:10–11; 28:18); μου (22:1; 24:13, 17, 20; 25:11; 26:3–4; 28:19); ἐγώ εἰμι (22:3–8; 25:10; 26:15). Soards, *Speeches in Acts*, 113, 115.

Literary Context

1. Both passages are preceded by journey accounts: Acts 21–26 is preceded by the journey to Jerusalem section, 19:21—21:16; and Acts 28:16–31 is preceded by the voyage to Rome account, 27:1—28:15. Both journey passages appear to set apart Acts 21:17—26:32 as a distinct and complete unit.[8] The voyage to Rome separates the two accounts of Paul at Rome (28) and Paul's arrest and defense (21–26).

Setting

2. A double reference to Paul's coming and arrival in Jerusalem and Rome is made (21:15, 17 and 28:14, 16). Both locations function as the destinations of Paul's journeys (19:21—21:16 and 27:1—28:15) and at both places, a defense is made for Paul and his mission.[9]
3. The contexts of both refer to Paul's condition under Roman custody (24:23; 28:16, 30–31) and two years of confinement (Caesarea 24:27; Rome 28:30).
4. The relative freedom of Paul under Roman custody is signified by the use of the verb κωλύω or a related adverbial form with the a. privative (μηδένα κωλύειν) adverbial form with a privative ἀκωλύτως 28:31).[10]

8. Acts 21:17–26 provides the immediate setting and background for the events concerning Paul's arrest and defense in Jerusalem (21:27—23:30) and his defense in Caesarea (23:31—26:32). See the function of the journey to Rome (27:1—28:15) as divine protection of the innocent Paul in G. B. Miles and G. Trompf, "Luke and the Antiphon: The Theology of Acts 27–28 in the Light of Pagan Beliefs about Divine Revelation, Pollution, and Shipwreck," *HTR* 69 (1976) 259–67. Do the divine beings in Acts 18:9–10; 23:11 and 27:23–24 function as deus ex machina to assure the reader of Paul's safe arrival in Rome (e.g., Heracles to the rescue in *Alcestis* by Euripides) or as agents of salvation for Paul and the readers? G. Trompf, "On Why Luke Declined to Recount the Death of Paul: Acts 27–28 and Beyond," *Luke-Acts: New Perspectives* (1984) 225–39. At Rome, a mission is accomplished, Alexander, "Reading Luke-Acts from Back to Front," 212–14; Paul's confidence, despite obstacles, D. Marguerat, "The Enigma of the Silent Closing of Acts," in *Jesus and the Heritage of Israel*, 294–97; on Gentile receptivity to Paul, see Tannehill, *Narrative Unity*, 2:335.

9. For further parallel features between Acts 28:16–31 and 21:17–26, see our comparison in chapter 2., the section "Opening Panel."

10. For ἀκωλύτως as adverbial form of κωλύω with a privative, see: ἀκωλύτως in Liddell and Scott, eds., *Greek-English Lexicon* (1978) 59; Zerwick and Grosvenor,

Paul's Audience

5. As in Acts 28:17, Paul makes his defense before prominent Jews: The Sanhedrin (23:26) and Herod Agrippa II (26:2).[11]

Defense Speech Structure

6. As noted earlier, the vocative of address Ἄνδρες ἀδελφοι and the use of the first person singular are found in Acts 21–26, 28.

The Charges of the Jews against Paul

7. In both passages, Paul defends himself against the charge(s) of his Jewish opponents (24:12–13; 25:8, 10; 26:2–4; 28:17, 19).

Paul, Innocent Like Jesus[12]

8. Paul is presented as a law-abiding Israelite like Jesus (22:3; 23:6; 24:14–15; 26:4–11, 22; 28:17–20; with Luke 2:21–24, 39–46; 4:16, 31; 13:10; 19:47—20:2; 23:14–16, 22; 24:26–7, 44–48).
9. Paul has done nothing against the people or the customs, recalling Jesus' trial (25:8, 10; 28:17, 19 with Luke 23:14–15).
10. The mention of Paul delivered into the hands of the Romans (28:17) recalls the prediction regarding Paul before his arrival in Jerusalem (21:11), and the passion of Jesus (Luke 18:32; 24:7, 20).

Grammatical Analysis of the Greek NT, 1:456. The adverb is a constant occurrence in legal documents in the second century C.E., *Vocabulary of the Greek Testament*, eds., Moulton and Milligan (Eerdmans, 1980) 20; Xavier Jacques classes ἀκωλύτως under κωλύω, regarding both terms as sharing the same root κωλύ, in X. Jacques, *List of New Testament Words* (Rome, 1969) 65. Gerhard Delling, "Das lezte Wort der Apostelgeschichte," *NovT* 15 (1973) 193–204; Frank Stagg calls κωλύω a catchword of ἀκωλύτως, occurring at crucial points in Acts, "The Unhindered Gospel," *RevExp* 71 (1974) 460–61; see also *BDAG*, 40, 580.

11. Paul also addresses the Jewish mob (Acts 22) and Felix the Roman (Acts 24), but in the above study the most common elements between Acts 21–26 and 28 will be underscored.

12. Dupont acknowledges the comparison of the trial proceedings of Paul with the passion of Jesus but again he does not investigate the significance of this observation in his study of Acts 21–26 and 28, "La Conclusion" 382. "In the Pauline Passion Narrative," Jack T. Sanders, "The Jewish People in Luke-Acts," *SBL* 1986 *Seminar Papers*, 127 (referring to Paul's arrest, trial, and imprisonment in Jerusalem and Caesarea).

11. Statements of Paul's not deserving the death penalty, are reminiscent of Jesus' trial (Acts 25:25; 26:31/Luke 23:15; Acts 28:18/ Luke 23:22).

12. The possibility of Paul's being released by the Romans is mentioned (Acts 26:32; 28:18), recalling Jesus' passion (Luke 23:16; Acts 3:13).

13. Paul is declared innocent by the parties examining him, reminiscent of Jesus' trial (Acts 23:9/Luke 23:4; Acts 25:25/Luke 23:15; Acts 26:31/Luke 23:15; Acts 28:18/ Luke 23:22).

The Nature and Purpose of Paul's Arrest

14. Reference to Paul's chains in made (Acts 21:33; 26:29; 28:20).

15. Paul mentions that he is arrested because of the hope of Israel/ resurrection (Acts 23:6; 24:15; 26:6–8; 28:20).[13]

16. Paul appeals to Caesar (25:11, 21, 25; 26:32; 28:19).

Paul and His Mission

17. Paul appeals to the law of Moses and to the prophets in his own defense (24:14) and in his preaching of Christ (26:22; 28:23).

18. Paul functions as a witness (μάρτυς or a derivative) see: 22:15 and 26:16 μάρτυς; 26:22; 23:11 and 28:23 διαμαρτύρομαι.

19. Paul's universal mission to Jews and Gentiles is referred to in both contexts (22:15, 21; 26:17, 20, 23, Paul's Damascus road commission; 28:23, 28–31, Rome).

20. A Jewish response of rejection or division occurs (rejection 22:22; division 23:7; 28:24–25a).[14]

13. It can be argued that the term ἐλπίς, used in Acts, is generally synonymous with the resurrection of the dead, Acts 23:6; 24:15; 26:6–8; O'Toole *Christological Climax*, 91–95, 121. Israel's messianic hope (Acts 23:6 as in 2 Macc 3:29; Acts 26:6; 28:20, *BDAG*, 320. Israel's hope of the resurrection is confirmed in the resurrection of Christ, Hooker, *Endings* 63.

14. The division of the Pharisees and Sadducees over Paul's belief in the resurrection (23:6–7) is similar to the division of the Jews at Rome over Paul's statement on salvation to the Gentiles (28:25–28).

21. Reference to spiritual perception as it concerns salvation in LXX Old Testament terminology (26:18; 28:26–27).[15]

The numerous commonalities stated in the above study indicate that Acts 28 and Acts 21–26 have a close literary relationship.[16] Several features in our points of comparison give some indication that Acts 28 recalls the events of Paul's arrest and defense (Acts 21–26). The reference to Paul's chains (14), the appeal to Caesar (16), Paul's plea of being a law-abiding Israelite (8, 9), the statement on the hope of Israel (15), and the general portrait of Paul under Roman custody defending himself against the charges of Jewish opponents (3, 5, 7–9) argue in favor of this aforementioned assertion. The brief allusions to Acts 21–26 found in Acts 28 would be comprehensible only for Luke's readers/auditors who could recall the accounts of Paul's arrest and trial in Acts 21–26.[17] There may be a number of reasons for this parallel relationship between the ending of Acts 28 ending and Acts 21–26, the middle of the narrative. One suggestion is that the innocence ascribed to Paul (and his work) in Jerusalem and Caesarea also applies to Paul at Rome. It seems from the narrative, that it was necessary to reaffirm Paul's innocence in Rome before he is to preach the gospel there. From 28:30–31 we notice that the implied author wants to leave Paul in Rome preaching the gospel to all openly and unhindered, yet Paul is still under arrest for alleged crimes against the Jewish people. This lingering problem for the author, could possibly jeopardize Paul's proclamation of the gospel at this new location. Although Paul has already been declared innocent

15. R. F. O'Toole, in his *Christological Climax*, 73, sees Acts 28:26–27 (Isa 6:9–10) as the best commentary on the meaning of "to open their eyes," Acts 26:18.

16. The above structural, linguistic, and thematic similarities between Acts 28:16–31 and Acts 21–26 should bring some qualification to O'Toole's statement that Paul's defense (Acts 22:1—26:32) needs to be distinguished from Acts 28:17ff because the latter passage does not contain a hearing scene or trial setting. See O'Toole, *Christological Climax*, 15. Our emphasis on the Jesus–Paul parallels in Acts 28:16–31 (as O'Toole has underscored in Acts 22–26) further substantiates the close relationship of Acts 28 and chaps. 21–26. See also our chapter 2, section "Passion Recital Speech," 43–45.

17. We refer to readers as auditors or "listeners" because public reading to a community of listeners was the primary mode of receiving information in antiquity (Luke 4:16; Acts 13:15, 27; 15:21; 2 Cor 3:14–15; 1 Thess 5:27; Josephus *Contra Apion* 2.175; Diodorus Siculus 15.10.1; Epictetus 3.23.6). Mention of "Let the reader understand" (Matt 24:15; Mark 13:14) is an editorial comment, we believe, directed *primarily* to the one who will read the document to the community.

several times in his defense speeches (Acts 22–26), the author's awareness of a new setting (especially Rome where Paul was "martyred under Nero," *Eccl. Hist.* 3.1.2) might have prompted this scene to once again defend or to reaffirm Paul and his mission.

There are several defense motifs in Acts 21–26 and 28 which recall another passage: Luke 23, the arrest and trial of Jesus. In points 8–13 of our comparison we have noted that both Paul and Jesus are law-abiding Israelites (8), have done nothing against the people or the customs (9), have done nothing deserving the death penalty (11), were delivered into the hands of the Romans (10), would have been released by the Romans (12), and were declared innocent by the Romans (13).

It seems clear that these Jesus–Paul parallels function as defense motifs and, with regard to Acts 21–26 and 28, they are used to defend Paul as one innocent like Jesus.[18] Paul undergoes similar experiences as Jesus did and is defended by Luke in a similar manner. Paul is not only identified with Christ but continues his work. The one who is innocent like Christ performs the work commissioned by Christ (22:15, 21; 23:11; 26:16–18, 23).[19] Therefore, it can be seen that the Jesus–Paul parallels in Acts 21–26 and 28 function as a defense of Paul and his work.

Acts 28 not only recalls certain features in the narrative of Luke–Acts, it also brings to a conclusion several concepts in Acts 21–26 (and elsewhere). The defense chapters of Paul also seek to lead Paul to Rome, yet not to Caesar, but to the Roman Jews where a climactic confrontation in the narrative occurs.[20] Paul's appeal to Caesar (25:10–12; 26:32) looks ahead to Paul's journey to Rome (27:24) and his arrival there

18. The following studies have demonstrated that one of the functions of the Jesus–Paul parallels is to defend Paul and his work: Mattill, "Jesus–Paul," 20, 37; O'Toole, *Christological Climax*, 22–25, 159–60; and "Parallels in Luke–Acts," 210–12; R. E. Cottle, "The Occasion and Purpose of the Final Drafting of Acts" (1967) 65–103, Cottle argues that the sources of these parallels are Acts and a Proto-Luke. V. Stolle states that the parallels help defend Jesus in Acts 21–26 because he is still vulnerable in the witness of Paul. Such a defense is indirect at best, especially in Acts 28, Stolle, *Der Zeuge als Angeklagter*, 215–42, 271–84.

19. See also Points 17–21 of our comparison of Acts 21–26 and Acts 28. O'Toole also mentions this additional function of disciples continuing the work of Jesus in his "Parallels in Luke–Acts," 211.

20. Jervell, *Luke*, 160. For Jervell, though, this final confrontation scene at Rome completes the early church's mission to the Jews which creates a renewed Israel of both believing Gentiles and Jews, *Apostelgeschichte*, 629.

(28:16–31).[21] It is in Rome, preaching to Jews and Gentiles (28:23–31), where Paul's missionary work, summed up in 26:22–23, finds its fulfillment. By preaching in Rome Paul has brought to completion his commission from Christ, as recited in Paul's defense speeches (Acts 22:15, 21; 23:11; 26:16–18, 23).[22]

It can be seen that the comparison of Acts 28 with chaps. 21–26 extends beyond 28:17–20 with allusions from Paul's arrest and defense extended throughout the pericope.[23] It is also to be noted that Acts 21–26 and 28 are not merely concerned with a defense of Paul, but also with a defense of his mission.[24] Yet both themes are interconnected since it is the missionary Paul who is defended.

In conclusion, we see that Acts 28 recalls the arrest and defense of Paul in chaps. 21–26 to show that the innocence ascribed to Paul and his work in Jerusalem and Caesarea applies to him also at Rome. Both Acts 21–26 and 28 also recall the arrest and trial of Jesus (Luke 23) which seems to function as a defense of Paul as one who is innocent like Jesus. Acts 28 brings to completion several concepts in Acts 21–26. The appeal to Caesar brings Paul to Rome to proclaim the gospel to the people and the Gentiles (26:22–23; 28:23–31) in fulfillment of Christ's commission stated in the defense speeches (22:15, 21; 23:11; 26:16–18, 23).

21. In a similar manner Paul's journey to Jerusalem leads Paul to his arrest and "passion" (Acts 19:21–21:16) paralleling the journey of Jesus to Jerusalem which leads Jesus to his arrest and passion (Luke 9:51—19:44), see Mattill, "Jesus–Paul," 30–37; O'Toole, "Parallels in Luke–Acts," 199, 207–8.

22. Dupont has also shown that Acts 28 functions as the conclusion of the history of Paul's trial proceedings. It underscores for the last time the contrast that sets the loyalty of Paul with regard to his people over against the blind stubbornness of his adversaries "La Conclusion," 380–83. Unfortunately, Dupont has restricted his analysis to Acts 28:17–22 and Acts 21–26. He has not shown the significance of Paul's preaching in Rome to both Jews and Gentiles (28:23–31) as a fulfillment, continuity, or completion of prophecies and related statements found in the defense speeches (22:15, 21; 23:11; 26:16–18, 22–23).

23. This raises some question about Schubert's suggestion that 28:17–20 should be classed with Acts 22–26 on the basis of the similarities common to both passages. The critique of Dupont in the preceding footnote would apply also to Schubert in his "Final Cycle," 10.

24. For a defense of Paul, see points 1–15 in the above comparative analysis. For a defense of Paul's mission, see points 16–20 in the above comparison.

The comparison of Acts 21–26 and 28 extends beyond 28:17–20 and is not only concerned with defending Paul but also his mission.[25]

Acts 28:16–31 and Other Pauline Missionary Settings

It can be argued from examining the scene of Paul at Rome, that we are confronted with a missionary situation. In Acts 28:23, the Jews gather to hear Paul preach from the law and the prophets. In v. 24, there is a divided response.

In vv. 26–27, there is an indictment pronounced on the unbelieving Jews. In v. 28, there is a turning to the Gentiles. As Dibelius and others have pointed out,[26] the above features of Paul at Rome (Acts 28) have close similarities with Paul's work in Antioch of Pisidia (13:44–48) and Corinth (18:5–6), revealing the common experience of Paul and the Christian mission in general. While other missionary encounters will be included in our study, the works cited above have sufficiently established a correspondence between Acts 28 and other missionary encounters of Paul.[27]

25. To argue with Dupont that Acts 28 functions as merely the conclusion of Paul's trial proceedings (Acts 21–26) in a linear-historical scheme, does not, we contend, give full consideration to all the Lukan patterns and images which convey a continuity of thought and a typical correspondence between the two passages, "La Conclusion," 380–83.

26. Dibelius, *Studies*, 149–50, 199 n. 16; Conzelmann, *Acts*, 227; Haenchen, *Acts*, 729–31; C. W. Stenschke, *Luke's Portrait of Gentiles Prior to Their Coming to Faith* (Mohr/Siebeck, 1999) 171–73, 237–38, 306–10, 340. See especially our discussion of Acts 13:46; 18:6; and 28:25–28 in the history of *Actaforschung* in chap. 1, "Lukan Parallels to Acts 28," 15–16.

27. The reference to a Christian community already existing in Rome (Acts 28:14, 15) presents no serious obstacles to our observation that Acts 28:23–31 functions as a typical missionary situation (as in Luke 4; Acts 13; 18; and 19). First of all, it is not the first time that Christians are mentioned before Paul's missionary encounter in a city. Reference is made to Christians in Ephesus 13:19, 26 before Paul's missionary situation in that city, Acts 19:8–10. Acts 19:8–10 and 28:23–31 share many common characteristics as missionary encounters. Christians are also mentioned before the "spread of the gospel . . . in the coastal regions" through Peter, Acts 9:32, 36 (quotes from the outline of Acts in Kümmel, *Introduction*, 155). Secondly, it is not clear why Luke gives these candid references to Christians. Most scholars highlight the importance of Paul bringing the gospel to (Ephesus and) Rome, Maddox, *Purpose*, 77; Lampe, *From Paul to Valentinus*, 7 n. 1. P. Menoud states that it is Paul who comes to Rome (and Ephesus). Paul is the chief missionary, the one invested by Christ Himself to function as a witness, the one most qualified to carry out Christ's command to proclaim to the world, Menoud, "Le Plan des Actes des Apôtres," *NTS* 1 (1954) 50. Support for Menoud's view

In this section we will be investigating Paul's missionary encounters in Antioch of Pisidia (13:44–48), Iconium (14:1–7), Thessalonica (17:2–3), Corinth (18:4–11), Ephesus (19:8–10), and Rome (28:16–31).[28] The reasons for including the above scenes in our study is because of the common elements they share: almost all contain a geographical location and a missionary setting with a summary account of Paul preaching, there is a confrontation with the Jews and a response, resulting in the turning to the Gentiles, usually concluding with a note on the success of the mission. These common features will now be investigated in a more detailed manner.

SETTING

1. All designate a geographical location (Antioch of Pisidia 13:14; Iconium 14:1; Thessalonica 17:1; Corinth 18:1; Ephesus 19:1; Rome 28:16) and a temporal setting (the sabbath, 13:14, 44; 17:2; 18:4; sabbath implied in 14:1 and 19:8; appointed day 28:23).[29]

---

is found in Wilson, *Gentiles*, 237–38. Haenchen and Conzelmann indirectly support Menoud by insisting that in Acts 28 the author deliberately hides the Roman church from view to have Paul introduce Christianity to Rome, Haenchen, "Acts as Source Material," in *SLA*, 278; Conzelmann, *Acts*, 227. Menoud and Wilson especially support our view that it is one like Jesus who completes the work of Jesus, by bringing the gospel to the Gentile world (Asia Minor, Greece, and Rome). Luke is obviously not concerned with how the gospel was first planted in the Roman empire (Acts 9:32, 36; 18:19, 26; 28:13–15). The author seems more concerned with how Paul, the chief missionary invested by Christ himself, carries out Christ's command to proclaim the gospel to the nations. See our discussion of Acts 28:14, 15 in chap. 1, "Historical Problems: Christian Community in Rome," 8–9.

28. The missionary settings in Berea (17:10–14) and related scenes are omitted because they do not share most of the common elements that the above six scenes contain. Dupont, following P. Schubert, "Final Cycle," 9 and P. Wendland (in Haenchen Acts 33), only examines four scenes: Pisidian Antioch, Corinth, Ephesus, and Rome, omitting Iconium and Thessalonica, "La Conclusion," 383–86.

29. All accounts, except that at Rome, mention Paul entering the synagogue to preach. Haenchen explains that "Paul in Rome is no longer a free man. He cannot, as he had in Antioch and Corinth, seek out the synagogues and preach there. He must therefore have the Jews come to his quarters . . ." *Acts*, 729; Fitzmyer agrees in his *Acts* 792. At Iconium (14:1) and Ephesus (19:8) Paul enters "the synagogues" to preach, in Pisidian Antioch (13:14, 44), Thessalonica (17:2), and Corinth (18:4). Paul preaches in synagogues "on the Sabbath," and there is no apparent reason to deny this same temporal setting at both Iconium and Ephesus, because it was the customary time when the Jews gathered in the synagogue. Paul at Rome is the only account where Paul preaches to the Jews "after they appointed (τάσσω) a day" to come to him (probably with Paul's consent, 28:23). The word τάσσω is used of divine appointment (13:48; 22:10), eccle-

Missionary Confrontation

2. All begin with a missionary situation in which Paul preaches to the Jews first (13:44; 14:1; 17:2–3; 18:4–5; 19:8; 28:23).[30]

3. A response of the Jews is reported (13:45; 14:1–2, 4–5; 17:4–5; 18:6; 19:9; 28:24–25a), in all cases unbelief or a divided response is stated.[31]

4. Paul's reaction to Jewish unbelief or indifference results in the extension of his ministry to the Gentiles (13:46–47; 18:6b; 19:9; 28:25–28).

Mission to Gentiles

5. Paul's ministry extends to the Gentiles (13:47–48; 18:6; 19:9–10; 28:28) with Scriptural support from Isaiah provided in several cases (Acts 13:47/Isa 49:6; Acts 28:26–27/Isa 6:9–10; and implicitly Acts 28:28/ Isa 40:5 and 49:6).[32]

---

siastical assignment (Acts 15:2 after debate) or imperial order/edict (Luke 7:8; Acts 18:2). In Matt 28:16 the same verb is used of Jesus who "directed" his disciples to meet on a Galillean mountain to hear his final words, *BDAG*, 991. For cognate (τακτός) with similar function, see Acts 12:21, τακτῇ δὲ ἡμέρᾳ ("on an appointed day," Herod Agrippa I took his seat at a spectacle honoring Caesar, see Josephus *Antiquities* 19.343–52), the Western text adds that "on this day," Herod was "reconciled with the Tyrians," Johnson, *Acts*, 215. We may conclude here that a *specific* day is set for the missionary encounter (Acts 28:23).

30. Paul is preaching to the Jews first (13:44; 17:2; 19:8; 28:23); and is preaching first to the Jews and God-fearing Greeks (14:1–2; 18:4–5). The following include a temporal note on preaching: "for three weeks" 17:2; "for three months" 19:8; "from morning until evening" 28:23. The following were noted in our chapter 2, pp. 49–50 as summary statements of Paul's preaching: Acts 17:2–3; 18:4–5; 19:8–10; 28:23, 31.

31. The divided response of the people of Iconium over Paul's preaching (σχίζω 14:4) is very similar to the Pharisees and Sadducees divided over Paul (σχίζω 23:7). Both of these passages have some similarities to the divided response of the Jews at Rome (ἀσύμφωνος 28:25), although the terminology of 28:25 is different and the divided response of 14:4 applies to Jews and Gentiles. To understand some of the social dynamics of conflict here, see Bruce J. Malina and Jerome H. Neyrey, "Conflict in Luke-Acts: Labeling and Deviance Theory," in *The Social World of Luke-Acts* (Hendrickson, 1991) 97–122.

32. Dupont also points out that Hab 1:5, quoted in Acts 13:41, functions in the same way as Isa 6:9–10 in Acts 28:26–27, as a menacing forewarning on the unbelieving Jews (*Salvation*, 18; and "La Conclusion," 384). Unlike the quote in Acts13:41, the prophetic text in 28:26–27 is connected more directly with salvation to the Gentiles, 28:28; see discussion in Craig A. Evans, *To See and Not Perceive*, 125–27.

Concluding Note on Success of Mission

6. The accounts conclude with a note on the success of the mission extended to Gentiles (13:48–49, 52; 18:11; 19:10; 28:30–31).[33]

It is noteworthy from the above comparison that Paul's missionary situation in Rome shares similar features with his earlier missionary encounters in Pisidian Antioch, Thessalonica, Corinth, and Ephesus. Following the other accounts, Acts 28 designates a geographical and temporal setting of Paul's mission (1). Acts 28, in agreement with the other passages, includes a missionary situation of Paul preaching to the Jews first (2) who respond in a typically divided manner (3–4). The mission is then extended to the Gentiles (5), concluding on a note of success (6).

The above data lend support to the idea that some continuity of action in the missionary activity of Paul and early Christianity is presented in the narrative. What has taken place at Rome regarding the confrontation with the Jews, their divisiveness, and the turning to the Gentiles is typical of the missionary activity in Asia Minor and Greece. Despite the arrest and trials of Paul, the missionary procedure of earliest Christianity is continued at Rome.[34]

33. Summary reports on the growth of the word containing λόγος τοῦ κυρίου or θεοῦ are: 13:49; 18:11; 19:10. Although the successful note of 13:48–49 is followed by the account of the Pisidian Jews stirring up persecution and driving Paul and Barnabas out of the city (v. 50), the chapter (Acts 13) concludes with the note: "And the disciples were filled with joy and with the Holy Spirit" (v. 52), reminiscent of Luke 24:52–53. So also at Rome, Paul "has proclaimed the triumph of the Gospel, not its defeat by a recalcitrant people," in Barrett, *Acts*, 2:1237.

34. From the continuous repetition of the patterns and themes enumerated above, which occur throughout the Pauline mission, there are sufficient reasons for asserting that Luke's narrative of Paul and his work transcends the historical or the biographical. It becomes more of a symbolical portrait of the Christian mission in the Roman world. What takes place in Acts 28 is typical of missionary activity almost everywhere in Acts. The mission of the church into the world (Luke 24:47; Acts 1:8) is personified in the work of Paul (Acts 13:47–48; 18:6; 19:9; 28:25–28). By this symbolic picture of Paul in mission, the author can describe the movement of Christianity from Jerusalem to the Gentile world in a personal way: by making it the story of Paul. This typical portrait of Paul's work might also provide a model or pattern of a continued world mission for the implied author and his readers. For further discussion on Paul as symbolic of Christianity in the history of *Actaforschung*, see chap. 1, "Historical Problems: Portrait of Paul," 9–12. For more explanation on Paul representing Christianity, see: chap. 4 "Relevance for Luke and His Readers/Auditors," 131–35. See also: Dibelius, *Studies*, 213; Haenchen, *Acts*, 628–31; 729–32. For additional reviews of Paul's portrait in

This typical portrayal of the Pauline mission may also indicate a procedure that is in accord with God's plan.[35] What Paul has encountered in Asia Minor, Greece, and Rome concerning Jewish rejection and Gentile receptivity is not only the normative experience of Christianity but is also a direct fulfillment of Scripture (Acts 13:47/Isa 49:6; Acts 28:26–27/ Isa 6:9–10). The Gentile mission of Paul is in obedience to the command of Christ (Acts 9:15; 22:15, 21; 26:16–18). Both themes of fulfillment of Scripture and obedience to Christ's command are often used by the author to indicate compliance with God's will.[36]

A characteristic of Acts 28 and the other missionary settings is the inclusion of summary statements concerning Paul's preaching to Jews and Gentiles (Acts 17:2–3; 18:4–5; 19:8–10; 28:23, 31). It has been stated in chapter 2 that these accounts presuppose Paul's sermon at Pisidian Antioch which is an extended account of Paul's missionary speeches (Acts 13:16–41).[37] Acts 13:16–41, like the other kerygmatic speeches (Acts 2; 3; 10), expounds the matter of Christ's suffering, death, and rising from the dead as the fulfillment of prophecy (2:22–35; 3:17–26; 10:36–43; 13:26–39). It is to the above contents that the Pauline preaching summaries allude.

Acts, see the case for the continued presence of Jesus in the work of Paul and the early church (perhaps an implicit assumption in Acts, as we see it), V. Stolle, *Der Zeuge als Angeklagter*, 283–84; and Paul, the cosmopolitan Christian gentleman, who arrives in Rome, the center of power and prestige, inviting others to join the ever-growing community of Christians, J. C. Lentz, *Luke's Portrait of Paul*, 4.

35. O'Neill describes the missionary procedure from Jerusalem to Rome as "divinely ordained," *Theology*, 177–79. See also Squires, *Plan of God*, 34–36, 137–39, 187–88.

36. See for example: Cadbury, *Making*, 303–6; Schubert, "Final Cycle," 1–4; Conzelmann, *Theology*, 149–69. This point would also make the patterns and procedures of the Pauline mission binding on Luke and his implied readers/auditors (insofar as it concerns a world mission).

37. An example of this kind of summary statement is Acts 17:2–3 where it says Paul argued from the Scriptures explaining that "it was necessary for Christ to suffer and to rise from the dead." In Acts 13:26–39 these points are developed more completely by Paul at Pisidian Antioch. See our chap. 2, "Summary Statement on Paul's Preaching," 48–52. Dupont describes Paul's inaugural address in Acts 13 as, "a genuine model of Paul's preaching to the Jews, ending as it does with a warning that, after announcing the message to the Jews it would turn to the Gentiles, so that the prophecies might be fulfilled," *Salvation*, 20. However, in chap. 2, p. 51, we have argued that the same message is presupposed in preaching to the Jews as well as Gentiles, (except for the speeches in Acts 14 and 17, where the Gentile audience appears to have no connection to the synagogue).

It has already been noted in our chapter 2 that Acts 13:46–47; 18:6; and 28:25–28 have a special formal relationship as apologies for the Gentile mission. All three accounts contain the elements of a Gentile apology: (1) a statement on Jewish unbelief, and (2) turning to the Gentiles.[38] Each of these elements will be examined in an attempt to understand the climactic qualities of Acts 28:25–28.

(1) Whereas the indictment on the unbelieving Jews is brief in Acts 13:46 and 18:6, a lengthy indictment in Acts 28:25–28 (from Isa 6:9–10) is pronounced on the unbelieving Jews.[39] Harnack and oth-

38. Although Acts 18:6 is not regarded as a Lukan speech in our study, it does contain these two elements of a Gentile apology. Luke 4:24–27, a Lukan speech, also fulfills this criterion. See, chap. 2, section on "Apologetic Speech," 54–58.

The two elements of Jewish unbelief and Gentile receptivity occur in many passages in Acts. (1) the Jewish refusal to believe the Christian proclamation (Acts 7:54, 57; 13:45–46, 50; 14:2; 17:5; 18:5–6; 19:8–9; 22:2, 22; 28:25–27). (2) The receptivity of the Gentiles to the gospel (Acts 10:44–45; 13:48; 15:7–8; 17:32b, 34; 18:8; 19:5, 9; 28:28–30. Moessner sees Jewish believers as the eschatological remnant who, along with growing numbers of Gentiles, call unbelieving Israel to repentance," in "Paul in Acts," *NTS* 34 (1988) 102. God is taking from among the Gentiles a "people for his name" (15:14–18), those who hear (ἀκούω) the prophet like Moses (Jesus) whom God has raised up (3:22–24; 7:37), Johnson, *Acts*, 70, 74, 129–30, 136–38, 264, 272.

39. This long indictment on Jewish unbelief in Acts 28 is comparable to the invective upon the Jews in the Stephen speech (Acts 7:51–53). In both accounts unbelief is portrayed as a hardening of the ears and heart (Acts 7:51; 28:26–27). In both accounts, the current unbelief of the Jews is interpreted as the traditional lack of obedience evidenced in Israel's history ("your fathers" Acts 7:51b–52; 28:25b). In both accounts there is a sweeping pronouncement upon the impenitent of Israel for their current and historic unbelief. See also: O'Toole, "Why Did Luke Write Acts?" 67, on Acts 28:25–28.

It must be added that this pronouncement of hardening in Acts 28:25–28, applies to the impenitent of Israel. Allowance should certainly be made for the possibility of a remnant of Israel obeying the gospel, as was evident earlier in Acts (2:41; 4:4; 6:7; 15:5; 21:20; 24:14). See B. Weiss, *Commentary*, 2:636–37. The universalistic statement implied in Acts 28:30 that Paul received "all who came to him" probably includes individual Jews as well as the Gentiles that would constitute the remnant of faithful Israel. See the cautious yet hopeful comments in Gaventa, *Acts*, 368–70.

Jervell argues that with the conclusion of Acts the mission to the Gentiles commences and the Jewish mission concludes since Israel (the people of God) has already been gathered: Jervell, *Luke and the People of God* (Augsburg, 1972) 55–56, 61–64; *The Unknown Paul* (Augsburg, 1984); *Apostelgeschichte*, 626–28. This view fails to address all of the data (see our chap. 3, pp. 74–76) and has other difficulties: see M. Moscato, "A Critique of Jervell's, Luke and the People of God," in *SBLSP II* (Scholars, 1975) 161–68; Wilson, *Gentiles*, 219–38; John T. Carroll, "Review of *The Unknown Paul*," *PSB* 7 (1986) 298–301; C. K. Barrett, "What Minorities?" in *Mighty Minorities?* (Oslo, 1995) 1–10. See also our chap. 1, p. 5 note 9. Although we see both Jewish and Gentile believers as included by Luke in the faithful remnant of Israel, the mission

ers see Acts 28:25–28 as a climactic pronouncement on the Jews who become more and more hostile until at last their heart was definitely hardened.[40] A case for the climactic nature of Paul's final statement of spiritual obtuseness on the *unbelieving* Jews can be made, on the basis of its climactic relationship with other similar passages, and because of its intrinsic climactic features.[41]

---

appears to *remain* open to "all" who will hear, both Jews and Gentiles (Acts 28:28–31; cf. 3:22,25).

40. Harnack, *Luke*, 133; Haenchen, *Acts*, 729; Dupont, *Salvation*, 141; O'Neill, *Theology*, 76; Johnson, *Acts*, 476; Tannehill, *Shape of Luke's Story*, 121–24, 159–65. In comparison to the receptivity of the Gentiles, the overall response of the Jews (as a group) to the Pauline mission was not favorable. See point 4 of our comparison on the Jewish response to Paul's mission as one of unbelief and divisiveness (Acts 13:45; 14:1–2, 4–5; 17:4–5; 18:6; 19:9; 28:24–25a). As a result, Israel's faithful remnant includes believing Jews along with a growing number of Gentiles who hear the prophet like Moses (3:22–26) and call upon the name of the Lord (15:14–18).

41. In Acts, the three pronouncements upon Jewish unbelief build up to a climax which is reached in Acts 28:25–28. (1) "Since you thrust it (the word) from you and judge yourselves unworthy of eternal life . . ." 13:46. (2) (And when they opposed and reviled him, he said to them) "Your blood be upon your heads!" 18:6, (a shorter but more emphatic denouncement on the unbelieving Jews). (3) "You shall indeed hear but never understand, you shall indeed see but never perceive, for the heart of this people has become dull and their ears are heavy of hearing and their eyes they have closed . . ." 28:26–27, (a longer, more emphatic, even final pronouncement, occurs in the narrative). See also Tannehill, *Narrative Unity*, 2:349–50; Marguerat, "The Enigma," 299–301.

In Acts 28:25–28 there is a certain intensity in vv. 26–27: "hear but never understand . . . see but never perceive." This intensity reaches a high point within the Isa 6 text: "their eyes they have closed." This high point forms the apex of a chiastic structure: a) "heart . . . b) ears . . . c) eyes . . . c') eyes . . . b') ears . . . a') heart . . ." See, Miesner, "Circumferential Speeches," 233, 236; Hauser, *Strukturen*, 38. In Acts 28:25b–28, however, Luke places greater emphasis on "hearing" (ἀκούω, ἀκοῇ vv 26–28; cf. 2:22; 3:22; 7:2; 15:13; 22:21) although allusions in 28:28 to Isa 40:5 "all flesh shall see" (Luke 3:6 ὁράω) are there. For more discussion, see discussion in n. 65 in our chapter two.

There is no evidence in the text to support the idea that Paul directs his statement of hardening here only to those who "disbelieved" and not to those who "were persuaded" v. 24. The utterance of Paul begins with a general statement of address: "The Holy Spirit was right in saying to your (ὑμῶν) fathers . . ." (v. 25b) without singling out either group. In chap. 2, "Apologetic Speech," 54–55, it was argued that both groups were present to hear Paul's hardening pronouncement and that after such a statement was made, they were in disagreement over it and began departing (v. 25). It was also discussed in chap. 2, p. 53. that Paul's statement of hardening may have been a major cause of their disagreement and departure.

Despite the scant reference to those who were persuaded (a doubtful term for conversion in Haenchen, *Acts*, 723) the overall response of the Jews at Rome was not favor-

(2) In all three apologies for the Gentile mission, the unbelief of the Jews provides the immediate occasion for the turning to the Gentiles (Acts 13:46–47; 18:6; 28:25–28).[42] By comparing Paul's final statement on the Gentiles in Acts 28:28 with the other Gentile apologies, and by examining the syntactical and thematic features of Acts 28:28, a case can be made for the climactic nature of Paul's announcement at Rome: "Let it be known to you then that this salvation of God has been sent to the Gentiles; they will listen."[43]

---

able: (1) some were persuaded; (2) others disbelieved; (3) all were in disagreement; and (4) all began leaving after Paul gave his hardening statement. The pronouncement on Jewish unbelief in vv. 26–27 confirms the unfavorable divided response of the Roman Jews as a group. See Marguerat, "The Enigma," 298–99. Karris argues that Luke purposely leaves the question of a Jewish mission open-ended in Acts 28, in "Missionary Communities," *CBQ* 41 (1979) 94. Spencer is also supportive of Karris here, *Journeying through Acts*, 250–51. We believe that the focus of the mission now appears to be on the Gentiles (28:28) although individual believing Jews will continue to be part of Israel's faithful remnant, which now includes a growing number of Gentiles. See our chap. 2, "Apologetic Speech," 56–58.

In point 4 of our comparison of Acts 28 with other Pauline missionary settings (chap. 3, p. 75) it was argued that the overall response of the Jews in all cases was one of unbelief or divisiveness (Acts 13:45; 14:1–2, 4–5; 17:4–5; 18:6; 19:9; 28:24–25a). Although Paul afterwards, "welcomed all who came to him,"(28:30), "'the days of retribution' upon an unrepentant people are straining to fulfillment," Moessner "Paul in Acts," *NTS* 34 (1988) 103.

42. The Gentile mission is further substantiated by the fulfillment of Scripture and the command of Christ. See chap. 1, "Gentile Mission," 4–6, and chap. 2, "Missionary Activity," 77.

43. The three apologies for the Gentile mission in the narrative of Acts form a rising order of importance regarding the idea of mission to the Gentiles. (1) "Behold we turn to the Gentiles," 13:46; (2) "From now on I will go to the Gentiles," 18:6; and (3) "Let it be known to you then that this salvation of God has been sent to the Gentiles; they will listen," 28:28. In Acts 28:28 the opening phrase γνωστὸν οὖν ἔστω calls attention to important material that follows as in several other Lukan speeches (Acts 2:14; 4:10; 13:38). The phrase τοῖς ἔθνεσιν ἀπεστάλη τοῦτο τὸ σωτήριον τοῦ θεοῦ (28:28) at the conclusion of Luke–Acts recalls similar terminology on God's salvation from the beginning of Luke–Acts (Luke 2:30; 3:6; cf. Isa 40:5). The theme of salvation for the Gentiles in Acts 28:28 is of prime importance in Luke–Acts (Luke 2:30; 3:6; 4:25–27; 13:29; 14:21; 21:24; 24:27; Acts 1:8; 2:39; 3:22–26; 9:15; 10:44—11:18; 13:46–47; 15:14–18; 18:6; 22:21; 26:16–23).

Acts 28:28 resolves the tension created by the problematic pronouncement on the Jews for spiritual blindness and deafness vv. 26–27. The crisis ends with the statement: God's salvation has been sent to the Gentiles ("all flesh will see," Isa 40:5; Luke 3:6), they will hear, v. 28! The climactic nature of Acts 28:28 (salvation to the Gentiles) is further developed in Dupont "La Conclusion," 366–80, 400–402. See also Talbert, *Reading Acts*, 227. As shown in our chapter two, Acts 28:25b-28 is an apologetic speech for the

In Paul's pronouncement on the Jews of Rome, Luke appears to make a final climactic statement on the Jewish conflicts and the Gentile mission in Acts: many of the Jews have become hardened to the gospel, the Gentiles have become receptive to the gospel.

In summary, we see that the scene in Acts 28 is portrayed as a typical Pauline missionary situation indicating the continuity and normative procedure of the Christian mission in accordance with God's plan. The extensive account of Paul preaching to the Jews in Pisidian Antioch (13:16–41) concerning Christ's suffering death, and resurrection from the dead as the fulfillment of prophecy, is presupposed in the preaching account of Acts 28:23 and 31 (as elsewhere 17:2–3; 18:5; 19:8). Acts 28:25–28, as a lengthy final pronouncement on the unbelief of the Jews and the turning to the Gentiles, functions as the climax of a series of apologies for the Gentile mission (13:46–47; 18:6). Therefore the relationship of Acts 28 with other Pauline missionary settings is established in terms of the common patterns employed and from their relationship in the middle of the narrative of Acts.[44]

Gentile mission with v. 28 (salvation to the Gentiles) as the concluding exhortation of the pronouncement upon the unbelieving Jews (vv. 26–27) with v. 25b as the opening panel, 54–58.

These findings support the view that Acts 28 is a deliberate and complete conclusion from a literary and theological standpoint, see Cadbury, *Making*, 323–25; Haenchen, *Acts*, 731–32; O'Neill, *Theology*, 60–62; Wilson, *Gentiles*, 236–38. See especially, our chap. 1, "Abrupt-Ending Question," 14.

44. Dupont argues that Acts 28 functions as the conclusion of the history of Paul's missionary activity (Acts 13–28), "La Conclusion," 383–86 but even as a history of Paul's missionary activity, some important intervening events occur, e.g., the Jerusalem Council (15) plus the Arrest and Defense of Paul (21–26). If we have a linear-temporal framework here (broadly outlined), it must be added that typical patterns and procedures are portrayed in Luke–Acts, showing a continuity of missionary activity and a normative procedure in accordance with God's plan (Luke 4; Acts 13; 18; 19; 28).

Countering this linear-temporal scheme, however, Beverly Gaventa, following Aristotle *Poetics* 18.1–3 (LCL 66–69), observes a dramatic plot structure in Acts: Prologue 1:1—2:47; Part I Preparation 3:1—9:43, Climactic Event 10:1—11:18 (Cornelius and household), Denouement 11:19—15:35; Part II Preparation 15:36—25:27, Climactic Event 26:1–32 (Paul before Agrippa), Denouement 27:1–28:31, "Acts," in *NIDB* 1:34; *Acts*, 55–56. We also observe a similar plot structure in the narrative of Paul's Journey to Rome: Complication, 19:21—21:16 (will Paul really "see Rome"?), Crisis, 21:17–36 (Paul is arrested by a *Roman* tribune, 21:33), Denouement, 21:37—28:31 with deus ex machina, 23:11; 27:23–24 (visions from God), to assure the audience/reader of Paul's arrival in Rome. See "The Dramatic Genre," in Puskas, *Introduction*, 126–38.

The Conclusion of Acts and the Beginnings of Acts

In recent studies, a detailed comparisons were made of Acts 1 and 28 on the basis of similar concepts and themes (e.g. kingdom of God, world-wide mission, the idea of "dwelling," the concept of "knowing").[45] A comparison of the beginning and conclusion of Acts has been made to understand the relevance of the enthroned Christ in the account of Paul at Rome.[46] Other studies in Luke–Acts have made frequent allusions to the relationship of Christ's commission (Acts 1:8) and Paul's mission in Rome (28:23–31).[47]

While there is insufficient evidence for viewing Acts 1 and 28 as parallel texts, they both share common elements and have a special literary relationship. In a comparison of Acts 28 with Acts 1, the following structural, linguistic, and thematic commonalities can be observed.

Teaching

1. The term at διδάσκω occurs in the opening and closing verses of Acts (1:1; 28:31) signifying Luke's interest in "teaching" especially in the activities of Jesus and Paul.

The Holy Spirit

2. The phrase πνεῦμα ἅγιον occurs in both contexts (1:2, 8; 28:25). In Acts 1 and 28, the Holy Spirit is actively involved in the pronouncements of Jesus (1:2) and Isaiah (28:25).[48] In Acts 1:8, the Holy Spirit is to empower the disciples for a worldwide mission, something which is presupposed in Acts 28.

45. Dupont, "La Conclusion," 388–90. See also: Mikeal C. Parsons, *The Departure of Jesus in Luke-Acts* (Sheffield, 1988) 156–59, 169, 255–58 and Arie W. Zwiep, *The Ascension of the Messiah in Lukan Christology* (Brill, 1997) 30–31, 99, 172–74.

46. R. H. Smith, "Theology," 531–32, 535. On Acts 1:6 and 28:30f, N. T. Wright mentions "the kingship of Israel's God in Rome," *New Testament and the People of God* (Fortress, 1992) 375.

47. For example, see: Dibelius, *Studies*, 3; Cadbury, *Making*, 323–24; Lampe, *Christians at Rome*, 7 n. 1; Alexander, "Reading Luke–Acts," 212–14. See our chap. 1, "Lukan Parallels: Acts 1 and Acts 28," 18.

48. In Acts 1:2, Jesus gave orders to the apostles "through the Holy Spirit"; in Acts 28:25, "the Holy Spirit" spoke to the fathers through Isaiah the prophet. The Lukan narrator also refers to the Spirit who once spoke to David (according to Peter in Acts 1:16) and Isaiah (Paul in 28:25). See also Ju Hur, *Dynamic Reading of the Holy Spirit in Luke–Acts* (Sheffield, 2001) 94–95, 109, 111, 141, 144–15 (Acts 1:8), 150, 277, 284 (Acts 1; 28).

The Kingdom of God

3. Four of the eight total occurrences, in Acts, of the phrases τῆς βασιλείας τοῦ θεοῦ and τὴν βασιλείαν are equally distributed in Acts 1:3, 6 and 28:23, 31.

What Is Known

4. In Acts 1, knowledge of the speculative matters of the times or seasons is withheld from Jesus' disciples οὐχ ὑμῶν ἐστιν γνῶναι χρόνους, 1:7). In Acts 28, knowledge of salvation to the Gentiles (γνωστὸν οὖν ἔστω ὑμῖν, 28:28) is revealed to Paul's listeners.[49]

World-Wide Mission

5. In Acts 1:8, Jesus tells his disciples "you shall be my witnesses" μάρτυρες. In Acts 28:23, Paul functions as a witness ("testifying" διαμαρτυρόμενος of the kingdom of God).
6. The geographical progression in Acts 1:8 from "Jerusalem . . . to the ends of the earth" has some application to Rome (Acts 28) which is the center of the Gentile world.[50]

49. This contrast was first pointed out in Dupont, "La Conclusion" 390.

50. Some caution should be taken in any attempt to equate the designation "ends of the earth" only with Rome (despite this apparent association in the Psalms of Solomon 8:15). The phrase "ends of the earth" from Acts 1:8 is also employed in Acts 13:47/Isa 49:6 to signify the Gentile world in general (where Rome is at the center). See: Dupont, *Salvation*, 12, 17–18, and Van Unnik, "'Book of Acts,'" 39. It must be noted, however, that the Lukan geographical perspective is from Jerusalem, not Rome. The mission is launched from Jerusalem (Luke 24:49; Acts 1:8) and the missionary activity is monitored from Jerusalem to which it returns before setting out again to farther regions (1:12—8:3; 9:1–2, 26–29; 11:2–18; 11:30—12:25; 15:1–29; 21:17—23:21). See Puskas and Crump, *An Introduction to the Gospels and Acts* (Eerdmans, 2008), chart 5.1. Geographical Expansion in Acts. Rome is also "one of the most distant points on the circumference of a Jerusalem-centered compass" (e.g., Acts 2:9–11) in Alexander, "Reading Luke-Acts," 212–14. Antioch of Syria is a temporary base of operation for two earlier missionary journeys (13:1–3; 14:26–28; 15:30–35; 18:22) but after Paul's third missionary journey, the attention returns to Jerusalem and eventually on to Rome. In Acts, Rome is a final destination (19:21; 23:11; 25:10–12, 21; 26:32; 27:24; 28:14, 16). See our survey in chap. 1, "Goal of the Progression of the Gospel from Jerusalem to Rome," 3–4.

On Lukan geography, see Conzelmann, *Theology of St. Luke* 149–69; F. V. Filson, "The Journey Motif in Acts," *Apostolic History*, 68–77; Moessner, *Lord of the Banquet*, 290–325; Fitzmyer, *Luke*, 1:164–71 (including a critique of Conzelmann); Scott, "Luke's Geographical Horizon," *Book of Acts*, 2:522–44.

7. Acts 1:8 presents us with the last words of Jesus which concern the church's world-wide mission, a similar theme in the last words of Paul (28:28).[51]

Concerning the theme of a world-wide mission, the relationship of Acts 28 to Acts 1 can be seen in the following manner: Paul, who is endued with the Holy Spirit (Acts 9:17–18; 13:2–3, 9; cf. 1:8), functions as Christ's witness in Rome (23:11; 28:23, 31; cf. 1:8), having brought the gospel to the Gentile world, to the "ends of the earth." In doing the above, Paul has brought Christ's commission (1:8) to its completion in Acts.

Concerning the theme of the kingdom of God in Acts 1 and 28, a comparison can be noted. In Acts 1, the resurrected Christ speaks to his disciples of the kingdom of God (v. 3). In Acts 28, Paul testifies to and proclaims the kingdom of God (vv. 23, 31). The speculative question of when Christ will restore the kingdom to Israel (1:6) is subordinated to the important concern of worldwide mission (1:8), a concern which is evident in Acts 28:28–31.

It was stated earlier that from a comparison of Acts 1 and 28, some conclude that the "relevance of the enthroned Christ" is proclaimed by Paul at Rome.[52] This position has some validity if it can be established that: (1) Christ assumed His heavenly throne as King at his exaltation (Luke 1:32–33; Acts 2:32–36; 13:32–34),[53] (2) the exaltation of Christ includes his resurrection and ascension (Luke 24:26; Acts 2:32–33; 5:30–31),[54] and (3) Christ's enthronement is presupposed in the account

51. See, Dupont, "La Conclusion," 390; Parsons also supports this connection, *Departure of Jesus*, 158.

52. The thesis in R. H. Smith, "Theology," 531–32, 535.

53. Christ is sometimes regarded as king in his earthly ministry (Luke 19:38; cf., Matt 21:5; Luke 23:2, 37), I. H. Marshall, *Luke: Historian and Theologian* (Zondervan, 1971) 89–91. In Acts, the title "king" is only used of the exalted Jesus in 17:7. Christ's authority is also made present through the Holy Spirit, by the power of his name, and in the very mission of his followers, George M. MacRae, "'Whom Heaven Must Receive Until the Time': Reflections on the Christology of Acts," *Int* 27 (1973) 155–65; his kingship over earth, however, is acknowledged by a limited community, Tannehill, "What Kind of King? What Kind of Kingdom?" in *The Shape of Luke's Story*, 50. See also the balanced study Mark Strauss, *David Messiah in Luke–Acts* (Sheffield, 1995) 337–56.

54. For a discussion of Christ's exaltation as including his resurrection and ascension, and an understanding of the implications of Christ's exaltation in terms of Davidic kingship, see: R. F. O'Toole, "Luke's Understanding of Jesus' Resurrection-Ascension-Exaltation," *BTB* 9 (1979) 106–14 and "Activity of the Risen Jesus in Luke–Acts," *Bib* 62 (1981) 471–97. For a survey of discussion, see Douglas Buckwalter, *The Character and*

of Paul's proclaiming the kingdom of God at Rome (Acts 1:3, 6; 28:23, 31).[55] Since each of the above points is not completely evident from a comparison of Acts 1 and 28 (the scope of our study), and each is not without some difficulty in the theology of Luke, the relevance of the enthroned Christ at Rome is at best an implicit theme in Acts 28.

In another study of Acts 1 and 28,[56] the association made between the restoring of the kingdom to Israel (1:6) and the hope of Israel (28:20), is in need of clarification. Although there may be an association here (in 1:6 and 28:20), one also needs to see their thematic relationship with Israel's hope in the resurrection of the dead (Acts 23:6; 24:15; 26:6–8; 28:20). To understand Acts 28:20 as pertaining to hope in the resurrection, and to compare it with Acts 1:6 (restoring the kingdom to Israel), assumes that: (1) Christ's exaltation to His heavenly throne involves the resurrection of Christ, and (2) Christ's enthronement is somehow connected with the concept of the kingdom of God in Acts 28. This last point is implicit at best.[57]

In conclusion, a comparison of Acts 1 and 28 indicates a correspondence between the activities of Jesus and Paul. Both Jesus and Paul speak, testify, or proclaim the kingdom of God which has appeared in the life and work of Jesus Christ. While Jesus withholds knowledge from the disciples concerning times or seasons, Paul makes known to his Jewish listeners that salvation has been sent to the Gentiles.[58] The ministries of

---

Purpose of Luke's Christology (Cambridge, 1996) 3–31. On Acts 28: "David's kingdom is being established so that all nations may seek the Lord," L. Goppelt, *Typos* (1982; Wipf & Stock, 2002) 118.

55. Smith, "Theology," 531–32. This last point (3) is assumed because it is not explicitly stated, and is thus the most difficult to establish of the three points stated above. With MacRae we agree that Christ's authority in Acts is made present in different ways, "Christology of Acts," 160–65. For a survey of the content of the preaching summaries in Acts, see our chap. 2, "Summary Statement," 50–51.

56. Dupont, "La Conclusion," 390. No explanation is given for the comparison of Acts 1:6 and 28:20 here.

57. We have pointed out in chap. 2, "Summary Statement," 51, that in the life and work of Christ, God's reign has appeared (or begun to appear), resulting in the salvation of Jews and Gentiles; Parsons favors this more inclusive understanding of the "hope of Israel," *Departure of Jesus*, 257. On Israel's hope confirmed in Christ's resurrection, see Morna Hooker, *Endings*, 63. For Acts 1:6 and its implications for God's reign, see Tannehill, *Narrative Unity*, 2:14–17; Hooker, *Endings*, 59.

58. See point 4 in our comparison of Acts 1 and 28, p. 83, dealing with the usage of γινώσκω.

Jesus and Paul are both characterized by teaching activity. Both Jesus and Paul make final declarations concerning a world-wide mission.

Acts 28 can also be seen as a fulfillment of Acts 1. Paul who is endued with the Holy Spirit functions as Christ's witness in Rome having brought the gospel to the Gentile world, "to the uttermost parts of the earth."

The Conclusion of Acts and the Conclusion of Luke

Luke and Acts since the early twentieth century have been regarded as parallel works.[59] It has been shown that the journey of Paul to Jerusalem (Acts 19:21—21:16) finds a close parallel in the journey of Jesus to Jerusalem (Luke 9:51—19:48).[60] It has been argued that just as Jesus' arrest, trial, crucifixion, and resurrection in Jerusalem completes Luke's

59. For example: Rackham, *Acts*, xlvii, 477–78; Morgenthaler, *Lukanische Geschichtsschreibung*, 1:180–94; Goulder, *Type*, 52–64; Talbert, *Literary Patterns*, 15–33; Mattill, "Jesus–Paul," 30–37; Radl, *Paulus und Jesus*; Peterson, *Literary Criticism*, 83–86; Tannehill, *Narrative Unity*, 1 and 2; Johnson, *Luke*; *Acts*; Barrett, *Acts*, 1 and 2; Fitzmyer, *Luke*, 1 and 2; *Acts*; Green, *Luke*, 6–21; D. S. McComiskey, *Lukan Theology in the Light of the Gospel's Literary Structure* (2004) 90–121.

Mikeal C. Parsons and Richard I. Pervo have raised questions regarding generic unity (e.g., are both general or apologetic history? Philosophical succession?), also theological unity, and narrative unity, in *Rethinking the Unity of Luke and Acts* (1993); Michael F. Bird focuses on the flashpoints of the debate after Parsons and Pervo and what's at stake for Lukan studies in "The Unity of Luke–Acts in Recent Discussion," *JSNT* 29 (2007) 425–48. Andrew Gregory shows that Irenaeus and the Muratorian Fragment (second century) each read Luke and Acts as two elements of one literary whole, "The Reception of Luke and Acts," *JSNT* 29 (2007) 459–72; C. K. Rowe (expanding on Gregory's work) argues that our earliest manuscript evidence and patristic usage provides no support for the idea that Luke's readers originally read/heard Luke and Acts together, "Literary Unity and Reception History," *JSNT* 29 (2007) 449–57. Joseph Verheyden's introductory article (3–56) and the supporting articles by Marguerat, Brawley, Radl, Moessner, Neirynck, and others demonstrate that there is still a general consensus regarding the unity of Luke–Acts even though the nature of that unity is still under debate, Verheyden, ed., *The Unity of Luke–Acts* (Leuven, 1999); Patrick Spencer responds to challenges in the areas of genre, narrative, theology, and reception history in "The Unity of Luke–Acts: A Four-Bolted Hermeneutical Hinge," *CurrBiblRes* 5:3 (2007) 341–46; L. T. Johnson, "Literary Criticism of Luke–Acts: Is Reception History Pertinent?" *JSNT* 28 (2005) 159–62.

60. Rackham, *Acts*, xlvii; Talbert, *Literary Patterns*, 16–17; Mattill, "Jesus–Paul," 30–33; Radl, *Paulus und Jesus*, 103–24; Moessner, *Lord of the Banquet*, 290–322; and "Jesus, Peter, Stephen, and Paul," 249–56; McComiskey, *Lukan Theology*, 108–11.

Gospel, so Paul's arrest, trial, and final vindication in Rome concludes Acts.[61]

In a well-known study by Paul Schubert, it was pointed out that Luke 24 and Acts 28 are parallel works in structure, form, and content.[62] Studies have also pointed out the linguistic similarities between Acts 28:17–19 and the passion of Jesus.[63] With the above parallels noted by others in Luke–Acts, there is good reason to suspect that the conclusion of Acts in its literary construction is not unlike the conclusion of Luke. By comparing Acts 28 with Luke 23–24 one might also detect the manner in which the implied author concludes a literary work. This comparison might further develope the typical correspondence between Jesus and Paul, and also seek to establish a promise-fulfillment relationship between the two passages.

The following structural, linguistic, and thematic parallels are detected in Luke 23–24 and Acts 28:16–31.

Passion Statements[64]

1. Both Jesus and Paul are accused of leading the people astray (Luke 23:14; Acts 28:17b).
2. Both Jesus and Paul are said to have been "handed over to the hands of" Romans/men (aorist passive of παπαδίδωμι with έίς τὰς χεῖρας. Luke 24:7; Acts 28:17c) in terminology characteristic of the Suffering Servant (Isa 53:6, 12 LXX).

61. Goulder, *Type*, 34–51; Talbert, *Literary Patterns*, 17–18; Mattill, "Jesus–Paul," 32–37; Peterson, *Literary Criticism*, 85; O'Toole, "Parallels in Luke–Acts," 199; David E. Aune views the Jesus–Paul parallels as the recurrence of similar events and patterns found in, e.g., Appian *Hannibalic Wars* 7.8.53, *New Testament in Its Literary Environment* (Westminster, 1987) 119; see also M. Skinner, *Locating Paul* (SBL, 2003) 157–60.

62. Schubert, "Luke 24," 185, also 166, 177. See the helpful studies of Mikeal Parsons, *Departure of Jesus in Luke–Acts*, 155–86, 255–69 and Arie Zwiep, *Ascension of the Messiah*, 28–33, 99, 172–73, 214–15.

63. Radl *Paulus und Jesus* 252–65. Note also the study on Acts 28 and Luke 24, in Dupont, "La Conclusion," 387–88. Here Barrett notes, "the passion of the servant of Christ is described in terms drawn from Christ's own," in his *Acts*, 2:1239. See also Hauser, *Struckturen*, 161–62; "In the Pauline Passion Narrative," Jack T. Sanders, "The Jewish People in Luke-Acts," 127 (referring to Paul's arrest, trial, and imprisonment in Jerusalem and Caesarea). Finally, see our chapter 2, "A Passion Recital Speech of Paul," 43–45.

64. The relationship of the passion of Jesus and Acts 28:17–19 has already been investigated in chapter 2, pp. 43–45.

3. Both Jesus and Paul are "examined" by the Romans (ἀνακρίνω Luke 23:14; Acts 28:18) who wanted "to release" them (ἀπολύω Luke 23:20; Acts 28:18a) because there was "no cause for death" in their cases (negative μή or ού) form with αἰτίαν/αἴτιον Θανάτου Luke 23:22; Acts 28:18).

4. It was because of the opposition of the Jews that Jesus and Paul encounter their fates (Roman crucifixion Luke 23:18–25; before Caesar Acts 28:19; cf. 27:24).

Similar Structure

5. Luke 24:36–53 and Acts 28:17–31 both have a similar structure with two corresponding scenes and an epilogue. In the first scene, both Jesus and Paul present themselves to their listeners (Luke 24:36–43; Acts 28:17–22). In scene two, both characters expound from the law and the prophets concerning Christ and declare a universal mission (Luke 24:44–49; Acts 28:23–28). Both accounts end with a concluding summary, vindicating Jesus and Paul (Luke 24:50–53; Acts 28:30–31).[65]

Divine Fulfillment and Continuity with the Prophets

6. Both Jesus and Paul expound from Moses and the prophets concerning Christ (Luke 24:27, 44–46; Acts 28:23).

Hardness of Heart

7. Both passages refer to unbelief (ἀπιστέω) Luke 24:41; Acts 28:24b) and hardness of heart (Luke 24:25; Acts 28:25b–27).[66]

65. This observation is from Dupont, "La Conclusion" 387–88. See our point 9, for further discussion on the concluding epilogues, 89.

The parallel between Luke 24 and Acts 28 further substantiates the claim that Acts 28 seeks to defend Paul and his work. See especially, chap. 3, "Acts 28 and Paul's Arrest and Defense," 71–72, and "Acts 28 and Other Pauline Missionary Settings," 76–81.

66. For an understanding of the semantic field of "hardness of heart" terminology and its synonymous relationship with the "refusal to see or hear," see: F. W. Danker, "Hardness of Heart: A Study in Biblical Thematic," *CTM* 44 (1972) 89–100; J. Gnilka, *Die Verstockung Israels: Isaias 6:9–10* (Kösel, 1961) 146–54; C. A. Evans, *To See and Not Perceive: Isaiah* 6:9–10, 121–26.

Universal Mission

8. Preaching (κηρύσσω) to the Gentiles/nations (ἔθνος) is a concern of both passages (Luke 24:47–48; Acts 28:28, 30–31).

Triumphant Conclusion

9. Both accounts end on a note of victory, with Jesus carried up into heaven and Paul carrying on a successful ministry unhindered (Luke 24:50–53; Acts 28:30–31).[67]

It is evident from points 1–4 that Jesus and Paul are portrayed as undergoing similar experiences. Both Jesus and Paul are accused of leading the people astray (1). Both are said to have been handed over to the hands of Romans/Roman men (2). Both Jesus and Paul are examined by Romans who wanted to release them because there was no cause for death in their cases (3). It was because of the opposition of the Jews that Jesus and Paul encounter their fates (4). It seems clear from the nature of the above parallels that the Lukan narrative seeks to defend both figures, by having Roman authorities declare them innocent (3) and by portraying their arrest with the imagery of the innocent Suffering Servant of YHWH (2).

What the Jesus–Paul parallelism seem to contribute to Acts 28 is an "irresistible apology for Paul" and his mission.[68] Paul is portrayed as

67. A comparison might also be made between Acts 13:52, when Paul and Barnabas were going to Iconium: "And the disciples were filled with joy and with the Holy Spirit," and Luke 24:52, when after the ascension of Jesus the disciples "returned to Jerusalem with great joy and were continually in the temple blessing God." See discussion on a tragic or triumphant conclusion to Acts in Mark Powell, *What Are They Saying about Acts?* (1991) 104–5. I would add to the debate that although Jewish responses to God's message/messengers can be viewed as tragic, Christ's mission to the world continues on a triumphant note. On this triumphant ending in Acts 28, see also: Rackham, *Acts*, xlvii, 478; Bruce, *Acts*, 510–11; Dupont, *Salvation*, 14–15; and "La Conclusion," 361; Witherington, *Acts* 815–16; Barrett, *Acts*, 2:1253; Darrell Bock, *Acts* (Baker, 2007) 40–41, 757. For a critique of triumphalism in Luke–Acts, see Beverly R. Gaventa, "Toward a Theology of Acts," *Int* 42 (1988) 153–57, "Luke is capable of sustaining elements of triumph and elements of failure in his narrative" 157; triumphalism "But is that really intended?" in Fitzmyer, *Luke*, 1:22–23; no triumphalism here from a "a persecuted minority fighting for its life!" W. H. Willimon, *Acts* (Westminster John Knox, 1988) 191.

68. Phrase borrowed from Mattill on Jesus–Paul parallels in general, "Jesus–Paul," 37; see also Mattill, "The Purpose of Acts: Schneckenburger Reconsidered," *Apostolic History*, 114–15, 120; O'Toole sees an apology for Paul as secondary to a Lukan intent to establish continuity between Luke and Acts, Jesus and his followers, "Parallels in

undergoing the same experiences as Jesus did, the Ideal Servant (points 1–4). Paul is accused of the same charges as Jesus (1, 4), is portrayed as a suffering servant like Jesus (2), and is declared innocent by Roman officials, as in the case of Jesus (3). The apologetic nature of the above Jesus–Paul parallels, and the fact that Paul is compared to Jesus, the Ideal Servant and Prophet of God, are two reasons for viewing the function of the Jesus–Paul parallels in Acts 28 as a defense of Paul.

Paul, the one who is innocent like Jesus, also does the work of Jesus. Paul follows Jesus' practice of appealing to the law and the prophets concerning the message of Christ (6). Paul's work is met by hardness of heart, a characteristic attitude of the Jews confronted with Christ, especially as it concerns the resurrection of Jesus from the dead (7).[69] Paul also brings to completion the commission of Christ to preach to all nations (8). From points 6–9 it is noted that both Luke 24 and Acts 28 contain common Lukan themes: fulfillment of Scripture concerning Jesus Christ,[70] unbelief and hardness of heart,[71] and the Gentile mission.[72]

Furthermore, it appears that in two of the above themes, Acts 28 is a continuation of Luke 24. In Luke 24:27 Christ interprets from Moses and the prophets concerning himself, while in Acts 28:23 Paul tries to convince the Roman Jews about Jesus from Moses and the prophets.[73] In Luke 24:47 Christ announces that repentance and forgiveness of sins should be "proclaimed" in his name to all nations, in Acts 28:30–31

Luke–Acts," 209–12.

69. The two on the way to Emmaus were "slow of heart" (βραδεῖς τῇ καρδίᾳ) to believe all that the prophets had spoken about Christ's suffering and resurrection-exaltation (Luke 24:25). The Jews at Rome have become deaf, blind, and their hearts made dull (ἐπαχύνθη γὰρ ἡ καρδία) because of their rejection of the proclamation about the risen-exalted Christ (Acts 28:23–28). For Paul's preaching on the risen-exalted Christ, see: Acts 13:30–37; 17:2–3, 32; 26:22–23; cf. Luke 24:26–27, 44–47; and Dupont, *Salvation*, 16–17, 28–29, 130–31. Examples of Jewish refusal to believe the Christian proclamation are Acts 7:54, 57; 13:45–46, 50; 14:2; 17:5; 18:5–6; 19:8–9; 22:22; 28:25–27. For further discussion on this matter, see our investigation of Acts 13:46–47; 18:6; 28:25–28, in chap. 3, "Acts 28 and Other Pauline Missionary Settings," 75–80.

70. For example: Luke 2:32; 18:31–33; 22:37; 24:27, 44–46; Acts 3:18; 8:35; 10:43; 13:27; 17:2–3; 18:28; 26:22–23; 28:23.

71. For example: Luke 2:34; 4:24–29; 10:21, 24; 16:31; 18:34; 19:42; 20:9–18; 22:67; 24:11, 25, 41; Acts 7:51; 13:27, 41, 46, 50; 14:2; 17:5; 18:6; 19:9; 28:24–25.

72. For example: Luke 2:32; 3:6; 4:25–27; 21:24; 24:47; Acts 2:39; 3:25; 9:15; 10:45; 13:46–47; 15:14–18; 18:6; 19:9–10; 22:21; 26:17–18, 23; 28:25–28.

73. See also Acts 17:2–3; 26:22–23.

Paul is "proclaiming" the kingdom of God and teaching about Jesus Christ to "all" who came to him (cf. 28:28).[74] In both cases Paul carries on the work of Jesus in his use of Scripture (6) and in following Christ's command to preach to the nations (8).

In the concluding verses of Acts, Paul is vindicated by carrying on a successful ministry at Rome unhindered (23:30–31). In the concluding verses of Luke's Gospel, Jesus is vindicated in his being carried up into heaven, with his disciples returning to Jerusalem with great joy (Luke 24:50–53). Both accounts end on a note of triumph (9).

In summary, it is noted that Luke 23–24 and Acts 28 may be viewed as parallel works, giving us a clue as to how the implied author concludes a literary work. Both texts contain passion statements, two corresponding scenes and an epilogue. Both passages have common themes such as: fulfillment of Scripture, hardness of heart, and the universal mission. Both Luke 24 and Acts 28 end on a note of triumph. From this comparison it can be concluded that the implied author probably had certain features of Luke 23–24 in view when he concluded the book of Acts.

It is also to be observed that a typical correspondence exists between the experiences and actions of Jesus and Paul. The author appears to utilize these parallels to defend Paul and his work, as one like Jesus who does the work of Jesus. In a promise-fulfillment scheme, Paul in Acts 28 brings to completion the command of Jesus in Luke 24 to preach in His name to all nations.

The Inaugural Sermon of Jesus and the Concluding Speech(es) of Paul

The significance of Luke 4:16–30 in Luke–Acts as a "keynote speech" of Jesus has been pointed out by Cadbury and others.[75] Donald R. Miesner has pointed out the similarities between Luke 4 and Acts 28 as the first and last addresses of Luke–Acts.[76] Our own position will

74. See also Acts 26:22–23.

75. Cadbury, *Making*, 61, 188–89; Smith, *Acts*, 78; Talbert, *Literary Patterns*, 19, 97–98; Goulder, *Type*, 55, 74; Dupont, "La Conclusion," 396–98; Fitzmyer, *Luke*, 1:526–30; David L. Tiede, *Prophecy and History in Luke-Acts* (Fortress, 1980) 19–63; Sanders, "From Isaiah 61 to Luke 4," in Evans and Sanders, *Luke and Scripture*, 46–69; Tannehill, "Luke 4:16–30," in *The Shape of Luke's Story*, 3–30.

76. Miesner, "Circumferential Speeches," 2:223–37. "The Nazareth episode can thus

be clarified as we analyze Miesner's study. Commenting on Luke 4, he states that its declaration of good news for people of all nations and the unreceptive attitude of Jesus' country men weave like a golden thread, throughout Luke–Acts, even to the final climactic speech in Rome at the end of Acts.[77]

Although Miesner's study is informative, his attempt to arrange Acts into a complete chiastic framework is less than successful.[78] At various points he overstates the features common to both Luke 4 and Acts 28.[79] Despite the above shortcomings, several of Miesner's obser-

---

be read as a direct counterpoint to Paul's final word in Acts 28," Alexander, "Reading Luke–Acts from Back to Front," 219–20; for an excellent survey of discussion on Luke 4, Acts 28 and other relevant texts, see Frans Neirynck, "Luke 4:16–30 and the Unity of Luke–Acts," in *The Unity of Luke–Acts*, ed., J. Verheyden (Leuven, 1999) 387–95.

77. Miesner, 223 (also 235 n. 3).

78. For example, Miesner includes the later Western reading of Acts 28:29 ("The Jews left, having much debate among themselves") to establish a chiastic relationship with v. 25 ("and since they were in disagreement with one another, they left"), Ibid., 230, 234. We have already argued in chap. 2, 54–55, that Acts 28:25a functions as the conclusion of Paul's apologetic speech (vv. 25–28) but was displaced at the beginning by Luke to underscore the dramatic effect of 28:28. For our discussion on the later Western reading of 28:29 see chap. 1, "Positions Taken on Various Verses," 25.

In support of his assertion that Acts 28:25–28 forms a complete chiasm, Miesner attempts to force several phrases into a parallel construction. This practice can be seen in his attempt to establish a parallelism between 28:25b and v. 28. On the basis of the use of divine names (v. 25b "Holy Spirit"; v. 28 "God") and the questionable parallel between a verb of speaking with a verb of hearing, because of their respective contexts (v. 25b "well spoke"; v. 28 "they will hear"; both having two different functions in the passage). Miesner divorces a phrase from its grammatical syntax (". . . of God; they will hear" v. 28) in an attempt to construct a parallel for v. 25b ("well spoke the Holy Spirit"), Ibid., 230, 233. Such a procedure is based on insufficient evidence, is grammatically questionable, and disrupts the sequence of thought in Acts 28:28 "this salvation of God" (cf. Luke 3:6/Isa 40:5). It is doubtful if many of the linguistic comparisons of Miesner can be regarded as chiastic parallelisms when the syntax and sequence of thought are disregarded, as noted above.

79. For example, Miesner compares Luke 4:18 "recovery of sight to the blind" with Acts 28:27 the blindness of the Jews. Ibid., 234. Although both passages are concerned with spiritual perception (Luke 4:18; Acts 28:26–27; cf. 26:17–18) there are differences in the understanding of blindness. In Luke 4:18, "the blind" (τυφλός) are identified with "the captives" and "the oppressed," those who are in need of God's help (Luke 4:18; 7:22–23; 14:13, 21), see Danker, *Jesus*, 58–59. Acts 28:27 applies "blindness" to those hardened by God because of unbelief (Luke 8:10; 10:21–24; 19:41–44; 24:16, 25; Acts 7:51; 19:9), see also Danker, "Hardness of Heart" 89–100. There is also need for further clarification in Miesner's comparative analysis, for example: what relationship does the phrase "no honor in his own country" (Luke 4:24) have with Paul's innocence

vations on the commonalities of the two chapters are noteworthy and will be utilized to some extent in our comparative analysis.[80]

The structural, linguistic, and thematic parallels to be noted in Luke 4 and Acts 28 are the following[81]

Setting

1. Both passages open with a geographical location (Nazareth, Luke 4:16; Rome, Acts 28:16) and a temporal setting (on the sabbath, Luke 4:16; on the appointed day, Acts 28:23).[82]
2. Both include the missionary setting with the Jews (in the synagogue, Luke 4:16; a calling together of prominent Jews, Acts 28:17, 23).[83]

Structure

3. Both accounts can be divided into two scenes. In scene one, both Jesus and Paul present themselves to their fellow countrymen, which prompts a favorable response from the listeners (Luke 4:16–22; Acts 28:17–22). In scene two, both Jesus and Paul speak of God's favor to Gentiles which prompts a negative response from the listeners (Luke 4:23–30; Acts 28:23–28).[84]

---

regarding his own nation (Acts 28:17): both Jesus and Paul were misunderstood? Do these verses form a synthetic or an antithetical parallelism? Miesner, 234.

80. Particularly in his table of parallels, Miesner, 234.

81. Only the Lukan features in Luke 4:16–30 (as distinct from Mark 6:1–6 and Matthew 13:53–58) will be compared with Acts 28.

82. As has been suggested earlier in chapter 3, 74–75, "appointed day" may have a similar function, as "sabbath" in terms of a designated day for a missionary encounter to take place (Acts 13:14, 44; 14:1; 17:1; 18:1, 4; 19:1; 28:16, 23).

83. It was Paul's normal missionary procedure to enter a synagogue and preach to the Jews first, but since Paul is a prisoner at Rome the Jews must come to him.

84. This observation is derived from Dupont, "La Conclusion," 398.

The assertion that Paul's address of salvation to the Gentiles (Acts 28:28) prompts the Jews to disagree among themselves and depart (28:25a) is based on the view that in v. 25 the participle εἰπόντος precedes the action of the adjacent main verb ἀπελύοντο, designating that the Jews "began departing, after he (Paul) made a statement" about Jewish unbelief and salvation to the Gentiles (vv. 26–28). It has been a situation that is typical of Paul's missionary experience. See our chap. 2, "Apologetic Speech," 54–55, for a detailed discussion.

Confrontation

4. Both portray the Jews at first as showing a polite interest in Jesus and Paul (Luke 4:22; Acts 28:22).

5. Both accounts refer to "preaching" with the verb κηρύσσω (Luke 4:18, 19; Acts 28:31), and use other similar witnessing terminology.[85]

6. Both portray the response of the Jews in terms of unbelief (Luke 4:28; Acts 28:24–25a).[86]

7. Reference is made to spiritual perception as it concerns salvation in LXX Old Testament terminology (Luke 4:18; Acts 28:26–27).[87]

8. Both accounts use the term ἀποστέλλω in terms of the sending of salvation (Luke 4:18 Jesus is "sent" to bring salvation to the needy; Acts 28:28 God's salvation is sent to the Gentiles through Paul).

Fulfillment of Scripture

9. Both passages are concerned with fulfillment of Scripture, quoting Isaiah the prophet (Luke 4:18–19/Isa 61:1–2; Acts 28:26–27/Isa 6:9–10).[88]

85. Such as εὐαγγελίζομαι (Luke 4:18) and διαμαρτύρομαι (Acts 28:23).

86. Paul Minear notes the above comparison, *To Heal*, 84; Dupont sees this attitude of unbelief in Nazareth as a characteristic one in Antioch of Pisidia, Corinth, and Rome (*Salvation*, 21).

87. O'Toole, *Christological Climax*, 73–74. While both passages are concerned with spiritual perception there are differences in the understanding of blindness, as mentioned in our critique of Miesner.

88. In Luke 4 and Acts 28, Luke cites passages from Isaiah the prophet in such a way as to identify the situation of Jesus and Paul with the situation of the prophet. The above provides some rationale for regarding Jesus and Paul as prophets in these two chapters (especially concerning Jesus, on the basis of Luke 4:17, 24). See the following, for the use of the Old Testament in Luke 4 and Acts 28, Richard Longenecker, *Biblical Exegesis in the Apostolic Period*, 2nd ed. (Eerdmans, 1999) 54, 80; F. Neirynck, "Luke 4:16–30," *Unity*, 387–95; Pao also sees a dramatic reversal between the use of Isa 61 in Luke 4 and Isaiah 6 in Acts 28, *Acts*, 106–10.

God's Concern for Gentiles

10. Both speak of Gentiles receiving favor from God: God's prophet is sent to the widow of Sidon, Naaman the Syrian is cleansed of leprosy (Luke 4:25–27): salvation to the Gentiles (Acts 28:28).

As in our previous analysis of Acts 28 and other missionary settings, similar parallels are detected: There is a geographical and temporal setting where the missionary encounter occurs (1, 2), there is a confrontation with the Jews who respond in unbelief (3–5), there is fulfillment of Scripture (6), and an expression of God's concern for the Gentiles (7). All of the above features occur to some degree in Paul's missionary encounters in Pisidian Antioch (Acts 13:14, 44–48), Iconium (14:1–7), Thessalonica (17:2–5), Corinth (18:4–11), Ephesus (19:8–10), and Rome (28:16–31).

With the similarities to Luke 4 and Paul's missionary encounters, the implied author seems to convey the idea that the unbelief of the Jews and receptivity of the Gentiles in Paul's ministry has a prototype in the ministry of Jesus at Nazareth. The normative experience of the Pauline mission has a precedent in the ministry of Jesus. The characteristic themes of the Pauline ministry find their germinal expression in the account of Jesus at Nazareth. The function of this analogy between Paul's mission in Rome and that of Jesus' ministry at Nazareth in the Lukan narrative may have been to argue in defense of Paul's missionary objectives and procedures on the basis of historical precedent and literary prototype.[89]

It has been noted earlier that Luke 4:24–27 may be classed with Acts 13:46–47 and 28:25–28 as an apology for the Gentile mission.[90] All of the above are forms of direct address containing the following

89. When we are talking about "historical precedent" we mean "something done or said that may serve as an example or norm to authorize or to justify a subsequent act of a similar or analogous kind." When we are talking about "literary prototype" we mean "an original model on which something is patterned," in *Merriam-Webster's New Collegiate Dictionary*, 11th ed. (2004) 976, 1000. On typological interpretation of OT in NT, see: Goppelt, *Typos* (Eerdmans, 1982) 1–20. See also biblical type scenes in Robert Alter, *Art of Biblical Narrative* (Basic Books, 1981) 47–52, 96–101; "type character" in Adele Berlin, *Poetics of Interpretation of Biblical Narrative* (Sheffield, 1983); patterns of similarity and repetition, based on the principle of analogy (two characters, events, etc.) in Sternberg, *Poetics of Biblical Narrative*, 365–440.

90. See our chap. 2, section "Apologetic Speech," 57.

key elements: unbelief of the Jews (Luke 4:24 implied; Acts 13:46a; Acts 28:26–27)[91] and turning to the Gentiles (Luke 4:26–27; Acts 13:46b-47; 28:28). While Luke 4 is less specific than Acts 13 and 28 on the Gentiles question, it does mention God's benefits extended to two non-Israelites (Luke 4:26–27). Although a statement of unbelief in Luke 4 is not as explicit as the other passages, v. 24 does provide a good commentary-on Israel's rejection of her own prophets (cf. Luke 6:22–23; 11:47–51; 13:33; Acts 7:51–53).

The apologies for the Gentile mission become more explicit in Acts. In 13:46–47 Paul speaks of turning to the Gentiles after the Jews have thrust the word of God aside. In Acts 28:25b-28, the most extensive apology is presented with a prophetic indictment on Israel (from Isa 6:9–10) and an announcement of salvation to the Gentiles. It has already been shown that Acts 28:25b-28 functions as a climactic conclusion to these series of apologies.[92]

Dupont, in his comparison of Luke 4 and Acts 28 also suggests that the last chapter of Acts brings to a conclusion Luke's history of salvation beginning with the ministry of Jesus in Luke 4.[93] If this is the case, it lends support to our view that Acts 28 draws to a conclusion key themes of Luke 4 in a progressive narrative scheme (from beginning to middle and end). Yet a reciprocal relationship also exists between the two chapters. The scene of Paul at Rome finds its prototype in Jesus at Nazareth, indicating that Paul is portrayed as one like Jesus who does the work of Jesus.

The Introduction of Luke's Gospel and the Conclusion of Acts

In past studies, relationships have been established between Acts 28 and the opening verses of Luke's gospel (1:1–4),[94] as well as Acts 28 and the

91. Dupont sees the theological problem of the privileges of Israel in relation to the pagan nations reflected in Luke 4:23–27, see "La Conclusion," 400.

92. See the discussion in our chap. 3, "Acts 28 and Other Pauline Missionary Settings," 78–80. See Dupont's discussion of Nazareth, Pisdian Antioch and Rome as three situations in Luke–Acts allowing variation on the same theme: God's salvation going to the Gentiles, "La Conclusion," 401.

93. "La Conclusion," 396–98.

94. Lake argues that the preface of Luke–Acts should reflect the leading ideas of what is found in the conclusion, if it was written after the completion of the work (as was generally the custom back then), Commentary, *BC*, 4:350. See a more cautious

opening chapters of the gospel (Luke 1–3).[95] Although close parallels appear to be lacking in Luke 1–3 and Acts 28, both share commonalities and have a noteworthy literary relationship.[96]

Concerning a comparison of the preface of Luke's gospel (1:1–4) and the conclusion of Acts, some caution must be taken in applying the preface too readily to the book of Acts. Yet if the author composed Luke and Acts as a two-volume work (Luke–Acts),[97] the preface of Luke 1:1–4 should have some relevance for Luke–Acts as a whole. Let us examine the text of Luke 1:1–4 drawing attention to those features in the passage which have relevance for Acts 28.[98]

> Since many have attempted to draw up a narrative (διήγησιν) concerning the events which have been accomplished among us, just as they were delivered to us by those who from the beginning were eyewitnesses (close to the facts) and servants of the word, it seemed good to me also, having followed all things closely from the beginning to write an orderly account (καθεξῆς) for you, most excellent Theophilus that you may know (ἵνα ἐπιγνῷς) the certainty (ἀσφάλεια) concerning the things of which you have been instructed (κατηχήθης).[99]

study of Luke's social and literary occasion in Loveday Alexander, *Preface to Luke's Gospel*, 187–212.

95. Dupont concludes that in Acts 28:28, Luke is alluding to the Isa 40:5 quotation that is found in Luke 3:6, *Salvation* 14–16, 57; P. S. Minear sees a link between the use of Isaiah in the prologue (Luke 1–2) and in the epilogue (Acts 28), "Birth Stories," in *SLA* 116–18; see also Alexander, "Reading Luke–Acts From Back to Front," 218–23.

96. While Dupont does briefly discuss the relationship of Luke 2:30–32 and 3:6 to Acts 28 at the conclusion of his study, he does not discuss in detail the significance of this relationship. Dupont also omits any comparison of the Prologue of Luke's Gospel with Acts 28, which has considerable import in understanding the conclusion of Acts as we will show in this section. See "La Conclusion," 402–4.

97. As a working assumption, we follow the axiom first emphasized by Cadbury concerning Luke–Acts as a two-volume work, *Making* 8–11. See also Green, *Luke* 7–8; Bovon, *Luke 1* (Fortress, 2002) 24–25; J. Verheyden, "The Unity of Luke–Acts: What Are We Up To?" 11–21, D. Moessner, "The Lukan Prologues in Light of Ancient Narrative Hermeneutics," 399–413, both in *Unity of Luke–Acts* (1999). Further discussion on "the unity of Luke–Acts" is found here in chap. 3, section on "The Conclusion of Acts and the Conclusion of Luke," 86.

98. For Luke 1:1–4 as the preface to Luke–Acts, see Cadbury, "Commentary on the Preface of Luke," *BC*, 2:491; Lake, Commentary, *BC*, 4:350; Cadbury, *Making*, 344–50; Alexander, *Preface to Luke's Gospel*; Talbert, *Reading Luke*, 7–11.

99. The above translation of Luke 1:1–4 is derived to some extent from the studies of Schuyler Brown, "The Role of the Prologues in Determining the Purpose of

In Luke 1:1, the "events (πρᾶγματων) accomplished among us" is probably best understood as the events in the Jesus' life, death and resurrection.[100] The "narrative" (διήγησιν) which "many have attempted to draw up" is probably a gospel of Jesus.[101] Luke states that the events of Jesus were "delivered (παρέδοσαν) to us from the beginning by eyewitnesses (αὐτόπται) and servants (ὑπηρέται) of the word."[102] These statements from Luke 1:1–2 seem to indicate a history of transmission: (1) the events of Jesus (2) are transmitted by eyewitnesses and servants

---

Luke–Acts," *SLA* 101–10; Danker, *Jesus*, 3–4, and especially the verse-by-verse analysis in Alexander, *Preface to Luke's Gospel*, 102–46, on αὐτόπται, 120.

100. In the preaching of Acts, for example, the gospel about Jesus is concerned with a recital of the major events (πρᾶγμα) of the life, death, and resurrection-exaltation of Jesus (Acts 2:22–24, 36; 3:13–15; 4:10; 10:36–42; 13:23–33). In 2 Macc 1:33–34 the word πρᾶγμα is used in a religious context and as "event" in Josephus *Life* 40; *Against Apion* 1.47; *BDAG*, 858–59.

The use of ἡμιν in the phrase "events accomplished among us" does not necessarily indicate that Luke and his readers/auditors are eyewitnesses of the events of Jesus, since in Luke 1:2 the "we" statement is distinguished from "eyewitnesses". It is better to regard the ἡμιν as signifying "the writer's conviction that his community is the center for the understanding of these events," Danker, *Jesus*, 3. "The events he relates extend to the time of his readers: all of them are in fulfillment of God's promises" L. T. Johnson, *Luke*, 27. On the significance of the "we" statements, see also our discussion in chap. 2, section on "Opening Panel."

101. It seems evident that by Luke's day (C.E. 80–90) others had begun to draw up accounts of Jesus (Luke 1:1, "many" πολλοὶ). The Gospel of Mark (65–75?) might be regarded as one example of "a narrative (διήγησιν) concerning the events (πραγμάτων)" of Jesus that was drawn up before Luke's attempt, although Mark is probably not alluded to in Luke 1:1. The verb, ἐπιχειρέω ("set one's hand to, endeavor, try") may indicate only attempted efforts. See Danker, *Jesus*, 3; Fitzmyer, *Luke*, 1:65–66, 291; Brown, "Prologues," in *SLA* 102–3; Johnson, *Luke*, 30 (more cautious); "Luke's use of the word 'many' here . . . is rhetorical; to vouch for the value of Luke's enterprise by its association with the tradition," Green, *Luke*, 38.

102. For the function of παραδίδωμι as the language of transmitting tradition see: παραδίδωμι in *BDAG*, 761–63; see also: Brown, "Prologues," in *SLA*, 103–7; Alexander, *Preface to Luke's Gospel*, 116–25.

The noun ὑπηρέτης is also applied to Paul in Acts 26:16 who is to function as a servant and witness of Christ, although Paul was not an "eyewitness" in the sense of one who was personally with Jesus, as were the Twelve (Luke 1:2; Acts 1:21–22). It is difficult to draw a sharp distinction between "eyewitnesses" and "servants of the word" because most eyewitnesses were also (or became) servants of the word (Acts 1:21–22). The meaning of αὐτόπται is best rendered "one who knows the facts" instead of "eyewitness" with its misleading forensic connotations, Alexander, *Preface*, 120; Marshall, *Luke*, 42; O'Toole, *Christological Climax*, 68 "eyewitnesses *who became* ministers of the word (see Acts 1:21–22 and 26:16)," in Johnson, *Luke*, 28; Bovon, *Luke*, 1:21.

of the word (3) to Lukan author and his community.[103] In a similar manner of tradition, Acts 28 forms a continuity with Jesus, the Twelve, and the early church in the proclamation of the word (Jesus, Luke 4:34; 8:1; disciples, 9:1–2; the Twelve, Acts 4:33; 5:4; the early church 8:4–5; 15:35; Paul 18:11; 19:8; 28:23, 31).[104] It is in the context of the above statements of Luke 1:1–2, that the phrase "that you might know the certainty (ἀσφάλειαν) concerning the things of which you were instructed (κατηχήθης)" can be understood as a defense or affirmation of Christianity, a concern which has been shown also in Acts 28.[105]

The comparison of Luke 1:1–4 with Acts 28 enables us to see how the activities of Paul at Rome function in relation to the history of transmission, implied in Luke 1:1–2.[106] Also, our contention that Acts 28 seeks to defend Paul and his work may find some support in Luke 1:1–4 which reflects some apologetic concern of the implied author.[107]

103. Luke and his readers seem to be distinguished from "eyewitnesses and servants of the word," Cadbury, "Preface," *BC*, 2:499–500, 510; Fitzmyer, *Luke*, 1:291.

104. The fact that Paul has an important part to play in the activity of proclaiming the word, qualifies him as a "servant of the word" (Luke 1:2; Acts 26:16). It can be noted from Luke 1:1–4 that a "servant of the word" is involved in the process of transmitting the traditions about the events (πράγματα) of Jesus. It is observed from Acts that Paul had a part in promoting the gospel of Jesus. For the association of πραγμάτων with τοῦ λόγου as the "events of Jesus" in "his story," (Luke 1:1–4), see Danker, *Jesus*, 3–4; Fitzmyer, *Luke*, 1:292; Green, *Luke*, 41–42.

105. In support of the above statement, it might be argued that Theophilus represents a type of Christian who has already been instructed but needs certitude (ἀσφάλειαν) concerning what they had come to believe, possibly due to some theological misunderstanding (not necessarily Gnostic), see: Talbert, *Luke and the Gnostics* (Abingdon, 1966) 56 n. 15; Brown, "Prologues," *SLA*, 107–8. Talbert sees the occasion as due to heresy, Brown adds to this a theological issue or problem; Theophilus, to whom the work is perhaps dedicated, may have been "a financial patron who sponsored the publication" and possibly Luke's "intended reader," (see Josephus *Life* 430; *Against Apion* 1:1) in Johnson, *Luke*, 28; With caution, Alexander explores the identity of Theophilus as real person, social superior, patron, outsider, publisher, concluding that "it would be dangerous to assume that Luke's point of view throughout his narrative was determined by a wish to please this particular reader," 200, *Preface*, 187–202.

106. This role of Paul and his immediate successors (e.g. the Ephesian elders, Acts 20:28–32) seems to form a temporal link between the Twelve and Luke's readers, see J. Lambrecht, "Paul's farewell-Address at Miletus (Acts 20:17–38)," *Les Actes des Apôtres*, 307–37; Talbert, *Reading Acts*, 180–84; Tannehill, *Narrative Unity*, 2:252–61.

107. As stated earlier, "that you might know (ἵνα ἐπιγνῷς) the certainty (ἀσφάλειαν) concerning the things of which you were instructed (κατηχήθης)." The mood of apologia conveyed in Luke 1:4 is also found at the close of Acts (28:31), Cadbury *Making*, 315; Mealand, "The Close of Acts," 589–97. But Brawley understands

A comparison of the introduction of Luke (Luke 1–3) and the conclusion of Acts reveals common features relevant for understanding the literary function of Acts 28.

1. Mention is made of the activity of the Holy Spirit in connection with prophets and prophetic utterances (Luke 1:67; 2:25–27; Acts 28:25b).[108]
2. The term ἀντίλεγω is used here in connection with opposition to Christ and his followers (Luke 2:34; Acts 28:19, 22; cf. 13:45).[109]
3. Reference to salvation (σωτήριον) for the Gentiles is made, in terms reminiscent of the book of Isaiah LXX (Luke 2:30, 32/Isa 40:5; 42:6; 49:6; Luke 3:6/Isa 40:5; Acts 28:28/Isa 40:5), a theme which Acts 28 brings to completion.[110]

In point one of the comparison, Acts 28:25b reflects the view that the Holy Spirit spoke to the prophets of old (David, Luke 4:25; Acts 1:16; Isaiah, Acts 28:25b). The implied author also has the Holy Spirit speaking to the followers of Jesus in a similar manner (Acts 8:29; 10:19; 11:12; 13:2), reflecting a continuity of the Spirit's activity in the two eras of time (i.e., the prophets and the way of Jesus). Luke 1:67 and 2:25–27 reflects the author's use of the Holy Spirit in connection with those in-

it in a less theological manner: "The preface to Luke anticipates the production of a narrative world that will offer certainty to readers," 39 in Brawley, *Centering on God*, 38–41.

108. Acts 28:25b states that "the Holy Spirit was right in saying to your fathers through Isaiah the prophet . . . ," Luke 1:70 has a similar statement, that God (v. 68) "spoke by the mouth of His holy prophets . . ." and Luke 1:55 adds that God (v. 46) "spoke to our fathers."

109. The reading of ἀντίλεγω in Luke 20:27 [ἀντι]λέγοντες is questionable because of insufficient textual support see, Metzger, *Textual Commentary*, 145–46. Johnson applies to Paul's situation the following words of Jesus: "The one who listens to you listens to me. The one who rejects you rejects me. The one who rejects me rejects the one who sent me" (Luke 10:16) in *Acts*, 467.

110. See Dupont, *Salvation*, 14–16, 57 where the relationship between Luke 3:6/Isa 40:5 and Acts 28:28/Isa 40:5 is especially examined. See also Litwak, *Echoes of Scripture*, 191; Pao, *Acts*, 40, 106–10. On Luke's mimesis (imitation, adaptation) of the Septuagint, see also: Baban, *On the Road Encounters*, 75–77; Luke's mimesis is similar to that of Philo and Josephus according to Plümacher, *Lukas als Hellenistischer Schriftsteller*, 38, 51, 57.

dividuals who announce the dawning of the new age.[111] This activity of the Spirit upon select individuals also anticipates the outpouring of God's Spirit "upon all flesh" (Acts 2:1–4, 14–21).[112]

In Luke 1–3 the activity of the Holy Spirit is mentioned in connection with the fulfillment of the prophetic words of promise. In Luke 1:67, Zechariah is filled with the Holy Spirit and prophesies (with echoes from the Psalms) that God's promised salvation has come to Israel (vv. 68–79). In Luke 2:25–27, it states that the Holy Spirit was upon Simeon, and that the promised Messiah was revealed to him through the Spirit. This experience prompts Simeon to bear witness to the dawning of God's promised salvation for Israel and the Gentiles (vv. 30–32, in phrases characteristic of the book of Isaiah). In Acts 28:25b, the words of the Holy Spirit spoken through Isaiah to disobedient Israel of old, find fulfillment in the disobedient Jews of Rome who have a spiritual heritage of callousness towards God's word ("your fathers").[113] In all of the above cases, the Holy Spirit plays a part in bringing to pass the words of the prophets in the new age.[114]

In point two of our comparison, the use of ἀντίλεγω in Luke–Acts is almost solely connected with Jewish opposition to Jesus and His followers.[115] In Luke 2:34 it is prophesied of the infant Jesus that He will be a sign that is "spoken against." This prophecy not only finds fulfillment in the passion of Jesus (Luke 22:63–65; 23:10, 18–25, 35–39) but also in the experience of Jesus' followers where the term ἀντίλεγω occurs

111. It is also includes Elizabeth, who is filled with the Holy Spirit and prophesies (Luke 1:41–44), Mary who would give birth to the Messiah through the Holy Spirit (Luke 1:30–35), and John (Luke 1:15) who is to announce the advent of the Messiah.

112. See Dupont, "La Conclusion," 391–96 for detailed analysis of the universalisms in Acts 2–3. See also Alexander on Acts 2:9–11 and related texts in her "Reading Luke–Acts from Back to Front," 212–14, 219.

113. See also Luke 11:47–48; Acts 7:51–52 for Luke's use of "your fathers" similar to the above manner.

114. For a discussion on the relationship between the Holy Spirit and the Gentile mission, see Wilson, *Gentiles*, 55. See also: Hur, *Dynamic Reading of the Holy Spirit in Luke–Acts* (Sheffield, 2001); R. P. Menzies, *Empowered for Witness* (Sheffield, 1994); M. Turner, *Power from on High* (Sheffield, 1996).

115. As stated earlier, footnote 109, a possible exception might be the phrase about Sadducean disbelief regarding the resurrection doctrine in Luke 20:27, οἱ [ἀντι]λέγοντες ἀνάστασιν μὴ εἶναι. Although ἀντι with λέγω is the more difficult reading in the text, it has poor external attestation, and is therefore a questionable reading.

again (Acts 13:45; 28:19).[116] In Pisidian Antioch, the Jews were filled with jealousy and "contradicted" what Paul said (Acts 13:45). In Rome, Paul mentions that when the Jews of Judea "opposed" his release, he was compelled to appeal to Caesar (28:19). The knowledge of the Jews at Rome concerning the Christian sect is restricted to the statement that everywhere it is "spoken against" (v. 22). Therefore the prophecy of the sign that is "spoken against" not only finds fulfillment in the passion of Jesus but in the life and activities of His followers who represent Christ and proclaim the message of Christ to all nations (Luke 24:44–47; Acts 13:26–39; 26:22–23; 28:23, 31).

In point three of our comparison, concerning Luke 2:30–32; 3:6; and Acts 28:28, two common features can be noted: (1) all three texts make use of the infrequent term σωτήριον which is only used elsewhere in the New Testament in Eph 6:17; (2) all passages recall or allude to the text of Isa 40:5 (LXX), καὶ ὄψεται πᾶσα σὰρξ τὸ σωτήριον τοῦ Θεοῦ, a text apparently not alluded to elsewhere in the New Testament.[117]

In Luke 2:30–32, the Nunc Dimittis, Jesus is spoken of as the embodiment of God's promised salvation for Israel and the nations.[118] Luke 3:6 is a direct quotation from Isaiah 40:5 and is a clear Lukan expansion of the Markan account (Mark 1:2–3).[119] Luke 3:6 further develops the previous reference in chap. 2, the salvation of God embodied in Jesus for Israel and the Gentiles (Luke 2:30–32) is announced by John the Baptist (3:6).[120] The association of this theme of universal salvation with Jesus is evident in His statements at Nazareth (Luke 4:25–27) and in Jerusalem after He had risen (24:47). Yet the actual fulfillment of the

116. For the close literary relationship of Jesus and his followers, see our chap. 1, "Portrait of Paul," 10–11, and 4, "Relevance for Luke," 131–35.

117. LXX quotation from A. Rahlfs (ed.) *Septuaginta*, 8th ed. (Stuttgart, 1905). See Isa 40:5 in Citati vel Allegati in Nestle-Aland *Novum Testamentum Graece* 27th ed. (Stuttgart, 1993) 791 where Isa 40:5 is cited in Luke 3:4–6 and allusions are made to it in both Luke 2:30 and Acts 28:28.

118. Allusions are also made here to Isa 42:6; and 49:6.

119. Luke also quotes more completely from Isa 40:3–5 deleting the allusions to Exod 23:20 and Mal 3:1, which are found in Mark 1:2–3, Danker, *Jesus*, 43–44; see also: Dupont, *Salvation*, 15; Wilson, *Gentiles*, 38–39; Fitzmyer, *Luke*, 1:460–61; Luke puzzlingly omits "glory of the Lord will be revealed" in Isa 40:5, Johnson, *Luke*, 64.

120. In support of the above, Danker argues that, for Luke , John does not prepare the way of the Messiah but the way of God's salvation for all flesh, *Jesus*, 44.

prophetic utterance "all flesh shall see the salvation of God" does not occur until the Gentile mission of Acts (2:39; 3:25–26; 10:44–11:18; 13:46–47; 15:14–17; 18:6; 28:25–28).

In the account of Paul at Rome the allusion to Isa 40:5 again occurs (Acts 28:28). As the final portrait of the universal mission in Acts, we see Acts 28:28 brings the Isaianic allusions of Luke 2:30–32 and 3:6 to a concluding climax: the salvation of God, embodied in Jesus, for Israel and the Gentiles, was carried to the Gentile world as far as Rome by Paul a representative of Jesus. Paul at Rome brings the universal significance of God' salvation in the person of Jesus, to its completion.[121]

Conclusion

In our comparative study of chapter 3, many patterns and relationships have been discovered which enable us to better understand the function and significance of Acts 28 in relationship to Luke–Acts.

1. In the comparison of Acts 28 with chaps. 21–26 there is a common concern to defend Paul and his work. This comparison with Acts 21–26 extends beyond 28:17–20 to include Paul's mission (28:23–31). The narrators concern to defend Paul in both passages makes it clear that the innocence ascribed to Paul and his work in Jerusalem and Caesarea also applies in Rome. From the allusions to the passion of Jesus in Acts 21–26 and 28 it seems clear that the author seeks to defend Paul as one who is innocent like Jesus.

In a linear-historical scheme, Acts 28 brings to a conclusion several themes in Acts 21–26. The appeal to Caesar brings Paul to Rome, where he proclaims the gospel to the people and the Gentiles (26:22–23; 28:23–31), in fulfillment of Christ's command stated in the defense

121. See also Dupont's comments on Luke 3:6 and Acts 28:28, *Salvation*, 13–16, also: Danker, *Luke*, 28; David W. Pao observes a dramatic reversal (in the Isaianic program) that occurs with the two Isaianic quotations used in Luke 3:4–6/Isa 40:3–5 (renewed hope of Israel's deliverance) and Acts 28:25–28/Isa 6:9–10 (Jewish recalcitrance but Gentile receptivity), in his *Acts and the Isaianic New Exodus*, 108. Gentile receptivity in Acts 28:28, however, does not exclude interested Jews since Paul "welcomed all πάντας who came to him" (Acts 28:30). As a result, a dramatic reversal of the Lukan hope expressed in Luke 3:4–6/Isa 40:3–5 that "all flesh" will see the salvation of God finds some resolution in Acts 28:28–31 where we find the hope of Israel's deliverance renewed in new ways in Acts. Litwak states that the hopeful theme of Isa 40:5 (addition of a remnant from the nations) echoed in Acts 28:28 builds upon Isaiah 6 (rejection by a majority of Israel, leaving a remnant), *Echoes of Scripture*, 191–92.

speeches (22:15, 21; 23:11; 26:16–18, 23). The author wants to show that Paul's imprisonment at Rome in no way hinders him from bringing to completion Christ's command to be a witness to the nations.

2. In the comparison of Acts 28 with other Pauline missionary settings, the data seems to signify that Paul's situation in Rome has been patterned after his missionary encounters in Pisidian Antioch, Thessalonica, Corinth, and Ephesus. What has taken place at Rome regarding the confrontation with the Jews, their divisiveness, and the turning to the Gentiles, is typical of Paul's missionary activity in Asia Minor and Greece. This portrayal designates a continuity and normative procedure of the Pauline mission in Acts. At key points in the linear development of the narrative, apologetic statements on the Gentile mission are made. These statements come to a climactic conclusion in the more extensive wording of Acts 28 (cf. 13:46–47; 18:6; 19:9; 28:25b-28).

3. The conclusion of Acts and the beginning of Acts show a correspondence between the activities of Jesus and Paul. Both Jesus and Paul speak, testify, or proclaim the kingdom of God, which has appeared in the life and work of Christ. Both Jesus and Paul make final declarations concerning a world-wide mission. Acts 28 can also be seen as a fulfillment of Acts 1. Paul, who is endued with the Holy Spirit, functions as Christ's witness in Rome, having brought the gospel to the Gentile world (Asia Minor, Greece, and Rome).

4. In our comparison of the conclusion of Luke's Gospel and the conclusion of Acts we have learned that both are parallel accounts, giving us a clue as to how the author concludes a literary work. Both passages have similar terminology, structure, and themes, which underscore Luke's special concerns in his two volume work. In this comparison the typical relationship between Jesus and Paul is especially underscored. The author here appears to use this typology to defend Paul as one like Jesus who does the work of Jesus. In a linear promise-fulfillment scheme, Paul in Acts 28 brings to completion the command of Christ in Luke 24 to preach to all nations.

5. Acts 28 shares several common elements with Luke 4. Both accounts occur in a typical missionary setting and both contain themes of Jewish unbelief and concern for Gentiles. With this comparison, the author may be showing his readers/auditors that the normative experience of the Pauline mission has a precedent in the ministry of Jesus and that many of the characteristic themes of the Pauline ministry find their

germinal expression in the account of Jesus at Nazareth. In doing the above, Luke seeks to defend Paul and his mission on the basis of historical precedent and literary prototype. In a linear-historical scheme, Acts 28 brings to a conclusion the apologetic statements on the Gentile mission which find their incipient expression in the account of Jesus at Nazareth (Luke 4:24–27; with Acts 13:46–47; 28:25b–28).

6. In the comparison of the introduction of Luke's Gospel and the conclusion of Acts, we have first compared Acts 28 with Luke 1:1–4, then with Luke 1–3. A comparison of the preface with Acts 28 shows us that (a) Paul functions as a "servant of the word" in relation to Luke's history of transmission implied in Luke 1:1–2; and (b) the apologetic mood at the close of Acts is also found in Luke 1:1–4.

A comparison of the opening chapters of Luke 1–3 with Acts 28 reveals several common features. In both passages the Holy Spirit plays a part in bringing to pass the words of the prophets in the new age (Luke 1:67; 2:26–27; Acts 28:25b). The opposition prophesied of the infant Jesus (Luke 2:34) finds fulfillment in the passion of Jesus (Luke 22–23) and also in the ministry of Paul (Acts 13:45; 28:19, 22). Acts 28:28 brings the universalisms in Luke 2:30–32 and 3:6, with their Isaianic allusions (Isa 40:5; 42:6; 49:6), to a concluding climax: the salvation of God, embodied in Jesus, for Israel and the Gentiles, was carried to the Gentile world as far as Rome by Paul, a representative of Jesus.

4

The Literary Function and Theological Significance of Acts 28:16–31

IN CHAPTER ONE, A SURVEY OF THE HISTORY OF RESEARCH on Acts 28:16–31 revealed the need to address several unsettled literary, structural, and thematic questions related to the function and significance of Acts 28 in Luke–Acts. In chapter two, an investigation of the structure and literary forms was undertaken, providing the groundwork for determining the function and significance of Acts 28. In chapter three, the parallels and patterns of Acts 28 were examined making an intratextual contribution toward an understanding of the function and significance of the text in Luke–Acts. In chapter four, the question of the literary function and theological significance of the text will be *directly* addressed, relying on the research of the three previous chapters. Chapter four, will seek to integrate and unify the research of the preceding chapters under the working hypothesis of our study: that in Acts 28:16–31 Luke is primarily concerned with defending Paul and his mission by presenting him as one like Jesus who does the work of Jesus.

With this picture of Paul at Rome as one like Christ engaged in Christ's mission, it will be argued that Luke brings together a variety of themes and motifs which form a grand conclusion to his twin-work. The above hypothesis will be substantiated by the function of the literary forms in Acts 28. A section on the relevance of this message for Luke and his implied readers or auditors (listeners) will also be included.

The Literary Forms of Acts 28:16–31 and Their Function

The nature of the literary forms and their function, as well as the relationship of the major themes in the narrative, were key problems discovered in our history of research in chapter one.[1] Although the literary function of the text is closely related to its theological significance,[2] we have sought to *first* look at the function of the literary forms before viewing the theological significance of the key themes in the narrative. In this manner, we can better perceive the distinct contribution that each makes with regard to our hypothesis of Paul at Rome as one like Jesus doing the work of Jesus.

Climactic Arrival in the City 28:16

Acts 28:16, the opening panel of our text, serves as the concluding climax to a series of prophetic announcements of Paul's journey to Rome (19:21; 23:11; 27:24; 28:14). These prophetic announcements in Acts are situated in such a way as to form a rising order of importance, which reaches its highest point when the double announcement of Paul's coming and arrival to Rome is made.[3] This climactic arrival in an important

1. See our chap. 1, "Questions Still to be Answered," 28–32.

2. The literary methods of the Lukan narrator serve his theology and his theology serves them, from Schubert, "Luke 24," 185. Our study also assumed the insights of the following works: Dibelius, *Studies*, 1–25; Cadbury, *Making*, 299–350; Haenchen, *Acts*, 90–110 and O'Toole, *Unity*, 11–14; Fitzmyer, *Acts*, 96–123; Barrett, *Acts*, 2:lxxiv-lxxxi. Insights from narrative criticism, rhetorical analysis, and social-scientific interpretation were also mentioned as they related to an understanding of Acts 28. See further discussion at the beginning of our chap. 1, "A Brief Survey," 1–2.

3. Note the climactic arrangement in the announcements of Paul's journey to Rome: (1) in Ephesus, Paul states: "I must also see Rome" after he has gone to Jerusalem, Acts 19:21; (2) as a prisoner in Jerusalem, Paul is assured by Christ in a dream or vision: "as you have testified of me in Jerusalem, so you must bear witness also of me in Rome" 23:11; (3) en route to Rome by ship in the midst of a storm, Paul is encouraged by another dream or vision which stated: "You must stand before Caesar" 27:24 (recalling the defense scenes of Paul, chs. 22–26); and (4) the last set of references are a dual announcement of Paul's coming and arrival to Rome: "And so we came to Rome . . . and when we came to Rome . . ." Acts 28:14, 16.

The double reference of Paul's coming to Rome has parallels to the dual announcement of his coming to Jerusalem (21:15, 17 also in "we" statement form). In both accounts, the "we" statements end when the destinations of Paul's journeys to Jerusalem and Rome are reached (21:18; 28:16). The dual announcements of Paul's coming and

city has parallels in Luke's Gospel. The announcements of Jesus' journey to Jerusalem in Luke's Gospel, also serve to make His arrival in Jerusalem climactic (Luke 9:51; 13:22, 33; 17:11; 19:11, 28, 41).[4] In the case of both Jesus and Paul, these announcements probably enhanced a sense of expectancy for Luke's readers/auditors. These references presumably sought to heighten the importance of the arrivals of Jesus and Paul at their respective places of destination.

Jerusalem and Rome both have significance for Luke. Jerusalem is the holy city of the Jews where the prophecies find their fulfillment. Rome is the center of the Gentile world, and the final goal of the Christian mission in Acts.[5] Just as Jesus has triumphed in Jerusalem

---

arrival to Rome mark the turning point in the journey to Rome motif (parallel also to Paul's journey to Jerusalem). The destination to which the announcements build up, has been reached: "And so we came to Rome."

It can also be seen that Paul's testifying in Rome (διαμαρτύρομαι, 28:23) fulfills the prophetic statement in Jerusalem to bear witness (διαμαρτύρομαι) concerning Christ in Rome (23:11). See also our chap. 2, "Arrival of Paul in Rome," 33–38, and chap. 1, "Positions on Various Verses: Acts 28:16," 19–20.

4. The announcements of Jesus' journey to Jerusalem are also situated in such a way as to form a rising order of importance, reaching its highest point when Jesus approaches the city. 1) "He set his face to go to Jerusalem" Luke 9:51. 2) "He went on his way . . . journeying toward Jerusalem" Luke 13:22. 3) I must go on my way today and tomorrow and the day following, for it cannot be that a prophet shall perish away from Jerusalem," Luke 13:33 (cf. Acts 23:11). 4) "On the way to Jerusalem, He was passing along between Samaria and Galilee, Luke 17:11. 5) "As they heard these things, he proceeded to tell a parable because he was near to Jerusalem Luke 19:11. 6) "After he had said this, he went on ahead, going up to Jerusalem," Luke 19:28. 7) "And as he came near and saw the city he wept over it, saying 'If you, even you, has only recognized on this day the things that make for peace! But now they are hidden from your eyes," Luke 19:41–42.

The coming of Jesus to Jerusalem marks the turning point in the journey motif (as in the case of Paul's arrivals in Jerusalem and Rome). The destination of the journey has been reached and Luke heightens the intensity at this point by including a lament of Jesus over the city (Luke 19:41–44). J. Green also notes Luke's use of the verb "to come near" ἐγγίζω (Luke 18:35,40; 19:29, 37, 41) "to slow the pace of the narrative and to dramatize the long-awaited arrival of Jesus," *Luke*, 689.

5. See the comments of the following works on the importance of Jerusalem and Rome in Luke–Acts: Dupont, *Salvation*, 13, 19, 24; R. H. Smith, *Acts*, 13–14, 387; J. C. O'Neill, *Theology*, 62–63; "Luke presents Paul as following in the footsteps of his master in his journey-calling to witness to the Kingdom of God," 299 in Moessner, *Lord of the Banquet*, 296–307; Peter Lampe writes "Paul in Rome being the crowning conclusion of world mission (28:22ff, 30–31)," *From Paul to Valentinus*, 7 n. 1; "All roads led not only *to* Rome but *from* Rome, from the Golden Milestone in the forum, to the 'ends of the earth' and thus 'to all nations,'" Charles Scobie, "A Canonical Approach to Interpreting

through His resurrection and ascension, Paul has triumphed in Rome through his open and unhindered preaching to all people.[6]

The notice of Paul's arrival in the capitol city of the Gentile world (28:16) marks the conclusion of a series of prophetic announcements concerning Paul's journey there (19:21; 23:11; 27:24; 28:14). Paul's arrival in Rome is significant for Luke, because Rome is the final goal of the Christian mission in Acts (Acts 1:8; 13:47; 23:11).[7]

A Passion Recital Speech, 28:17–20

It has been argued earlier that Acts 28:17–20 is a passion recital speech defending Paul as one who is innocent like Jesus.[8] While 28:17–20 does not occur in a typical trial setting as in Acts 22–26, there are sufficient reasons for our text to have a similar function of defending Paul and his cause.[9] In Acts 28:17–20 there are also several clear allusions to the passion of Jesus, concentrated in a few verses which form a complete address.

The allusions to the passion of Jesus in Acts 28:17–20 are (1) the arrests of Jesus and Paul are viewed as being "delivered into the hands of"

Luke," in *Reading Luke*, 344. Loveday Alexander assesses the data and argumentation of various positions, favoring Rome "one of the most distant points on the circumference of a Jerusalem-centered compass" (e.g., Acts 2:9–11) in her "Reading Luke–Acts from Back to Front," *Acts in Its Ancient Literary Context*, 212–14. D. P. Moessner argues that "Rome is the symbolic center of the great pagan power at 'the end of the earth'" in his "'Completed End(s)ings' of Historiographical Narrative," 220–21.

6. J. C. O'Neill, ibid.; Luke 24 and Acts 28 as God's affirmation of Jesus and Paul, Peterson, *Literary Criticism*, 85–86.

7. It has been mentioned earlier that Acts 1:8 and 13:47 do not speak exclusively of Rome but of the Gentile world in general, yet Rome does have special importance for Luke in the Gentile mission (19:21; 23:11; 27:24; 28:14, 16). See our discussion of Acts 1:8 and 13:47 in our chap. 1 "Acts 28 and the Beginning of Acts," 18.

8. See our chap. 2, "Passion Recital Speech," 43–45. On Jesus–Paul parallels see O'Toole, "Disciples Continue the Work of Jesus," chap. 3 in *Unity*, 62–94; "'Be Imitators of Me," 155–61; and his "Parallels in Luke–Acts," 195–212; also: Radl, *Paulus und Jesus* (1975) 252–65; Mattill, "Jesus–Paul," (1975) 15–46; Praeder, "Jesus–Paul" 23–39 (similarities and differences noted, 37).

On Stephen's final words (Acts 7) recalling Jesus' passion function in a similar way as Paul's passion recital speech to the Jews of Rome (28), see Cadbury, *Making*, 231, 310; O'Toole, "Parallels in Luke–Acts," 195–99, 203–9; Trompf, "Luke and the Death of Paul," 231–2; Moessner, "Jesus-Peter, Stephen, Paul," 227–34.

9. See our list of seventeen similarities between Acts 21–26 and 28 with our evaluation of the data in our chap. 3, section on "Paul's Arrest and Defense."

Gentiles;[10] (2) The Romans "who examined" Jesus and Paul declared that there was "no cause for death" in them;[11] (3) Luke says of Paul and Jesus that the Romans wanted "to release" them;[12] (4) It was because of the opposition of the Jews that Paul and Jesus encountered their fates;[13] and (5) As Paul's passion recital includes the hope of the resurrection (Acts 28:20; cf. 23:6; 24:15; 26:6–8) so also does the passion of Jesus (Luke 23:42–43, life after death; 24:6–7, 46–47, passion predictions fulfilled).

From the above data it seems clear that the Lukan narrative presents Paul as one who underwent the same kind of experience as Jesus did and who was regarded as innocent like Jesus. In this closing scene, the experiences of Paul are identified with those of the suffering Messiah. Would not such a comparison create a sense of credibility and divine sanction upon the one who preached Christ at Rome to both Jews and Gentiles?[14]

Summary Statements of Preaching, 28:23, 30–31[15]

Acts 28:23, 30–31 constitute the conclusion of a series of preaching summaries beginning with Jesus (Luke 4:43–44; 8:1; 9:11; 20:1), continued by his disciples (Luke 9:6; 10:8–11; cf. 8:39), carried on by the early church (Acts 4:31, 33; 5:42; 8:4–5, 12, 25, 40), and brought to a culmination by Paul (9:27, 29; 14:7; 15:35; 17:2–3; 18:5, 11; 19:8; 28:23, 30–31).

The climactic features of the preaching summaries of Acts 28:23 and vv. 30–31, can be established because of 1) distinctive, 2) syntactical, 3) contextual, and 4) thematic considerations.

1. Acts 17:2–3, Acts 28:23, and Acts 28:30–31 can be distinguished from the other preaching summaries in terms of content and

10. Acts 28:17c; Luke 24:7, aorist passive of παραδίδωμι with εἰς τὰς χεῖρας.

11. Acts 28:18; Luke 23:14, aorist participle of οανακρίνω; Acts 28:18b; Luke 23:22, αἰτίαν or αἰτίον θανάτου.

12. Acts 28:18a; Luke 23:20, ἀπολύω.

13. Acts 28:19, appearance before Caesar; Luke 23:18–25, crucifixion.

14. Concerning the function of the Jesus-Paul parallels as an effective apology for Paul, see: Mattill, "Purpose of Acts," 114–15, 120, and "Jesus-Paul," 37.

15. Preaching summaries are those Lukan summaries characterized by such witnessing terminology as: preaching, teaching, bearing witness, persuading. The common message conveyed by this terminology is that in the divinely-willed events of Christ's life, suffering, death, and resurrection, God's kingdom has dawned for the salvation of all nations. See our chap. 2, "Summary Statement," 51.

structure. All three summaries contain a temporal and local setting, are concerned with expounding Christ,[16] and are followed by a statement of response to the preaching.[17] The differences which mark off these three summaries from the other preaching accounts are significant with regard to the climactic nature of two of them: Acts 28:23 and 28:30–31.

2. The syntactical arrangement of words and phrases in Acts 28:23 and vv. 30–31 contribute to their climactic nature. The preaching activity described in these summaries is intensified by the use of uncommon prepositional and adverbial phrases which modify the witnessing verbs.

In Acts 28:23, Paul testifies and tries to convince his hearers concerning Christ "from morning until evening". This latter phrase underscores the remarkable persistency of Paul's witness to the Roman Jews.[18] Another prepositional phrase in v. 23 qualifies the manner of Paul's persistent attempt to convince his listeners about Jesus "from the law of Moses and from the prophets". This phrase underscores the thoroughness of Paul's witness to the Roman Jews.[19]

In Acts 28:30–31, Paul is preaching and teaching "with all boldness and without hindrance." The term παρρησία generally specifies the manner of Christian proclamation in Acts: boldly and frankly.[20] In Acts 28:31, the term is linked with the hapaxlegomenon ἀκωλύτως to qualify the manner and extent of Paul's witness at Rome: boldly and unhindered.[21]

16. Acts 17:2 and 28:23 expound Christ from the Scriptures, i.e., from the law of Moses and from the prophets.

17. In Acts 17:4 and 28:24 a divided response is mentioned, in Acts 28:30–31 a favorable outcome for two whole years is at least indicated.

18. No other missionary situation in Luke–Acts designates such a long period of witnessing to Christ. The only possible exception is the gathering at Troas from evening until daybreak, Acts 20:7–12. This gathering, however, is not for a missionary situation, but for Christian fellowship.

19. Although appealing to Moses and the prophets concerning Christ is not uncommon in Luke–Acts (e.g. Luke 24:27, 44–46; Acts 26:22–23), it does contribute to the thoroughness and intensity of Paul's witness at Rome "from morning until evening."

20. Acts 4:31; 9:27–29; 18:26; 19:8. Often mentioned in (defiant) contrast to situations of danger or imprisonment, Rapske, *Book of Acts*, 3:310–12.

21. An adverb is a strange word with which to end a book, but Luke did just that. In fact, the two-volume work, Luke-Acts, is brought to a dramatic close and epitomized in an adverb." Stagg, *Acts*, 1.

3. There are elements in the immediate context of Acts 28:23 and vv. 30–31, which provide the occasion for these accounts, and establish the importance of these preaching summaries in the narrative.

In Acts 28:17–28, the occasion and significance of the preaching account in v. 23 is highlighted. In v. 20, Paul's passion recital speech concludes with Paul's desire to speak with his Jewish listeners. In v. 22, the Jews desire to hear from Paul and his views. The occasion is then provided for the meeting when Paul tries to convince them concerning Christ (v.23). What results from this preaching account is a divided Jewish response (v. 24) which then provides the occasion for Paul's statement on the mission to the Gentiles (vv. 25–28).

Acts 28:30–31 functions as a concluding summary of the entire account of Paul at Rome. It ends the scene with a generalized report of Paul's activities in Rome for two whole years. Acts 28:30–31 also concludes the proclamation of the gospel in Luke–Acts, historically (from Jesus and the Twelve to Paul and others) and geographically (from Judea, Samaria, and Asia Minor, to Greece and Rome).

4. The preaching summaries of Acts 28:23 and 30–31 elaborate on a variety of key Lukan themes which are concentrated in these verses. The witnessing terminology in Acts 28:23 and 28:30–31 is used extensively throughout Luke–Acts.[22] Major Lukan themes are repeated in both summaries of Acts 28. One theme is the kingdom of God.[23] Another theme is Jesus Christ as the object or content of Christian proclamation.[24] In the summary of Acts 28:23 where Paul testifies to the kingdom of God and tries to persuade the Jews about Jesus from the law of Moses and from the prophets, the following conclusion can be drawn: "This aligns all of Paul's speeches with Luke's theology and

22. In Acts 28:23 see διαμαρτύρομαι (e.g. Acts 4:33; 8:25; 10:42; 18:5; 20:21, 24; 23:11) and πείθω (Acts 13:43; 18:4;19:8; 26:28). In Acts 28:30–31 note κηρύσσω (Luke 4:44; 8:1, 39; Acts 8:5, 12; cf. εὐαγγελίζομαι (e.g. Luke 8:1; Acts 5:42) and διδάσκω (Luke 20:1; Acts 5:42; 15:35; 18:11). See chap. 2, "Summary Statement," 51, for extensive discussion on the witnessing terminology.

23. Luke 4:43; 8:1; 9:2, 11, 60; 16:16; Acts 1:3; 8:12; 19:8; 20:25.

24. Luke 8:39; Acts 4:33; 5:42; 8:5, 12, 35; 9:20; 10:36, 42; 11:20; 18:5, 25. The Jesus-kerygma speeches in Acts should also be included (Acts 2:14–36; 3:11–26; 4:8–12; 10:34–43; 13:16–41).

summarizes it in a final climax."[25] It has been mentioned in chapter two, that the use of ἀκωλύτως in Acts 28:31 with its catchword κωλύω convey the idea of the final triumph of Christianity over various religious, racial, and political obstacles.[26]

In terms of the theme of fulfillment of prophecy, the preaching summaries of Paul at Rome (a) fulfill specifically the prophecy of Christ that Paul would bear witness to Christ in Rome (Acts 23:11), and (b) fulfill generally Christ's command to preach to all nations.[27]

In the four points of investigation noted above, it has been shown that the preaching summaries of Paul at Rome (28:23 and vv. 30–31) function climactically. It was argued on the basis of their distinction with other preaching summaries, their syntactical arrangement, their immediate context in the narrative, and the key Lukan themes to which they allude.

An Apologetic Speech on the Gentile Mission, 28:25–28

Acts 28:25–28 functions with 13:46–47 as an apologetic speech on the Gentile mission because of their similar formal, structural, and thematic features.[28] The pattern most characteristic in these speeches is that of 1) unbelief of the Jews and 2) turning to the Gentiles. Acts 13:46–47 sets the tone of Paul's missionary encounters with the Jews, while Acts 28:25–28 provides the climactic conclusion of these encounters.[29]

25. Luke 24:27, 46–47; Acts 2:39; 3:18; 10:43; 13:27–32; 17:30–31; 20:27; 23:6; 24:14–15; 26:6–8, 22–23. The above quote and scriptural references are from Schubert, "Final Cycle," 9.

26. Religious and racial obstacles (Luke 9:49–50; 11:52; Acts 8:36; 10:47; 11:17) and political restrictions of Rome (Acts 24:23; 27:43) are overcome. See: Stagg "Unhindered Gospel" 451–62, and *Acts* 1, 12–17, 266; Fitzmyer, *Acts* 791, 797; "The prisoner proclaims ἀκωλύτως without (legal) hindrance from the governing authorities *and* by the full (spiritual) power of God," Skinner, *Locating Paul*, 169; Delling, "Letzte Worte," 196–201.

27. Luke 24:47; Acts 1:8; 22:21; 26:17–18.

28. See chap. 2, "An Apologetic Speech on the Gentile Mission," 56–57. Acts 18:6, although it contains reference to Jewish rejection and turning to the Gentiles, does not have the characteristics of an apologetic speech and: is therefore classed with 19:9 and other similar missionary statements, see also chap. 3, section on "Acts 28 and Other Pauline Missionary Settings."

29. In chap. 3, "Acts 28 and Other Missionary Settings," 78–80, the climactic features of Acts 28:25–28 were discussed. As an apology for the Gentile mission, Acts 28:25–28 shares with Acts 13:46–47 and 18:6 the two characteristics of that literary

Both speeches also have a relationship to statements attributed to Jesus in Luke's Gospel. Acts 13:46–47 and 28:25–28 find their germinal expression in the speech of Jesus at Nazareth (Luke 4:24–27) where God's favor upon certain Gentiles (vv. 26, 27) and the unbelief of the Jews (vv. 24, cf. 28–29) are mentioned. These statements of Jesus (Luke 4:24–27) provide a historical precedent and a literary prototype for the missionary procedures of Paul as stated in Acts 13:46–47 and 28:25–28.[30]

In summary, we have sought in this section of chapter four, to present the literary forms of Acts 28 as they function for Luke in presenting Paul as one like Jesus who does the work of Jesus.

1. The arrival of Paul in Rome (as in the case of Jesus in Jerusalem) is climactic, the result of a series of announcements which preceded the arrival. As Jesus triumphed in Jerusalem, Paul triumphed in Rome. 2. In Acts 28:17–20 the experiences of Paul are recounted in terms reminiscent of Jesus, identifying the Apostle with the innocent suffering Messiah who performed God's will. 3. Acts 28:23, and vv. 30–31 constitute the conclusion of a long series of preaching summaries beginning with Jesus. Both summaries have climactic features because of distinctive, syntactical, contextual, and thematic considerations. Both preaching accounts of Paul at Rome are in fulfillment of Christ's command (Acts 23:11; also Luke 24:27; Acts 1:8; 22:21; 26:17–18). 4. Acts 28:25–28 functions as the climax of the Gentile apologies in Acts (13:46–47; 18:6), all of which find their germinal expression in the speech of Jesus at Nazareth (Luke 4:24–27), a speech which establishes a historical precedent and provides a literary prototype for Paul's missionary procedures in Acts.

form (1) a statement on Jewish unbelief and (2) turning to the Gentiles. In chap. 3, it was shown that both of the two features above are climactic in Acts 28:25–28. In the three statements on Jewish unbelief, it was argued that the condition of the Jewish listeners, reflected in these statements, became progressively worse until they were definitely hardened as a group against the gospel (Acts 28). In the three statements on turning to the Gentiles it was shown that Acts 28:28 was the most explicit and intense declaration of the apologies, recalling universalistic phrases from Luke 2–3, and key Lukan passages on the Gentile mission.

30. Luke 4:24–27 could also be viewed as a prophetic statement of what would take place in Paul's ministry. For further discussion see chap. 3, "Inaugural Sermon of Jesus," 93–96.

The Theological Significance of Acts 28:16–31

It has been stated that with the picture of Paul at Rome as one like Jesus engaged in the work of Jesus, Luke brings together a variety of themes and motifs in a climactic fashion. Theological significance is a vital component of our study. This section will seek to elaborate upon the above assertion by first investigating the identity of Paul in Acts 28 and then Paul's missionary activity in the pericope.

The Identity of Paul in Acts 28:17–20

Although it is difficult to distinguish the image of Paul from the activity he does, this unit will deal more specifically with the portrait of Paul in 28:17–20 and additional verses that may help to convey his identity and role in our pericope (vv. 16, 30–31).

Paul Is Defended As a Faithful Israelite Like Jesus

In chapter one, it was discussed that 28:17–20 was used to support the theme of a Jewish apology in Acts 28.[31] It will be shown here that this theme is used to present Paul as a faithful Israelite like Jesus. The following is evidence from Acts 28 for the above theme:

1. "I have done nothing against my people," 28:17;
   "I had no charge to bring against my nation," v. 19 (cf. 24:17; 25:10; 26:4).[32]
2. "I have done nothing against the people or the customs of the fathers," 28:17 (cf. 25:8, 10).[33]

31. See our chap. 1, "Jewish Prophecies, Heritage," 6–7.

32. The above two statements recall what was said by Paul in the defense speeches. Before Festus, Paul said: "to the Jews I have done no wrong" (25:10). Before Felix, it was said: "I came (to Jerusalem) to bring my nation (τὸ ἔθνος μου) alms and offerings" (24:17). Before Agrippa, Paul said: "my manner of life from my youth . . . among my own nation . . . is known by all Jews" (26:4).

33. This statement is reminiscent of Paul's defense speeches. Before Festus, it was said: "neither against the law of the Jews (Ἰουδαῖος), nor against the temple, nor against Caesar, have I sinned . . . to the Jews I have done no wrong" (25:8, 10). See the positive statements on Paul observing the law and the customs of the fathers (22:3; 24:14).

3. "Because of the hope of Israel I am bound in these chains," 28:20 (cf. 23:6; 24:14; 26:6, 8).[34]

From the above verses in Acts 28, and the corresponding parallels from Paul's defense speeches, it is clear that Paul, and the Christianity he represents, is defended as obedient to the faith of Israel.[35]

This theme of Christians as the faithful ones of Israel is evident throughout Acts. The founding leaders of Christianity are portrayed as faithful Israelites.[36] A great number of devout Jews, priests, and Pharisees become believers of Jesus the Messiah.[37] Christ and his followers are portrayed as fulfilling the Jewish Scriptures.[38]

In Luke's Gospel, Jesus is portrayed as the ideal model of a true and faithful Israelite. His birth and childhood were in fulfillment of prophecy and according to the custom of the law of Moses.[39] His life and

34. Before Agrippa, Paul said: "I stand trial for the hope in the promise made by God to our fathers . . . that God raises the dead" (26:6, 8). Before the Pharisees and Sadducees, Paul said: "with respect to the hope and the resurrection of the dead I am on trial" (23:6). Before Felix, Paul stated that: "I worship the God of our fathers . . . having a hope in God which these themselves accept, that there wil1 be a resurrection of both the just and the unjust" (24:14).

35. It is with this Lukan concept of Christianity as the faithful remnant of Israel, that we can understand why, in Acts 28, Paul the faithful Israelite pronounces a statement of hardening on impenitent Israel. Jewish indifference to Paul's preaching is not due to anything Paul has done or said. Paul has done nothing against his people and stands for the hope of Israel, 28:17–20. Jewish indifference to Paul's preaching is due instead, to the traditional disobedience of the Jews reflected in the unbelief of their fathers to the message of the prophets (Acts 28:25b-28; cf. Luke 6:22–23; 11:47–50; 13:33–34; Acts 7:51–53). As a result, Luke has Paul, the faithful Israelite, making a prophetic pronouncement on the Jewish indifference regarding his message. See also: O'Neill, *Theology*, 76 n. 1; Franklin, *Christ the Lord*, 114–15; a dramatic reversal: "it is not the apostle to the Gentiles, but the chosen people in Rome who are judged," Marguerat, "Enigma of the Silent Closing," 295–96.

36. Peter and John, Acts 3:1; 5:12, 25; 5:42; James, and others 21:17–20; Paul, 16:3–4; 18:18; 20:16; 21:18–28; 23:6; 24:14; 26:6–8; 28:20.

37. Acts 2:5 devout Jews, 41; 4:4; 6:7 priests; 15:5 Pharisees; 21:20 Jews who believe and are zealous for the law (and misinformed about Paul's ministry, v. 21).

38. For example: Acts 2:14–21/Joel 2:28–32; Acts 3:22–26; Acts 13:47/Isa 49:6; Acts 24:14; 26:22–23.

39. The birth of Jesus is announced as the fulfillment of Jewish Scriptures Luke 1:31–33/Isa 7:14; 2 Sam 7:12–16; Luke 1:46–55/1 Sam 2:1–10. He was born of the lineage of David (Luke 1:32–33; 2:4; 3:31) and reared by Jewish parents according to Jewish custom (Luke 2:21–24, 27, 39, 41–43, 46). See Jesus as a son of Israel in Jervell, *Theology of Acts*, 29–30.

ministry were in compliance with the customs of the law of Moses.[40] The life and work of Jesus fulfilled the Scriptures.[41]

In his two-volume work, Luke not only portrays the early church and Paul as faithful Israelites, he patterns them after Jesus, the supreme example of a true and faithful Israelite. This observation is especially evident in the Jesus-Paul parallels. By comparing the Jewish portrait of Paul with that of Jesus we see that Paul like Jesus: lived according to the law from his youth,[42] preached in synagogues,[43] affirmed the Pharisaic doctrine of the resurrection,[44] and used the Jewish Scriptures to explain the necessity of Christ's suffering, death, and resurrection.[45]

In Acts 28, we note that Paul, like Jesus in Luke 23, is presented as a law-abiding Israelite (Acts 28:17–20; cf. Luke 23:14–16, 22). Paul, as well as Jesus, has done nothing against the people or the customs (Acts 28:17, 19; cf. Luke 23:14–15). Paul, like Jesus, is falsely charged by the unbelieving Jews (Acts 28:17, 19; cf. Luke 23:2, 4, 14).[46] In Acts 28:23, Paul expounded from the law of Moses and the Hebrew prophets as Jesus himself had done (Luke 24:27, 44).

From the observations we have made from Acts 28 and Luke–Acts as a whole, it seems apparent that Paul is defended as a faithful Israelite like Jesus, who had done nothing against the people, the law of Moses, or the customs of the fathers.

40. Jesus preached in the synagogues of Palestine on the sabbath (Luke 4:15, 16ff, 31–33; 6:6; 13:10). Upon entering Jerusalem Jesus taught daily in the temple (19:47; 20:1; 21:37–38; 22:53). Jesus communed with Pharisees (7:36–50; 14:1 and even had followers from the Sanhedrin (23:50–51). Jesus affirmed the Pharisaic doctrine of the resurrection (14:1, 14; 20:34–39) and was regarded as a prophet of Israel by himself and others (4:22, 24; 13:33; 24:19).

41. His birth (Luke 1:31–33/2 Sam 7:12–16; Luke 1:46–55/1 Sam 2:1–10), His work and ministry (Luke 3:6/Isa 40:5; Luke 4:18–19/Isa 61:1–2); His Lordship (Luke 20:41–44/Ps 110:1); His passion, death, and resurrection (Luke 24:27, 44–47; Acts 2:24–28/Ps 16:8–11; Acts 2:34/Ps 110:1; Acts 3:22–23/Deut 18:15–16; Acts 4:11/Ps 118:22; Acts 8:32–33, 35/Isa 53:7–8; Acts 13:33–36/Ps 2:7; Isa 55:3; Ps 16:10; Acts 17:2–3; 26:22–23; 28:23).

42. Jesus, Luke 2:21–24 (as an infant); 2:41–43, 46; Paul, Acts 22:3; 23:6; 26:4–5.

43. Jesus, Luke 4:15, 16–30, 31–33; 6:6; 13:10; Paul, Acts 13:5, 14–43; 14:1; 17:1–4, 10, 17; 18:4, 19, 26; 19:8.

44. Jesus, Luke 14:1, 14; 20:34–39; Paul, Acts 17:18, 32; 23:6–8; 24:15, 21; 26:8, 23.

45. For example: Jesus, Luke 24:27, 44–48; Paul, Acts 17:2–3; 26; 22–23; 28:23.

46. For Paul, see also: Acts 21:21; 25:8, 10.

Paul is presented as innocent before Rome like Jesus

It seems evident from Acts 28:16, 17–19, 30–31 that a favorable relationship of Paul (and Christianity) with Rome is conveyed. This theme of a Roman apology in Acts 28 was discussed at the beginning of our study.[47] It will be argued here that Paul is defended as innocent before Rome in a similar fashion as Jesus was in Luke 23.

Specific statements of favorable actions toward Paul in Acts 28 are found in v. 18 where Romans pronounce Paul innocent: "When they (the Romans) had examined me they wanted to release (ἀπολύω) me because there was no cause for the death penalty (μηδεμίαν ἀιτίαν θανάτου) in my case." In the face of Jewish opposition, Paul appeals to the Roman authorities, v. 19, "I was compelled to appeal to Caesar" (cf. 25:8–12, 21, 25; 26:32). In the following verses, Paul is given relative freedom while under Roman capitivity. In v. 16, Paul was permitted to stay by himself with the soldier that guarded him (cf. 24:23).[48] In vv. 30–31, Paul lived in Rome two whole years at his own rented lodging (perhaps a private residence?) and welcomed all who came to him (i.e., he had liberty to receive visitors). He was "preaching . . . and teaching . . . quite openly and unhindered" by and under Rome.[49]

This portrait of Paul and the early church's fair treatment under Rome is seen elsewhere in Acts. Paul and others are granted certain privileges as Roman citizens.[50] Roman officials are pictured as unconcerned with religious debates among Jews (including the Messianists/ Christians).[51] Paul is rescued from death on two occasions by Romans.[52] When Paul is taken into Roman custody, his innocence is declared by all

47. See our chap. 1, "Fair Treatment under Rome," 7–8.

48. Paul was allowed a degree of liberty before his case was heard, he was permitted to live as a private resident under the custody of a guard, Bruce, *Book of Acts* (1988) 504.

49. See the following passages connected with κωλύω, a term sharing a common root with ἀκωλύτως, which deals with the overcoming of certain political obstacles under Rome, Acts 24:23; 27:43. On Roman tolerance generally, see Hauser, *Strukturen*, 141.

50. Paul and Silas are released from prison, Acts 16:37–39; Paul is exempt from a scourging, 22:25–29.

51.Gallio's judgment on the dissension between Paul and the Jews in Corinth, 18:12–16. Talbert, *Reading Acts* (2005) 162–63.

52. Paul is rescued from a Jewish lynch-mob, 21:30–32; and a Roman centurion prevents the marines from killing Paul along with other prisoners, 27:42–43.

the Roman officials involved.[53] Roman officials are among the Gentiles converted to Christianity.[54]

In the case of Jesus in the Third Gospel, fair treatment under Rome is mentioned by Luke. At his arrest and trial, certain Jews accuse Jesus of sedition before Pilate, but Pilate pronounces him innocent of the charges:

1. "I find no guilt (αἴτιον) in this man," Luke 23:4.
2. "I did not find this man guilty (αἴτιον) of any of your charges," v. 14.
3. "He has done nothing worthy of death," (οὐδὲν ἄξιον θανάτου) v. 15.
4. "I find no cause for death (οὐδὲν αἴτιον θανάτου) in him, after I have chastised him I will release him," (ἀπολύσω), v. 22.

At His crucifixion, a Roman centurion declared, "certainly this man was innocent" Luke 23:47. According to Luke it was the influence of the chief priests,[55] and the clamor of the city mob incited by them,[56] that compelled Pilate against his own judgment to pass the death sentence on Jesus (Luke 23:21–25). Thus the crucifixion of Jesus is viewed as a serious miscarriage of Roman justice.[57]

In comparing the Roman apology of Paul with that of Jesus, the following similarities can be noted.[58] Paul like Jesus has amicable contacts with a Roman centurion (Acts 27:3, 43; cf. Luke 7:2–10). Paul like Jesus appears on trial before Roman procurators (Felix, Festus, cf.

53. Claudius Lysias, 23:9; Felix, 24:22–23; Festus 25:18–19, 25; Agrippa (in harmony with Rome) 26:31–32.

54. Cornelius, Acts 10; Sergius Paulus, 13:7–12; Publius 28:7–10; a god-fearing centurion impresses Jesus with his faith Luke 7:1–10.

55. Luke 22:67–71; 23:1–5, 13–14.

56. Luke 23:18–23.

57. "(Jesus) whom you delivered up and denied in the presence of Pilate when he had decided to release him" Acts 3:13–14.

58. For comparisons of the trials of both Jesus and Paul, see: Mattill, "Jesus–Paul," 32–37 and O'Toole, *Christological Climax*, 22–25; and his "Disciples Continue the Work of Jesus," chap. 3 in *Unity*, 62–94; "'Be Imitators of Me as I am of Christ,' *BTB* 8 (1978) 155–61; "Parallels between Jesus and His Disciples," *BZ* 27 (1983) 195–212; and further studies: Radl, *Paulus und Jesus*; Mattill, "Jesus–Paul," 15–46; Praeder, "Jesus–Paul," 23–39; Moessner, "Jesus–Peter, Stephen, Paul," *NovT* 28 (1986) 220–56; Hauser, *Strukturen*, 138, 161–62, 164–65, 233–34.

Pilate). Paul is asked questions by Felix which are similar to those asked by Pilate of Jesus (Acts 23:34–35; cf. Luke 23:6–7). Roman governors declare Paul innocent as in the case of Jesus (Acts 23:9/Luke 23:4; Acts 25:25/Luke 23:15; Acts 26:31/Luke 23:15/ Acts 28:18/Luke 23:22).[59]

In Acts 28, Paul like Jesus is examined by the Romans (ἀνακρίνω Acts 28:18; cf. Luke 23:14) who wanted "to release" him (ἀπολύω Acts 28:18a; cf. Luke 23:20) because there was "no cause for death" in his case (negative μή or οὐ form with αἰτίαν or αἴτιον θανάτου, Acts 28:18; cf. Luke 23:22). It was because of opposition by certain Jews that Paul, like Jesus, was delivered into the hand of Romans (before Caesar, Acts 27:24 with 28:19; cf. crucifixion, Luke 23:18–25).

From the above study we have shown that Jesus and Paul (and others, such as Silas) received fair treatment under Rome. In Acts 28, Paul is portrayed as one innocent before Rome in terms reminiscent of Jesus' hearing before Pilate.

Paul is portrayed as a prophet like Jesus[60]

In Acts 28, we note the following characteristics which enable us to see Paul portrayed as a prophet:

59. The above comparisons are derived, to some extent, from Mattill "Jesus–Paul," 33–34. They intend to defend Jesus and Paul, but not necessarily to legitimize Roman policies in general.

To counter notions of pro-Roman flattery here, R. Cassidy reminds us of prophetic utterances (Luke 1:52–53), teachings of Jesus (21:12ff; 22:25–26), zealot contacts (6:15; Acts 1:13), and defiant actions (Acts 4:20–21; 5:29) that appear to be critical of authorities like Rome and examples of corruption (24:26), indifference (24:27) and cruelty (Luke 13:1ff; 23:22ff) regarding Rome's treatment of Jesus and his followers, *Jesus, Politics, and Society*, 20–76, 126–35; see also our chap. 1, "Fair Treatment under Rome," 7–8. These texts should raise questions about any suggestion that Luke–Acts seeks to flatter or appease certain sympathetic or even believing Roman officials (e.g., Theophilus?). P. Walaskay, who sees a Roman apology here *for the church* not a secular official, would agree that the contents of Luke–Acts presuppose an audience more interested in the sacred story of Jesus and his followers in the Roman world, '*And so we came to Rome*' (1983) 18–22, 59–62; *Acts* (1998) 242–47.

60. See the following works for a presentation of Paul as a prophet. E. E. Ellis, "The Role of the Christian Prophet in Acts," *Apostolic History*, 56, 61; P. S. Minear, *To Heal and To Reveal*, 142–47; R. F. O'Toole, *Christological Climax*, 66–68. W. Schmeichel, "Christian Prophecy in Lucan Thought: Luke 4:16–30," *SBLSP* (Scholars, 1976) 293–94; Moessner, *Lord of the Banquet*, 305–7; "Paul and the Pattern of the Prophet like Moses in Acts," *SBLSP* 22 (1983) 203–12; "Paul in Acts," *NTS* 34 (1988) 96–104; Johnson, *Acts*, 12–14, 471–72; "Luke uses the Scriptures of Israel in this passage to present the message of Paul, an Israelite prophet," 183 in Litwak, *Echoes of Scripture*,

1. Paul in quoting from the book of Isaiah, identifies his situation with that of the prophet.
2. Paul's pronouncement of hardening on the unbelieving Jews of Rome (28:25–28) functions very much like a prophetic announcement of judgment on Judah (cf. Isa 29:9–10).[61]
3. Paul is pictured as standing for the hope of Israel (τῆς ἐλπίς τοῦ Ἰσραὴλ), a hope which the prophets anticipated.[62]
4. Paul appeals to the law of Moses and the prophets (28:23; cf. 26:22–23) in his preaching.

Elsewhere in Acts we see that Paul and the early church are portrayed as prophets. Reference is made to Christian prophets in Judea.[63] Paul and others are designated as prophets.[64]

Christians who prophesy function as prophets.[65] In Luke's Gospel, John the Baptist and others are referred to as prophets.[66] In Luke–Acts,

see 180–200, for further discussion.

61. Ellis views the use of Acts 28:25–28/Isa 6:9–10 as a prophetic declaration of divine judgment (cf. Acts 13:11), "Christian Prophet," *Apostolic History*, 56; see also Craig Evans, *To See and Not Perceive*, 121–26; Pao also notes a dramatic reversal accomplished by the two different Isaianic quotations used in Luke 3:4–6/Isa 40:3–5 (hope of Israel's deliverance) and Acts 28:25–27/Isa 6:9–10 (Jewish recalcitrance and Gentile receptivity) in his *Acts and the Isaianic New Exodus*, 105–10.

62. Acts 24:14–15; 26:6–7; 28:20; cf. ὑπομονή Ἰσραὴλ, LXX Jer. 14:8; 17:13; see: O'Toole, *Christological Climax*, 89–95.

63. Acts 11:27–28; 21:10, Agabus and others.

64. In Acts 13:1, Paul is called a prophet. In Acts 26:16–18, the call of Paul is described in language characteristic of the call of a prophet (cf. Ezek. 2:1–3; Jer. 1:7–8). Paul is to do the work of a prophet (Acts 26:16–18; cf. Isa 35:5; 42:7; 61:1). In Acts 26:22–27, Paul's teaching is associated with the prophets. Paul declares that he says "nothing but what the prophets and Moses said would come to pass" (26:22), and then asks King Agrippa, "do you believe the prophets?" (v. 27). See O'Toole, *Christological Climax*, 66–68, which deals with the prophetic imagery of Acts 26.

65. The Ephesian disciples (19:6) and the daughters of Philip (21:9), in fulfillment of Acts 2:17–18/Joel 2:28–32.

66. John is to be a prophet of the Most High, Luke 1:76; a prophet like Elijah, 7:16, 26–27; 20:6; Zechariah prophesies, Luke 1:67; and Anna is called a prophetess, 2:36.

Jesus is regarded as a prophet. Jesus refers to himself as a prophet,[67] and is identified as one by others.[68]

In Acts 28, what can be said of Paul (and other Christians) can be said of Jesus:

1. Jesus at Nazareth quotes from the book of Isaiah, and identifies the words of the prophet with his situation, Luke 4:18–19/Isa 61:1–2 (cf. Isa 58:6),
2. The indictments of Jesus on unbelieving Jews are very similar to prophetic announcements of judgment (e.g. Luke 11:42–52; cf. Isa 33:1). In Luke 8:10, Jesus quotes from Isa 6:9–10 (as Paul does in Acts 28:25–28) which is applied to His unbelieving listeners (as in the case of Paul).[69]

67. At Nazareth, Luke 4:24, and nearing Jerusalem, 13:33–34. See the discussion on these texts in O'Toole, *Luke's Presentation of Jesus*, 29–33.

68. Jesus is rumored to be Elijah or one of the old prophets raised from the dead, Luke 9:7–8, 19. Jesus is called "a prophet mighty in deed and word" Luke 24:19 and a prophet like Moses, Acts 3:22–23; 7:37; Johnson, *Luke*, 16–21; O'Toole, *Luke's Presentation of Jesus*, 33–42, 51–52.

69. For more discussion of *the actions* of Jesus as a prophet, see O'Toole, *Luke's Presentation of Jesus*, 42–54.

Regarding the Isaiah 6 prophecy, "At Luke 8:10 Luke minimizes Mark's (4:12) predestined Isaianic rejection of the Jews so that the Jews might have every chance to accept the gospel before Paul, quoting fully Isaiah 6:9f, rejects them as a whole (Acts 28:26–28)," Mattill, "Purpose of Acts," *Apostolic History*, 119–20. Danker in *Luke*, 84, is more hopeful on this point stating that "Luke is looking forward to Pentecost when the leaders of Israel will be faced with their crime; forgiveness will be available to the repentant, and for them hardness of heart was to cease." Even in Acts 28, Moessner adds: "as with the prophets of the Old Testament, along with the pronouncement of certain judgment comes the implicit, 'Unless you repent,'" 103, in "Paul in Acts," *NTS* 34 (1988) 96–104; N. T. Wright agrees that both judgment and renewal are found in the prophecy of Isaiah 6 and that this has relevance for Luke–Acts, *Jesus and the Victory of God*, 236; Bovon points out "there is slight hope for the salvation of Israel expressed in the last phrase . . . 'and I shall heal them,'" in his "Studies in Luke–Acts," *HTR* 85 (1992) 189–90.

Although there is the possibility of a softening of Mark in Luke 8:10 to provide some opportunity for a favorable response of the Jews, there are "few takers" by the end of Acts. It has already been argued (in chap. 3, "Missionary Settings," 78–81) that Acts 28:26–28 appears to be a climactic indictment on the unfaithful members of Israel in Acts. It is not clear that Luke 8:10 and Acts 28:25–28 have a direct linear relationship of commencement and completion. Acts 28:25–28, however, as an apology for the Gentile mission has a closer linear relationship with Luke 4:24–27 in terms of the surfacing of a mission to the Gentiles in Luke's Gospel and its development in Acts. The lengthy statement of hardening in Acts 28:25–28 recalls numerous passages of Jewish stubbornness

3. The work of Jesus as prophet and Messiah is connected with the hope and consolation of Israel (Luke 2:25–32, 36–38; 24:19–21; Acts 4:10–12).
4. Jesus appeals to the law of Moses and the prophets in his teaching (e.g. Luke 24:27, 44).

In summary we see that what can be said of Paul and the early church as prophets also applies to Jesus, Luke's ideal model of a prophet. Throughout Luke–Acts, Jesus is referred to as a prophet. The portrait of Paul as a prophet in Acts 28 parallels Luke's portrait of Jesus the ideal prophet. It is this ideal model of Jesus the prophet that Paul is patterned after in Acts 28.

Paul Is Portrayed As a Suffering Servant Like Jesus[70]

The following characteristics in Acts 28 appear to designate Paul as a suffering servant:

1. The παραδίδωμι motif is used in the account of Paul: "I was delivered (παραδίδωμι) into the hands of Romans" (Acts 28:17; cf. 21:11). LXX Isa 53:6 "The Lord delivered (παραδίδωμι) him up for our sins."[71] LXX Isa 53:12 "His life was delivered up

---

and rejection, in which Luke 8:10 is included (Luke 2:34; 4:24–27; 6:22–23, 26; 8:10; 11:47–51; 13:23–30, 33–34; 14:24; 19:27, 46; 20:9–18; 21:20–24; 23:28–31; 24:27; Acts 3:23; 4:25–28; 7:35–53; 13:40–41, 46; 18:6; 19:9). On linear progression of the way of salvation see Robinson, *Der Weg Des Herrn*, 30–34,43; Moessner, *Lord of the Banquet*, 294–307.

If Luke 8:10 appears to soften Mark's hardening statement to give more opportunity for Jewish repentance, Acts 28: 25–28 is definitely a climactic pronouncement on the unrepentant of Israel. It is not clear if Luke 8:10 and Acts 28:25–28 have any direct relationship in terms of Jewish stubbornness and rejection in Luke–Acts. See also, Gnilka *Verstockung*, 13–18, 119–50; As we mentioned, there remains of faithful remnant of Israel with a growing number of Gentiles, see Tiede, *Prophecy and History*, 121–22, 151; Evans and Sanders, *Luke and Scripture*, 208–11; Evans, *To See and Not Perceive*, 121, 126; Moessner, "Paul in Acts," *NTS* 34 (1988) 102–4.

70. For the portrait of Paul and Jesus as the Servant of Isaiah, see: Danker *Luke* 70–90; O'Toole *Christological Climax*, 68–69, 109–10, and his excellent study "How Does Luke Portrary Jesus as Servant of YHWH," *Biblica* 81 (2000) 328–46, "Jesus, through Paul . . . actualizes the mission of the Servant of YHWH" (339); O'Toole, *Luke's Presentation of Jesus*, 95–112.

71. All passages cited from the Septuagint are based on the text edited by A. Rahlfs, *Septuaginta*, 8th ed. (as stated earlier). See discussion of παραδίδωμι and Jesus as Servant of YHWH in O'Toole, *Luke's Presentation of Jesus*, 100–103.

(παραδίδωμι) unto death . . . he was delivered up (παραδί-δωμι) because of their iniquities."

2. At his trial, Paul is "led" in (ἄγω, Acts 25:6, 23; cf. Isa 53:7–8) and declared innocent (Acts 25:18, 25; 26:31–32; cf. Isa 50:9; 53:9) in a way similar to the Suffering Servant.[72] The servant motifs from Isaiah 42:1, 6–7; 49:6 are applied to Paul: he is a chosen (ἐκλογῆς) vessel (Acts 9:15), who will open the eyes of the blind (26:18) and be a light to the nations (13:47; cf. 26:23).

The above servant motifs used of Paul are employed earlier by Luke in the account of Jesus. In Luke–Acts, Jesus is the Suffering Servant, after which Paul is patterned:

1. The παραδίδωμι motif is used in the account of Jesus: "The Son of Man must be delivered into the hands of sinful men" (Luke 24:7; cf. 9:44;18:32; Acts 3:13).
2. Jesus like the Suffering Servant is "led" to his fate (ἄγω Luke 22:54; 23:1; cf. Isa 53:7–8) but declared innocent (Luke 23:4, 14–15, 22; cf. Isa 50:9; 53:9).
3. In addition to the above, Jesus is given the technical title-of "servant" (παῖς, παιδός), derived from the servant passages in LXX Isaiah (Acts 3:13, 26; 4:25, 27, 30; cf. Isa 42:1; 49:6; 52:13).
4. Jesus is explicitly identified as the Suffering Servant of Isaiah 53 in Acts 8:32–33, 35.

The servant motifs from Isa 42:1, 6–7 and 49:6 used of Paul in Acts, are first applied to Jesus in Luke's Gospel. The infant Jesus is spoken of as "a light for revelation to the Gentiles and for the glory to thy people Israel" (Luke 2:32). It is in the work of Jesus that "all flesh shall see the salvation of God" as announced by John the Baptist (Luke 3:6). At His transfiguration, Jesus is designated God's chosen (ἐκλέγομαι) Luke 9:35.

The above data has shown that the servant motifs that Luke applies to Paul were first applied to Jesus in Luke's Gospel. Jesus is the Suffering Servant of YHWH after whom Paul is patterned in Acts.

We have shown in this section that the key themes of the Jewish and Roman apologies, and the prophet and servant motifs are con-

72. See O'Toole, *Christological Climax*, 23; and *Luke's Presentation of Jesus*, 103.

nected with the image of Paul as one who is innocent like Jesus and undergoes similar experiences as Jesus did. These themes were mostly derived from Acts 28:17–20 and were primarily concerned with Paul's identity and role in the text.

The Missionary Activity of Paul in Acts 28

This section will seek to examine the activity in which Paul is engaged: specifically his preaching activity and the Gentile mission. We will show how these activities are in continuity with the practices of Jesus and are in fulfillment of His commands. The above themes are derived from Acts 28:23–31 which is primarily concerned with Paul's missionary activity at Rome.

The Preaching of the Gospel by Paul at Rome Concludes a Continuity of Witness from Jesus to the Twelve and Paul

In chapter one it was discussed how the preaching summaries (Acts 28:23, and especially vv. 30–31) were utilized in support of viewing Acts 28 as the goal of the progression of the gospel from Jerusalem to Rome.[73]

Despite the support for Rome as the final destination of Paul (Acts 19:21; 23:11; 27:24) some caution should be taken in viewing Rome as the particular geographical goal of the proclamation of the gospel in Acts, since Acts 1:8 and 13:47 ("to the ends of the earth") seem to refer to the Gentile world in general. Nevertheless, it has been shown in chapter two, that there not only is a geographical progression from Jerusalem to Rome conveyed,[74] but a historical continuity of witness from Jesus to Paul.[75]

73. See our chap. 1, "Progression," 3–4; see also: chap. 2, section on "Summary Statement on Preaching," 50–51.

74. Jesus: in Galilee and Judea (Luke 4:31, 44), in Jerusalem (Luke 19:47—20:1); the early church in Jerusalem (Acts 4:31, 33; 5:42; 9:28–29), Samaria (8:4–5, 25), the coastal regions (8:40); Paul (and others) in Antioch (15:35), Asia Minor (13:49; 14:1, 6–7; 19:8, 10) Greece (17:2–3; 18:5, 11) and Rome (28:23, 30–31).

75. A continuity of witness beginning with Jesus (Luke 4:43–44; 8:1; 9:11; 20:1), continued by His disciples (9:6; 10:8–11; cf. 8:39), carried on by the Twelve and others (Acts 4:31, 33; 5:42; 8:4–5, 12, 25), and brought to a culmination by Paul (9:27, 29; 15:35; 17:2–3; 18:5; 19:8; 28:23, 30–31). When we are talking about "witness" in the above context, we are not restricting our study to the technical usage of μαρτύρομαι (and its equivalents) as the apostolic witness to the risen Christ (although there are excep-

In our investigation of the literary forms in chapter four, the climactic features of Acts 28:23 and 28:30–31 were established. Both summaries are distinct in content and structure from the others. Both summaries have a significant location in the narrative of Acts 28:16–31.

Acts 28:23, 30–31 elaborate on key themes in Luke–Acts: proclaiming and bearing witness to the kingdom of God, persuading and teaching about Jesus Christ from the law and the prophets. In Acts 28:30–31, the use of ἀκωλύτως, and its catchword κωλύω, convey the idea of the final triumph of Christianity over religious, racial, and political obstacles.

In terms of fulfillment of prophecy, the preaching summaries of Paul at Rome (a) fulfill specifically the prophecy that Paul would bear witness to Christ at Rome (23:11), and (b) fulfill generally Christ's command to preach to all nations (Luke 24:47; Acts 1:8; 22:21; 26:17–18).

The above conclusions of our investigation on the function of the summary statements, has direct application to the theological significance of our study.

The preaching accounts in Acts 28 provide the conclusion of a historical continuity of proclamation that began with Jesus and his disciples in Palestine, was continued by the Twelve and others in Judea and Samaria (Stephen, Philip), and was brought to a culmination by Paul and his associates (e.g., Barnabas) in the Gentile world. This continuity of witness provides us with an important history of transmission scheme in Luke–Acts.

---

tions to this usage, Luke 21:13; Acts 8:25; 20:24; 22:20; 28:23). The phrase "witnessing terminology" will be used in a broader sense of preaching, teaching, persuading, and bearing witness to the dawning of God's reign in the life and work of Christ. Such terminology is generally applied to Christ, the Twelve (also Stephen, Philip, Barnabas), and Paul. See chap. 2, "Summary Statement," 50–52, for further discussion on this subject. Without classifying Luke–Acts as biographical genre, Loveday Alexander reviews the discussion on the succession motif in Greco-Roman biographies, favoring the influence of a succession pattern similar to the Socratic tradition to understand Luke's efforts to incorporate Paul's story with that of both Jesus in the Third Gospel and the Twelve in the first half of Acts, "Acts in Ancient Intellectual Biography," *Book of Acts*, 1:31–63; also her *Preface*, 210–12. To better understand Luke's theme of continuity of witness in the context of early Christianity, see "the preservation of apostolic traditions," in Puskas, *Introduction*, 241–43. Although Luke–Acts shares certain generic similarities, it does not embrace all of early catholicism's characteristics of the second and third centuries, in response to criticisms of, e.g., Barrett, *Acts* 2:xciii-xcvii; Bock, *Acts*, 39–40.

The preaching summaries at Rome (28:23, vv. 30–31) serve as a climactic conclusion to the gospel proclamation from Jesus and the Twelve (with others), to Paul. In these summaries of Acts 28 there are several key Lukan themes and significant witnessing terminology. The preaching accounts at Rome also fulfill the commands of Christ to be His witness to the nations.

The Concluding Speech at Rome on the Gentile Mission Fulfills Christ's Command

The view that Acts 28 presents a concluding account of the mission to the Gentiles was discussed in chapter one. The importance of this theme in our text is especially evident in Acts 28:25–28.

It has been pointed out in chapter two that Acts 28:25–28 functions with 13:46–47 and Luke 4:24–27 as an apologetic speech on the Gentile mission, all of which are concerned with the following themes: (1) unbelief of the Jews (Luke 4:24, 28f; Acts 13:46b; 28:26–27) and (2) the turning to the Gentiles (Luke 4:26–27; Acts 13:46c; 28:28). In our chapter 3, dealing with the Pauline mission (see "Missionary Settings," 96), it was shown how Acts 28:25–28 functions as the climactic conclusion to these themes of Jewish unbelief and turning to the Gentiles (Acts 13:46–47; 18:6; 19:9).

It has been mentioned in our chapter one, that one particular interpretation regarded the mission to the Gentiles as prompted by Jewish unbelief in Acts 28 and elsewhere.[76] This position is argued on the basis of the Gentile apologies (13:46–47; 28:25–28) and other passages in the Pauline mission (18:6; 19:9). But the unbelief of certain Jews is only one immediate cause for the Gentile mission,[77] another immediate cause

76. See, for example: E. Zeller, *Contents*, 2:85, 105–6; A. Harnack, *Missions*, 49 n. 1; J. Weiss, *Christianity*, 2:661; and Haenchen, *Acts*, 100–102, 729–30; J. T. Sanders, *The Jews in Luke-Acts* (Fortress, 1987) 261–62, 298; G. Wasserberg, *Aus Israels Mitte*, 71–115; see chap. 1, "The Gentile Mission," 4–5.

77. Dupont's view in his study on Acts 28 that no cause and effect relationship exists between Jewish unbelief and the Gentile mission ("La Conclusion," 403) fails to reckon with the fact that, the unfavorable response of a growing number of Jews is presented as a real, even frustrating, problem for Paul and his missionary colleagues (13:46–47; 18:6; 19:9; 28:25–28). Therefore these passages in mission appear to express or at least imply such a relationship. Here we exclude (for the present) the theme of unrepentant Israel as the fulfillment of Scripture which can be argued as the ultimate cause for a mission to the nations.

is that of persecution of the church, for example.[78] The ultimate causes for the Gentile mission are the Old Testament prophecies applied to the work of Christ and His church,[79] and the commands of Jesus Christ Himself.

Old Testament prophecies supporting a Gentile mission, which are connected with Christ's universal work include:

1. "A light for revelation to the Gentiles" is applied to Jesus the infant (Luke 2:32/Isa 42:6–7; 49:6).
2. John announces that "all flesh shall see the salvation of God", which looks ahead to the life and work of Christ (Luke 3:6/Isa 40:5).
3. Christ is proclaimed as the ground and means by which "all the families of the earth shall be blessed" (Acts 3:25/Gen. 22:18).[80]

Prophecies from the Old Testament connected with the Gentile mission of the church are:

1. The mission of Paul (and the church) is to proclaim Jesus as "a light for the Gentiles" (Acts 13:47/Isa 49:6; [Acts 26:18]; cf. Luke 2:32).

78. Acts 8:1, 4–5.

79. This view is in partial agreement with Dupont who states that both Jewish unbelief and the Gentile mission are the fulfillment of prophecy, "La Conclusion" 402–3. Although the above assertion is certainly true, the statements in the Pauline mission (e.g. 13:46–47; 18:6) speak of Jewish unbelief as also prompting the Gentile mission. The data might best be explained in the following manner. Passages referring to the Gentile mission due to Jewish rejection express the experience of the missionaries in the narrative time. Gentile mission and Jewish unbelief as "fulfillment of prophecy" are interpretations for the implied reader/auditor by the narrator who sought to explain and substantiate this experiential phenomenon in terms of Old Testament prophecies. Harnack gives a similar explanation in a more historical manner in his *Mission* 36–72; see also J. Weiss *Christianity* 384; "the occasion but not the cause for the mission to the Gentiles was allegedly commanded in the Old Testament" (Acts 13:47), Barrett, *Acts* 1:657; David Peterson, "The Motif of Fulfillment and the Purpose of Luke–Acts," *Book of Acts*, 1:100; Jewish unbelief fulfills the Scriptures and justifies the Gentile mission, Evans, *To See and Not Perceive* 126.

80. We would agree with Dupont against Jervell (*Luke*, 58–59) that the "seed" (σπέρμα) of Acts 3:25 is Christ, Dupont, "La Conclusion," 395.

2. Appeal to the book of Amos is made at the Jerusalem assembly concerning the receptivity of the Gentiles in the new age (Acts 15:14–18/Amos 9:11–12).
3. Paul is commissioned by Christ to preach to Israel and the Gentiles in a manner similar to the prophets (Acts 26:16–18/Ezek 2:1–4; Isa 42:7, 16).

Further basis for the Gentile mission, which compliments the fulfillment of Scripture explanation, are the commands of Christ to preach to the nations:

1. The commission in Jerusalem given to his disciples and the church (Luke 24:47–49; Acts 1:8).
2. The commission given to Paul by Christ (Acts 9:15–16; 22:15, 21; 26:16–20, 23).

From the above analysis we note that the ultimate grounds for the Gentile mission are found in the Old Testament prophecies fulfilled in the work of Christ and his church, and the commands of Christ Himself. In almost every passage, reference to salvation for the nations is connected with Christ. He brings about God's universal salvation in his life and work, and commands his disciples to proclaim this salvation to the nations. Therefore the ultimate basis for the Gentile mission is in the life and work of Christ who fulfills the Old Testament prophecies and commands others to proclaim to the nations what he has done.

In Acts 28:28 (τοῖς ἔθνεσιν . . . τὸ σωτήριον τοῦ θεοῦ) we detect a close correspondence with passages concerned with the life and work of Christ: Luke 2:30–32 (τὸ σωτήριόν σου . . . εἰς ἀποκάλυψιν ἐθνῶν) and 3:6 (πᾶσα σὰρξ τὸ σωτήριον τοῦ θεοῦ).[81] All of the above terms are derived essentially from Isaiah 40:5 (LXX).[82] Therefore the statements of Paul at Rome concerning salvation to the Gentiles is a fulfillment of the universal work predicted of Christ. In uttering this statement at Rome (Acts 28:28); and putting it into effect (28:30–31),

81. This pattern of correspondence is argued especially in W. C. Robinson, *Der Weg*, 39; and in Dupont, *Salvation*, 14–16; and "La Conclusion," 402, 404.

82. As cited from A. Rahlfs (ed.) *Septuaginta* 8th ed.; Litwak, *Echoes of Scripture*, 191–92.

Paul completes the work of Christ as announced in Luke 2:30–32 and 3:6, albeit it in a new direction.[83]

In this section of chapter four, we have shown how in Acts 28, a number of themes and motifs are brought together in a climactic fashion with the portrait of Paul at Rome as one like Jesus who does the work of Jesus. In Acts 28:17–20 (and also in vv. 16, 30–31) various themes such as the Jewish and Roman apologies, the servant and prophet themes find a unifying factor in the identity of Paul as one who is like Jesus. On the basis of parallels between Acts 28 and Luke 23, Paul is defended as a faithful Israelite like Jesus and is declared innocent by Romans as in the case of Jesus. In a comparison of Acts 28 with Luke 4 (and Luke 2; 11; 24), Paul is portrayed as a prophet like Jesus. An investigation of the παραδίδωμι motif and other servant themes implied in Acts 28, indicate that Paul is also portrayed as a suffering servant like Jesus. The above themes are connected primarily with the identity of the one who came to Rome to do the work of Jesus, and are confined mostly to 28:17–20.[84]

83. In chap. 3, "Acts 28 and Other Pauline Missionary Settings," 78–81, the climactic features of Acts 28:28 were argued on the basis of its climactic relationship with other Gentile apologies, its contrasting relationship with Acts 28:26–27, and its thematic associations with Luke 2:30–32 and 3:6. David W. Pao observes a dramatic reversal (in the Isaianic program) that occurs with the two Isaianic quotations used in Luke 3:4–6/Isa 40:3–5 (renewed hope of Israel's deliverance) and Acts 28:25–28/Isa 6:9–10 (Jewish recalcitrance but Gentile receptivity), in his *Acts and the Isaianic New Exodus*, 108. Gentile receptivity in Acts 28:28, however, does not exclude interested or receptive Jews since Paul "welcomed all (πάντας) who came to him" (Acts 28:30). As a result, a dramatic reversal of the Lukan hope expressed in Luke 3:4–6/Isa 40:3–5 that "all flesh" will see the salvation of God finds some resolution in Acts 28:28–31 where we find the hope of Israel's deliverance renewed in new ways in Acts. Litwak states that Isa 40:5 (the addition of a remnant from the nations) in Acts 28.28 builds upon Isaiah 6 (rejection by a majority of Israel, leaving a remnant), *Echoes of Scripture*, 191–92.

84. While it has been pointed out that the gospel proclamation (Acts 28:23, 31) and Gentile mission (vv. 25–28) constitute the climactic features of the narrative, vv. 17–20 plays an important role in identifying Paul as the one like Jesus who does the work of Jesus. Our concluding narrative of Acts 28 seems to function in a manner similar to a peroration or epilogue in classical rhetoric. It recapitulates major points of the speeches (and other relevant texts) as shown in our comparative analyses (chap. 3), and seeks to stir the audience to action with a portrait of Paul triumphing over obstacles. Hauser refers to Acts 28 as a "peroratio," *Strukturen*, 6; see "Acts 28 as Epilogue to Luke–Acts," in Alexander, "Reading Luke–Acts from Back to Front," 223–29.

On ancient rhetoric, see George A. Kennedy, *New Testament Interpretation through Rhetorical Criticism* (University of North Carolina Press, 1984) 62–63, 114–40 and his

In Acts 28:23–31, such themes as the gospel proclamation and the Gentile mission are the activities of Paul who does the work of Jesus. From an analysis of the preaching summaries in Luke–Acts, the gospel proclamation of Paul at Rome constitutes the climactic conclusion of an activity begun by Jesus, continued by the disciples and the early church, and culminated by Paul in his Gentile mission. Paul's final statement on the Gentile mission (Acts 28:25–28) constitutes a climactic conclusion to the Gentile apologies in Luke–Acts (Luke 4:24–27; Acts 13:46–47). This Gentile mission is in fulfillment of Old Testament prophecy concerning Christ and His Church, and is commanded by Christ Himself.

Thus we see in Acts 28 a concluding account of Paul as one like Jesus (vv. 17–20) who completes the work of Jesus in a climactic manner (vv. 23–31). To understand the complete message of Acts 28:16–31, the identity of Paul cannot be separated from his activity. Therefore vv. 17–20 should not be ignored in an exegesis of Acts 28:16–31. Acts 28:17–20 has the function of introducing and identifying the one who at Rome brought the work of Jesus to a climactic conclusion (vv. 23–31).

The Relevance of Acts 28:16–31 for Luke and His Readers/Auditors[85]

The narrative portrait of Paul at Rome as one like Jesus who does the work of Jesus may have had relevance for Luke and his implied read-

---

Classical Rhetoric and its Christian and Secular Tradition from Ancient to Modern Times (1980); see also W. Wuellner, "Where is Rhetorical Criticism Taking Us?" *CBQ* 49 (1987) 448–63; W. S. Kurz, "Hellenistic Rhetoric in the Christological Proof of Luke–Acts," *CBQ* 42 (1980) 171–95; B. L. Mack, *Rhetoric and the New Testament* (Fortress, 1990); A. J. Woodman, *Rhetoric in Classical Historiography* (Croom Helm, 1988); "Luke–Acts and Rhetoric," in Witherington, *Acts*, 39–51. For a rhetorical analysis of the entire Pauline corpus, see Charles B. Puskas, *The Letters of Paul: An Introduction* (Liturgical, 1993).

85. Regarding Lukan *Sitz im Leben* see, "It is hazardous to move from the presence of a theme . . . to the situation of the readers" (89) in L. T. Johnson, "On Finding the Lukan Community: A Cautionary Essay," in 1979 *SBLSP*, 67–100; "the purpose of Luke–Acts is reflected in the narrative rather than in some polemical, paraenetic, or other tendency to be abstracted from it," Nils Dahl, *Jesus and the Memory of the Early Church* (Augsburg, 1976) 88; on implied readers, see Walter Ong, "The Writer's Audience is Always a Fiction," in his *Interfaces of the Word* (Cornell, 1977) 53–81; also Kurz, *Reading Luke-Acts*, 9, 186; but Wayne Booth reminds us that by shaping their words into the narrative, "authors are in effect exercising careful control over the reader's degree of involvement in or distance from the events of the story, by insuring that

ers/auditors in the following three ways: (1) to defend the life and work of Paul; (2) to establish some historical continuity with the past; and (3) to provide a model or pattern for a world-wide mission of the church.

It has been stated that the Jesus-Paul parallels provide an "irresistible apology for Paul." If controversies connected with Paul's death and teaching were issues for the author and his implied readers/auditors, a defense of Paul would be relevant.[86] Such an apology might convey the following message: although the life and work of Paul were controversial, Paul did not deviate from the life and teachings of Christ, but was in harmony with them. In chapter three, our comparisons of Acts 28 with: Acts 21–26, Luke 23–24, and Luke 1:1–4, established the apologetic tone of the account of Paul at Rome. In chapter four, we demonstrated that the identity of Paul in Acts 28 as a faithful Israelite, a suffering servant, a prophet, and one who is innocent before Rome, functions as a defense of Paul as one like Jesus.

Luke's narrative appears to address issues of identity and continuity with the past. From Luke 1:1–2 it can be observed that Luke views himself and his implied readers/auditors as standing in a historical relationship with Jesus, "eyewitnesses and servants of the word" (the

---

the reader views the materials with the degree of detachment or sympathy felt by the implied author, *The Rhetoric of Fiction* (Chicago, 1961) 200; R. Scholes and R. Kellogg show that the development of narrative in the western world is without sharp distinctions between oral or written, verse or prose, fact or fiction, in narratives *The Nature of Narrative* (Oxford University Press, 1966) 3–13, 57–81, also in Beverly Gaventa, "Toward a Theology of Acts: Reading and Rereading," *Int* 42 (1988) 149–53; Joel B. Green states that Luke's theology in *the world of Luke* must grapple with three levels: the world it assumes, the world it actualizes in the narrative, and the world as Luke wanted it to be, in his *Theology of St. Luke* (Cambridge University Press, 1995) 4–5.

86. Quote from Mattill, "Jesus–Paul," 37. An example of the controversy connected with Paul's *teaching*, might be found in Acts 21:21, where rumors have been circulated among certain Jewish believers in Jerusalem that Paul teaches all the Jews of the diaspora to turn away from Moses, telling them not to circumcise their children or live according to their customs. An example of the controversy connected with Paul's *life* might be the fact that Paul comes to Rome, a prisoner accused of crimes against the Jewish people (e.g. Acts 24:5–8) and is later condemned to die there (possible allusions to Paul's death are in Acts 20:25, 38). In support of these observations, see O'Toole, "Why Did Luke Write Acts?" 71. "Doubtless, Paul's execution in Rome cast a shadow on any church founded by him," in O'Toole, *Christological Climax*, 160; On Acts 20:17–38 assuming Paul's death, see Pervo, *Dating* 23–24, 379. See also our discussion of the defense motifs in Acts 28 and their significance for Luke in chap. 3, "Acts 28 and Acts 21–26," 71–73.

Twelve, Paul, and others), and finally their own situation.[87] This historical connection is also supported by the pattern of continuity detected in the preaching summaries: beginning with Jesus, the Twelve, the early church, and continued by Paul and others.[88] This emphasis would certainly be relevant for Luke's implied readers/auditors, if they were mostly Gentile followers of Christ living in the late first century who had some questions or issues regarding their origins and heritage.[89]

Luke's emphasis on historical continuity with the church's past would be significant for an audience facing some kind of identity crisis and seeking stability with a reminder of its historic roots and traditions, if they indeed faced such issues.[90] A defense of Paul and his work also

87. For further discussion of this line of development or progression of witness, see chap. 3, "Acts 28 and the Introduction to Luke's Gospel," 97–99.

88. See chap. 4, section on "Summary Statements on Paul's Preaching," 110–11. Continuity with the past is also evident in the comparisons of Paul and Jesus in chap. 3, 89–91.

89. Despite the challenges of establishing a plausible Lukan *Sitz im Leben*, Barbara Shellard surveys the theories about "Luke's Intended Audience" and argues for a "mixed audience of Jews and Gentiles like Rome" (55) in her *New Light on Luke* (Sheffield, 2002) 37–55; Relevant to our discussion, is the suggestion of Beverly Gaventa that "he (Luke) seeks to instruct believers, particularly Gentile believers, in the fundamentals of their tradition," in her "Acts of the Apostles," *NIDB*, 1:35–6. More specifically, Bruno Bauer (1850), sees Acts addressing readers who "had lost touch with the Jewish heritage of the faith and needed to have it explained to them," from *Die Apostelgeschichte* 120–22, cited in Gasque, *Criticism*, 76. Also, "Luke's Church was inquisitive about its origins," Wilson, *Gentiles*, 249; Bock considers "the new community's emerging separate identity," *Acts* 37–38, (social context) 42–43. Robert L. Brawley focuses on Christian self-identity in his *Luke-Acts and the Jews*, 39, 71–72, 143–44, 159; Luke's readers are different from the readers of Mark and Matthew in Harold Riley, *Preface to Luke* (Mercer, 1993) 131–42. David Aune states "By ca. A.D. 50, Christianity was a religious movment needing definition, identity, and legitimation," *Literary Environment*, 137–38; Arguing for Acts as an early 2nd century writing, Richard I. Pervo examines, e.g., the ecclesiastical structures and functions, sources, theology, anachronisms, view of the other, in his *Dating Acts*, 309–46. In Puskas, *Introduction*, this author sought to reconstruct a history of early Christianity from the New Testament (NT) and other relevant documents only after first examining the Greco-Roman and Jewish world (1–59), the literary forms and characteristics of the NT (109–58); see also here: Lukan Christianity (214–17) and the features of emerging Christian orthodoxy (223–52).

90. Conzelmann suspects that the author of Luke and Acts seeks to address some "theoretical basis of the church" with the presentation of the unity of the apostolic tradition. Conzelmann, "Luke's Place in the Development of Early Christianity," *SLA*, 308; so also Brown, "Prologues," *PLA*, 103–4. Avoiding theories of community crises reflected in the texts, see the sociological analyses of the narrative data (e.g., class, education, ideologies) in Vernon K. Robbins, "The Social Location of the Implied Author

contributes to Luke's attempt at finding some sense of identity and continuity with the Church's heritage. For Luke and his readers/auditors a defense of Paul as one like Jesus would confirm the historical continuity from Jesus to Paul, and would establish Paul as an important historical link between Jesus and Luke's audience. In the narrative situation of the Ephesian elders before Paul who commends to them the faith (Acts 20:17–37), Luke may have imagined himself and his readers/auditors, although living at a later time period (A.D. 80–90) from that of the Ephesian disciples of Paul (ca., A.D. 58). In terms of type and model, Paul's divinely-willed mission provides a compelling model for Luke and his readers/auditors, since Paul who does Christ's work at Rome also represents Christianity.

Paul is also symbolic of Christianity in the Lukan narrative.[91] What Christ predicts of Christians (Luke 12:8–12; 21:12–19) is what Paul experiences (Acts 22–26).[92] Paul is the advocate of "the Way, which they call a sect" (Acts 24:14–15). At Rome, the "views" of Paul are identified with the Christian "sect" (28:22). Paul identifies himself as a Christian in his discourse with Agrippa (Acts 26:28–29). The mission of the church into all the world (Luke 24:47; Acts 1:8) is typified in the mission of Paul (Acts 13:47–48; 18:6; 19:9; 28:25–28).[93]

The church's pattern for world-wide mission is exemplified in the life and work of Paul: proclaiming the gospel to the Gentiles.[94] Movement to the Gentiles is a typical pattern throughout Paul's mission in Acts, a procedure in fulfillment of Christ's command, and one which

---

of Luke–Acts," *Social World*, 305–32; and his "Luke–Acts: A Mixed Population Seeks a Home in the Roman Empire," *Images of Empire*, 202–21; Jerome H. Neyrey, "Luke's Social Location of Paul," in *History, Literature and Society*, 251–79; also observing certain "social context" clues see Witherington, *Acts*, 54–56; Gaventa, *Acts*, 49–52; and "Acts," *NIDB*, 1:34–37; Bock, *Acts*, 42–43.

91. See for example the following works: Rackham, *Acts*, 506; Dibelius, *Studies*, 213; O'Toole, *Christological Climax*, 14, 147; and "'Be Imitators of Me," 157–59; for further discussion on Paul as symbolic of Christianity, see chap. 1, "Portrait of Paul," 11.

92. O'Toole, "'Be Imitators of Me,'" 158–59; and *Unity*, 84.

93. See, Haenchen, *Acts*, 729–32. The fact that Paul is also an important historical link between Jesus and Luke's readers (as mentioned earlier) further substantiates the view that Paul's life and work seems to be some type of model and pattern for Christians (who seem to be the readers envisioned by the author of Luke–Acts).

94. See our chap. 3, "Acts 28 and Other Pauline Missionary Settings," 73–78, for further discussion on the above pattern.

completes the work of Christ.[95] The portrait of Paul at Rome as one like Jesus who does the work of Jesus has relevance for the implied author and his readers/auditors, to (1) defend the life and work of their great predecessor who did the work of Christ, (2) establish some continuity with their Christian heritage going back to Paul, the Twelve, and Jesus, and (3) provide the readers/auditors (followers of Jesus) with some kind of pattern and program for world mission.[96]

95. The Jesus-Paul parallels also argue in favor of viewing Paul's work as a model and example for Christians. See chap. 1, "Portrait of Paul," 10–11, chap. 4, "Acts 28 and the Conclusion of Luke," 86–91, and chap. 4, "Missionary Activity," 125–27.

96. Did not the implied author Luke–Acts envision readers who were in need of some specific instruction and general direction concerning the importance and necessity of a world-wide mission by including these commands of Jesus (Luke 24:47; Acts 1:8; 9:15; 13:47; 22:21; 26:16–18)? The narrative of Luke–Acts has some connection with "a growing Gentile community in need of self-identity and direction as a result of Jewish and pagan antagonism . . . the author appears to be influenced by Pauline Christianity," Puskas, *Introduction*, 215. On Acts and the Letters of Paul, see Pervo, *Dating Acts*, chap. 4.

Conclusion

IN CHAPTER ONE, IT WAS DISCOVERED THAT THE AREAS most in need of investigation were those concerned with the literary function and theological significance of Acts 28:16–31. In chapter two, the foundational questions of the structure of the text and the nature of the literary forms were pursued. In chapter three, the literary, structural, and thematic relationship of Acts 28 to Luke–Acts were explored. Chapter four, on the basis of the research in the previous chapters, sought to establish the literary function and theological significance of the text. It was concluded that in Acts 28:16–31, the Lukan narrator is primarily concerned with defending Paul and his work as one like Jesus who does the work of Jesus. With this focus, the implied author brings together several key themes and motifs which form a grand conclusion to the two-volume work. Such a presentation of Paul would be relevant for the implied author, who probably viewed the church of his day as successors of Paul and sought to identify his readers/auditors not only with Paul and his work, but also with Jesus and his work (e.g. allusions to Luke's Gospel, Jesus–Paul parallels)

In our study of Acts 28:16–31 we have shown that the Lukan author defends Paul. A similar apologetic tone was noted in comparisons of Acts 28 with chapters 21–26 (the arrest and defense of Paul), and with Luke 1:1–4 (implying an apologetic concern). In a comparison with Luke 23 we noted that the innocence of Paul is vindicated in Acts 28 by presenting Paul as undergoing the same kind of experiences as Jesus did. In our analysis of Acts 28 and Luke 4, we have argued that Paul and his mission are defended by means of historical precedent and literary prototype in the ministry of Jesus at Nazareth.

It was demonstrated in Acts 28, that Paul is defended as one who is like Jesus. He is presented as a faithful Israelite like Jesus, innocent before Rome like Jesus, a prophet and suffering servant like Jesus (see especially vv. 17–20). It has also been shown that Paul at Rome is vindicated as one who does the work of Jesus. The preaching of the gospel at Rome concludes a progression of proclamation from Jesus to the Twelve and Paul. The concluding account of Paul and the Gentile mission completes the work of Christ and fulfills his commands (see especially 28:23–31).[1] In Acts 28 it was pointed out that there were several features which make the text a climactic conclusion to Luke–Acts.

Paul's coming and arrival in Rome (28:14,16) serve as the concluding climax of a series of prophetic announcements concerning Paul's journey to Rome.[2] It was shown that these announcements are located in such a way so as to form a rising order of importance, reaching their highest point in the dual announcement of Paul's coming and arrival in Rome. For the Lukan author, Rome is the final goal of the Christian mission in Acts.[3]

Paul's concluding speech on the Gentile mission (28:25–28) functions as the climax of a series of Gentile apologies (13:46–47; 18:6) going back to the implicit statements of Jesus (Luke 4:24–27). In Acts 28:25–28, a climactic pronouncement on the unbelieving Jews and a definitive statement on the mission to the Gentiles are made by Paul in the conclusion of Luke–Acts.[4]

The preaching summaries of Paul at Rome (28:23, and 30–31) function climactically because of their distinctive content, syntax, and place in the narrative.[5] Both summaries also elaborate upon the Lukan

1. It was also stressed in chap. 4 that the identity of Paul (28:17–20) could not be separated from the missionary activity of Paul (vv. 23–31), 130–31.

2. Acts 19:21; 23:11; 27:24. See chap. 3, footnote 44, for the function of these texts in the dramatic plot structure of Acts 19:21—28:31.

3. The double reference to Paul's coming and arrival in Jerusalem (21:15, 17) has parallels to the dual announcement of Paul's coming to Rome. Both sets of announcements are climactic, containing "we" statements which end when the destination of Paul's journeys to Jerusalem and Rome are reached (21:18; 28:16).

The coming of Jesus to Jerusalem (Luke 19:41–44) also marks the climax in the journey motif of Luke's Gospel (Luke 9:51; 13:22, 33; 17:11; 19:11, 28). The coming of Jesus to Jerusalem signifies the highest point of interest in the journey motif of Luke's Gospel (as in the cases of Paul's arrival in Jerusalem and Rome, in Acts). See also our chap. 4, "Climactic Arrival in the City," 107–9.

4. Individual Jews who believe will continue to be a part of the faithful remnant of Israel, comprised now of a growing number of Gentiles who heed "the prophet" like Moses and "call on God's name" (Acts 3:22–24; 15:14–18). For discussion of the climactic characteristics of Acts 28:25–28, see chap. 3, "Acts 28 and Other Pauline Missionary Settings," 78–81.

5. For a discussion on the climactic features of the preaching summaries, see chap. 4, "Summary Statements," 110–13.

themes of: bearing witness to the kingdom of God and persuading others about Jesus from the law and the prophets. In Acts 28:30–31, the use of ἀκωλύτως, and its catchword κωλύω, convey the idea of the final triumph of Christianity over religious, racial, and political obstacles.[6] In terms of fulfillment of prophecy, the preaching summaries of Paul at Rome fulfill (a) specifically the prophecy to bear witness to Christ in Rome (23:11), and (b) in a general way Christ's command to preach to all nations.[7]

In the portrait of Paul at Rome defended as one like Jesus who does the work of Jesus, the author brings to a climactic conclusion several major concerns in his two-volume work.[8] Therefore Acts 28:16–31 functions not only as the conclusion of Acts but of Luke–Acts as a whole, as we have indicated in chapter three.

As successors of Paul, Luke and his church may have found in this great figure an important link to Jesus and the early followers.[9] They are in a line of continuity from Jesus to Paul. They are to continue the work begun by Jesus and carried on by the Twelve, others witnesses, and Paul, the work which fulfills Israel's prophecies (e.g., Isa. 40:5; 49:6): world-wide proclamation of the gospel. Such a message would be of value for readers/auditors living in the late first century, who may have been searching for self-identity with the death of Paul and in need of some continuity with the past.

The account of Paul at Rome not only provides Luke and his implied readers/auditors with historical identity, it also serves as a mis-

6. Triumph over religious and racial barriers (Luke 9:49–50; 11:52; 18:16; Acts 8:36; 10:47; 11:17) and political obstacles (Acts 24:23, 27:43) is achieved here. See, Stagg, "Unhindered Gospel," 451–62; Fitzmyer, *Acts*, 791, 797. See also our chap. 4, "Summary Statements," 110–13.

7. Luke 24:47; Acts 1:8; 22:21; 26:17–18.

8. The results of our investigation confirm the view of a growing majority of scholars that Acts 28 functions as a deliberate and complete conclusion which therefore makes the question of an abrupt ending a superficial one. M. Skinner, "Locating Paul," 169 n. 51. "The 'plan for his narrative has reached its goal'...Acts 28 formally and 'finally' secures that grasp through a concluding event (τελευτή) 'from which . . . nothing of necessity must follow,'" in D. P. Moessner "Diodorus Siculus and the End of Acts," *Die Apostelgeschichte*, 218–21. See our discussion of this alleged problem in chap. 1, "The Abrupt Ending Question," 13–14.

9. See especially Luke 1:1–2 and Acts 20:17–37, Puskas, *Introduction*, 214–17, and our nuanced study at the end of our chap. 4, "Relevance of Acts 28 for Luke and His Readers," 131–35.

sionary model. The mission of Paul in Acts sets forth an agenda of world-wide mission for the church. In Acts 28, Luke seems to be telling his readers/auditors: to be identified with Christ and his church, one must also do the work of Christ and his church.

Abbreviations

ABBREVIATIONS OF BIBLICAL BOOKS, ANCIENT TEXTS, periodicals, and reference works used in the contents of our study are derived from the list in *The SBL Handbook of Style (*Peabody, Mass.: Hendrickson Publishers, 1999). The following work has also been consulted: *The Chicago Manual of Style*, 15th ed. (Chicago: University of Chicago Press, 2003). Both of the above titles have been consulted on style and related matters.

When an extensive list of passages are cited, which are only from the Acts of the Apostles, chapter and verse designations without the book title "Acts" will be employed: e.g. "Corinth (18:4–11), Ephesus (19:8–10), and Rome (28:16–31)."

All English translations of quotations from the New Testament, Old Testament, and Apocrypha are from the *New Revised Standard Version of the Bible*, 1989, unless noted otherwise, e.g., AT or author translation.

Certain frequently cited works with special bearing on the subject matter are abbreviated in our study. They are the following:

AB	The Anchor Bible
ANRW	*Aufstieg und Niedergang der römischen Welt*
Apostolic History	W. W. Gasque and R. P. Martin, eds., *Apostolic History and the Gospel: Studies in Honor of F. F. Bruce*
BDAG	Walter Bauer, Frederick William Danker, W. F. Arndt, and F. W. Gingrich, eds. *A Greek-English Lexicon of the New Testament and Other Early Christian Literature.* Revised and edited by F. W. Danker. 3rd edition
BR	*Biblical Research*
Book of Acts 1	Bruce W. Winter, and Andrew D. Clarke, eds., *The Book of Acts in its Ancient Literary Setting*
Book of Acts 3	Brian Rapske, *Paul in Roman Custody*

BC	F. J. Foakes-Jackson and Kirsopp Lake, eds., *The Beginnings of Christianity: Part I. The Acts of the Apostles*
BETL	Bibliotheca ephemeridum theologicarum lovaniensium
Bruce, *Acts GT*	F. F. Bruce, *The Acts of the Apostles, The Greek Text with Introduction and Commentary*. 3rd rev. and enlarged ed.
Bruce, *Book of Acts*	F. F. Bruce, *The Book of the Acts*. Rev. ed. New International Commentary of the New Testament
BZNW	Beihefte zur Zeitschrift für die neutestamentliche Wissenschaft
Cadbury, *Making*	Henry J. Cadbury, *The Making of Luke-Acts*
CBQ	*Catholic Biblical Quarterly*
Danker, *Jesus*	Frederick W. Danker, *Jesus and the New Age According to St. Luke, A Commentary on the Third Gospel*
Dibelius, *Studies*	Martin Dibelius, *Studies in the Acts of the Apostles*
Dupont, "La Conclusion"	Jacques Dupont, "La Conclusion des Actes et son rapport a l'ensemble de l'ouvrage de Luc"
Dupont, *Salvation*	Jacques Dupont, *The Salvation of the Gentiles*
ETL	*Ephemerides theologicae lovanienses*
ExpT	*Expository Times*
Fitzmyer, *Luke 1*	Joseph A. Fitzmyer, *The Gospel according to Luke I–IX*
Fitzmyer, *Acts*	Joseph A. Fitzmyer, *The Acts of the Apostle*
Gasque, *Criticism*	W. W. Gasque, *A History of the Criticism of the Acts of the Apostles*
GBS	Guides to Biblical Scholarship
Goulder, *Type*	M. D. Goulder, *Type and History in Acts*
Green, *Luke*	Joel B. Green, *The Gospel of Luke*
Haenchen, *Acts*	Ernst Haenchen, *The Acts of the Apostles*
Harnack, *Date*	Adolf Harnack, *The Date of Acts and the Synoptic Gospels, New Testament Studies 4*
Hauser, *Strukturen*	Herman J. Hauser, *Strukturen der Abschlusserzahlung der Apostelgeschichte (Apg 28:16–31)*
HDB	*Hasting's Dictionary of the Bible. A Dictionary of the Bible.* Ed. by James Hastings, 5 vols, 1898–1904. New York: Scribners, 1905.
ICC	The International Critical Commentary
IDB	George A. Buttrick, ed., *Interpreter's Dictionary of the Bible*, 4 vols.

Int	*Interpretation*
Jervell, *Apostelgeschichte*	Jacob Jervell, *Die Apostelgeschichte*
Jervell, *Luke*	Jacob Jervell, *Luke and the People of God: A New Look at Luke-Acts*
JBL	*Journal of Biblical Literature*
JSNT	*Journal for the Study of the New Testament*
JSNTSup	Journal for the Study of the New Testament Supplement Series
KEK	Meyers Kritisch-Exegetishcer Kommentar über das Neue Testament
LCL	Loeb Classical Library
LXX	The Septuagint. The Jewish Scriptures in Greek
Mattill, "Jesus-Paul"	A. J. Mattill Jr., "The Jesus-Paul Parallels and the Purpose of Luke-Acts: H. H. Evans Reconsidered"
Metzger, *Textual Commentary*	Bruce M. Metzger, *A Textual Commentary on the Greek New Testament.* 2nd ed.
MPG	*Patrologiae cursus completus series graeca,* 161 vols., ed. by J. P. Migne.
MPL	*Patrologiae cursus completus series latina,* 221 vols., ed. by J. P. Migne.
NCB	New Century Bible.
NICNT	New International Commentary on the New Testament
NIDB 1	*The New Interpreter's Dictionary of the Bible A-C.* Edited by Katherine Doob Sakenfeld et al.
NovT	*Novum Testamentum*
NovTSup	Novum Testamentum Supplements
NTS	*New Testament Studies*
NTTS	New Testament Tools and Studies
O'Neill, *Theology*	J. C. O'Neill, *The Theology of Acts in Its Historical Setting,* 2nd ed.
O'Toole, *Unity*	Robert F. O'Toole, *The Unity of Luke's Theology: An Analysis of Luke-Acts*
PRSt	*Perpsectives in Religious Studies.*
PSB	*Princeton Seminary Bulletin*
Puskas, *Introduction*	Charles B. Puskas, *An Introduction to the New Testament*
PLA	C. H. Talbert, ed. *Perspectives on Luke-Acts*

SBT	Studies in Biblical Theology
Schubert, "Luke 24"	Paul Schubert, "The Structure and Significance of Luke 24"
Schubert, "Final Cycle"	P. Schubert, "The Final Cycle of Speeches in Acts"
SHS	Scripture and Hermeneutics Series
SNTSMS	Society for New Testament Studies Monograph Series
SBLSP	*Society of Biblical Literature Seminar Papers*
SBLMS	Society of Biblical Literature Monograph Series
Smith, "Theology"	R. H. Smith, "The Theology of Acts"
SBT	Studies in Biblical Theology
SLA	L. E. Keck and J. L. Martyn, eds. *Studies in Luke-Acts: Essays Presented in Honor of Paul Schubert*
SUNT	Studien zur Umwelt des Neuen Testaments
Talbert, *Reading Acts*	Charles H. Talbert, *Reading Acts: A Literary and Theological Commentary on the Acts of the Apostles*, rev. ed.
Tannehill, *Narrative Unity 2*	Robert C. Tannehill, *The Narrative Unity of Luke-Acts: A Literary Appreciation, Vol. 2: The Acts of the Apostles*
TLG	*Thesaurus Linguae Graecae*
TynBull	*Tyndale Bulletin*
Wilson, *Gentiles*	Stephen G. Wilson, *The Gentiles and the Gentile Mission in Luke-Acts*
WUNT	Wissenschaftliche Untersuchungen zum Nuen Testament
ZNW	*Zeitschrift für die neutestamentliche Wissenschaft und die Kunde der* älteren *Kirche.*

Bibliography

IF ONLY ONE OR TWO ENTRIES ARE LISTED UNDER AN edited collection of articles, full bibliographical information is provided; otherwise, only the name(s) of the editor(s) and the title of the work will be given with the entry. Full information of edited works are found under the name(s) of the editor(s).

Texts and Tools

Aland, Kurt, Matthew Black, Carlo M. Martini, Bruce M. Metzger, editors. *The Greek New Testament.* 4th rev. ed. Stuttgart: Bibelgesellschaft, 1998.

Aland, Kurt. *Synopsis Quattuor Evangeliorum.* 12th ed. Stuttgart: German Bible Society, 1983.

Bauer, Walter, Frederick William Danker, W. F. Arndt, and F. W. Gingrich, editors. *A Greek-English Lexicon of the New Testament and Other Early Christian Literature.* Revised and edited by W. F. Danker. 3rd ed. Chicago: University of Chicago Press, 2000.

Blass, Friedrich W., and Albert Debrunner. *A Greek Grammar of the New Testament and Other Early Christian Literature.* Translated and revised by Robert. W. Funk with supplementary notes of A. Debrunner. Chicago: University of Chicago Press, 1961.

Hatch, Edwin, and Henry A. Redpath. *A Concordance to the Septuagint and Other Greek Versions of the Old Testament.* 3 vols. Oxford: Clarendon Press, 1897. Reprinted, Grand Rapids: Baker, 1980.

Hawkins, John C. *Horae Synopticae: Contributions to the Study of the Synoptic Problem.* 2nd ed. Oxford: Clarendon, 1909, 1968.

Holmes, Michael W., editor and translator. *The Apostolic Fathers: Greek Texts and English Translations.* 3rd ed. Grand Rapids: Baker Academic, 2007.

Jacques, Xavier. *List of New Testament Words Sharing Common Elements.* Rome: Biblical Institute Press, 1969.

———. *List of Septuagint Words Sharing Common Elements.* Subsidia Biblica 1. Rome: Biblical Institute Press, 1972.

Kittel, Gerhard, and Gerhard Friedrich, editors. *Theological Dictionary of the New Testament.* 10 vols. Translated and edited by Geoffrey W. Bromiley. Grand Rapids: Eerdmans, 1964–1974.

Lampe, Geoffrey William Hugo. *A Patristic Greek Lexicon.* Oxford: Clarendon, 1961–68.

Liddell, Henry George, and Robert Scott. *A Greek-English Lexicon.* Oxford: Clarendon, 1925–1940. Revised edition by Sir Henry Stuart Jones with Roderick McKenzie, 1940, with Supplement, 1968. London: Oxford University Press, 1978.

Mattill, A. J., and Mary B. Mattill. *A Classified Bibliography of Literature on the Acts of the Apostles.* NTTS 7. Leiden: Brill, 1966.

Merriam-Webster's New Collegiate Dictionary. 11th ed. Springfield, MA: Merriam-Webster, 2004.

Metzger, Bruce M. *A Textual Commentary on the Greek New Testament.* London: United Bible Societies, 1971.

———. *A Textual Commentary on the Greek New Testament.* 2nd ed. Stuttgart: United Bible Societies, 1994.

Morgenthaler, Robert. *Statistik des Neutestamentlichen Wortschatzes.* Zürich: Gotthelf, 1958.

Moulton, William F., and Alfred S. Geden. *A Concordance to the Greek Testament.* 4th rev. ed. by Harold K. Moulton. Grand Rapids: Eerdmans, 1980.

Novum Testamentum Graece. 27th ed. by Eberhard and Erwin Nestle, Barbara and Kurt Aland, Johannes Karavidopoulos, C. M. Martini, B. M. Metzger. Stuttgart: Bibelgesellschaft, 1993.

Rahlfs, Alfred, editor. *Septuaginta: id est vetus testamentum graece juxta LXX interpretes.* Stuttgart: Würtemberg Bible Society, 1935. Rev. ed. by Robert Hanhart. 2 vols. in one. Stuttgart: Deutsche Bibelgesellschaft, 2006.

Strack, Hermann L., and Paul Billerbeck. *Kommentar zum Neuen Testament aus Talmud und Midrash.* 6 vols. Munich: Beck, 1922–1961.

Zerwick, Max, and Mary Grosvenor. *A Grammatical Analysis of the Greek New Testament. Vol. Gospels-Acts.* Translated and adapted by M. Grosvenor from Zerwick, *Analysis Philologica Novi Testaments Graeci.* 3rd ed. Rome: Biblical Institute Press, 1974.

Commentaries on the Gospel of Luke

Bovon, François. *Luke1: A Commentary on the Gospel of Luke 1:1—9:50.* Hermeneia. Translated by Christine M. Thomas. Minneapolis: Fortress, 2002.

Bock, Darrell Lane. *Luke 1–9:50.* Baker Exegetical Commentary of the New Testament 3A. Grand Rapids: Baker, 1994.

———. *Luke 9:51—24:53.* Baker Exegetical Commentary of the New Testament 3B. Grand Rapids: Baker, 1996.

Creed, John Martin. *The Gospel according to St. Luke.* London: Macmillan, 1930.

Danker, Frederick W. *Jesus and the New Age according to St. Luke—A Commentary on the Third Gospel.* St. Louis: Clayton, 1974.

———. *Luke.* 2nd ed. Proclamation Commentaries. Philadelphia: Fortress, 1987.

Ellis, E. Earle. *The Gospel of Luke.* Century Bible. London: Nelson, 1966.

Fitzmyer, Joseph A. *The Gospel according to Luke I–IX.* AB 28. Garden City, NY: Doubleday, 1981.

———. *The Gospel according to Luke X–XXIV.* AB 28A. Garden City, NY: Doubleday, 1985.

Green, Joel B. *The Gospel of Luke.* NICNT. Grand Rapids: Eerdmans, 1997.

Grundmann, Walter. *Das Evangelium nach Lukas*. Theologischer Handkommentar zum Neuen Testament 3. Berlin: Evangelische Verlaganstalt, 1971.
Johnson, Luke Timothy. *The Gospel of Luke*. Sacra Pagina 3. Collegeville, MN: Liturgical, 1991.
Karris, Robert J. *Invitation to Luke: A Commentary on the Gospel of Luke with Complete Text from The Jerusalem Bible*. Garden City, NY: Image, 1977.
Kremer, Jacob. *Das Lukasevangelium*. 2nd ed. Neue Echter Bibel: Neuen Testament 3. Würzburg: Echter, 1988.
Loisy, Alfred F. *L'Evangile selon Luc*. Paris: Nourry, 1924.
Marshall, Ian Howard. *The Gospel of Luke*. New International Greek Testament Commentary. Grand Rapids: Eerdmans, 1978.
Nolland, John. *Luke*. 3 vols. Word Biblical Commentary 35A-C. Dallas: Word, 1989–93.
Plummer, Alfred. *A Critical and Exegetical Commentary on the Gospel according to St. Luke*. 9th ed. ICC. New York: Scribner, 1910.
Radl, Walter. *Das Evangelium nach Lukas. Kommentar*. Vol. 1. Freiburg: Herder, 2003.
Schürmann, Heinz. *Das Lukasevangelium. Kommentar zu Kap. 1,1–9,50*. Herders Theologischer Kommentar zum Neuen Testament 3. Erster Teil. Freiburg: Herder, 1969.
Talbert, Charles H. *Reading Luke: A Literary and Theological Commentary*. Rev. ed. Macon, GA: Smyth & Helwys, 2005.
Tannehill, Robert C. *The Gospel of Luke*. Vol. 1 in *The Narrative Unity of Luke–Acts: A Literary Appreciation*. 2 vols. Foundations and Facets. Minneapolis: Fortress, 1986.
———. *Luke*. Abingdon New Testament Commentary. Nashville: Abingdon, 1996.
Tiede, David L. *Luke*. Augsburg Commentary of the New Testament. Minneapolis: Augsburg, 1988.

Commentaries on Acts

Ammonii Alexandrii. *Fragmenta in Acta Apostolorum in Commentariorum in Vetus et Novum Testamentum Fragmenta*. Patrologiae cursus completus, series graeca 85. Edited by J. P. Migne. Paris: Migne, 1864.
Arator. *De Actibus Apostolorum*. Patrologiae cursus completus, series latina 68. Edited by J. P. Migne. Paris: Migne, 1866.
Bauernfeind, Otto. *Die Apostelgeschichte*. Theologischer Handkommentar zum Neuen Testament 5. Leipzig: Deichertsche, 1939.
Barrett, C. K. *A Critical and Exegetical Commentary on The Acts of the Apostles, Vol 1: I–XIV*. ICC. Edinburgh: T. & T. Clark, 1994.
———. *A Critical and Exegetical Commentary on The Acts of the Apostles, Vol 2: XV–XXVIII*. ICC. Edinburgh: T. & T. Clark, 1998.
Bedae Venerabilis. *Super Acta Apostolorum*. Patrologiae cursus completus, series latina 92. Edited by J. P. Migne. Paris: Migne, n.d.
Beyer, Hans W. *Die Apostelgeschichte*. Das Neue Testament Deutsch. 5th ed. Göttingen: Vandenhoeck & Ruprecht, 1949.
Bock, Darrell L. *Acts*. Baker Exegetical Commentary of the New Testament. Grand Rapids: Baker, 2007.

Bruce, Frederick, Fyvie. *The Acts of the Apostles.* The Greek Text with Introduction and Commentary. 3rd rev. and enlarged ed. Grand Rapids: Eerdmans, 1990.

———. *The Book of the Acts.* Rev. ed. New International Commentary of the New Testament. Grand Rapids: Eerdmans, 1988.

Burnside, William F. *The Acts of the Apostles: The Greek Text.* Cambridge: Cambridge University Press, 1916.

Calvin, John. *Commentary on Acts of the Apostles.* 2 vols. Translated by H. Beveridge. Grand Rapids: Eerdmans, 1949.

Cassiodori, M. Aurelii. *Complexiones in Actus Apostolorum.* Edited by J. Garetius. Patrologiae cursus completus, series latina 70. Edited by J. P. Migne. Paris: Migne, 1865.

Chrysostom, John. *The Homilies on the Acts of the Apostles.* Part II: *Homilies XXIX–LV.* Oxford: John Henry Parker, 1852.

Conzelmann, Hans. *Die Apostelgeschichte.* Handbuch zum Neuen Testament 7. Tübingen: Mohr/Siebeck, 1963, 1972.

———. *The Acts of the Apostle: A Commentary.* Translated by James Limburg, A. Thomas Kraabel, and Donald H. Juel. Hermeneia. Minneapolis: Fortress, 1987.

Culy, Martin M., and Mikeal Carl Parsons, *The Acts of the Apostles: A Handbook on the Greek Text.* Waco, TX: Baylor University Press, 2003.

Dillon, Richard J., and Joseph A. Fitzmyer. "Acts of the Apostles." In *The Jerome Biblical Commentary*, 2:165–214. Englewood Cliffs, NJ: Prentice-Hall, 1968.

Dunn, James D. G. *The Acts of the Apostles.* Narrative Commentaries. Valley Forge, PA: Trinity, 1996.

Fitzmyer, Joseph A. *The Acts of the Apostles.* AB 31. New York: Doubleday, 1998.

Foakes-Jackson, Frederick. J. *The Acts of the Apostles.* Moffat New Testament Commentary. London: Hodder and Stoughton, 1931, 1960.

Gaventa, Beverly Roberts. *The Acts of the Apostles.* Abingdon New Testament Commentaries. Nashville: Abingdon, 2003.

Grotius, Hugo. *Annotations In Acta Apostolorum Et Epistolas Apostolicas.* [with] *Annotationum In Novum Testametum pars Tertia Ac Ultima.* Paris: Viduæ Theod, Pepingué, & Stephan Macroy, 1650.

Haenchen, Ernst. *The Acts of the Apostles.* Translated by Bernard Noble, et al. Philadelphia: Westminster, 1971.

Harnack, Adolf. *Die Apostelgeschichte.* Beitrage zur Einleitung in das Neuen Testament III. Leipzig: Hinrichs, 1908.

Holtzmann, Heinrich Julius. *Die Apostelgeschichte.* Handkommentar zum Neuen Testament. Tübingen: Mohr/Siebeck, 1901.

Jacquier, Etienne. *Les Actes des Apôtres.* Paris: Lecoffre, 1926.

Jervell, Jacob. *Die Apostelgeschichte.* KEK. 17th ed. Göttingen: Vandenhoeck & Ruprecht, 1998.

Johnson, Luke Timothy. *The Acts of the Apostles.* Sacra Pagina 5. Collegeville, MN: Liturgical, 1992.

Krodel, Gerhard A. *Acts.* Augsburg Commentary on the New Testament. Minneapolis: Augsburg, 1986.

———. *Acts.* Proclamation Commentaries. Minneapolis: Fortress, 1981.

Loisy, Alfred. *Les Actes des Apôtres.* Paris: Nourry, 1920.

Lüdemann, Gerhard. *Early Christianity according to the Traditions in Acts: A Commentary*. Translated John Bowden. Minneapolis: Fortress, 1989.

Macgregor, G. H. C. "The Acts of the Apostles." In *Interpreter's Bible* 9. Edited by George A. Buttrick. Nashville: Abingdon-Cokesbury, 1954.

Malina, Bruce J., and John J. Pilch. *Social-Science Commentary on the Book of Acts*. Minneapolis: Fortress, 2008.

Marshall, Ian Howard. *Acts*. Tyndale New Testament Commentaries 5. Grand Rapids: Eerdmans, 1980.

Munck, Johannes. *The Acts of the Apostles*. AB 31. Garden City, NY: Doubleday, 1967.

Neil, William. *The Acts of the Apostles*. New Century Bible, Greenwood, SC: Attic, 1973.

Pervo, Richard I. *Acts: A Commentary*. Hermeneia. Minneapolis: Fortress, 2008.

Oekumenius. *Commentaria in Acta Apostolorum*. Patrologiae cursus completus, series graeca 118. Edited by J. P. Migne. Paris: Migne, 1893.

Rackham, Richard Belward. *The Acts of the Apostles*. 1901. Reprinted, Grand Rapids: Baker, 1978.

Roloff, Jürgen. *Die Apostelgeschichte*. Göttingen: Vandenhoeck & Ruprecht, 1988.

Sadler, Michael F. *The Acts of the Apostles*. London: Bell, 1906.

Smith, Robert H. *Acts*. Concordia Commentary. St. Louis: Concordia, 1970.

Spencer, Franklin Scott. *Journeying through Acts: A Literary-Cultural Reading*. Peabody, MA: Hendrickson, 2004.

Stagg, Frank. *The Book of Acts*. Nashville: Broadman, 1955.

Talbert, Charles H. *Reading Acts: A Literary and Theological Commentary on the Acts of the Apostles*. Rev. ed. Macon, GA: Smyth & Helwys, 2005.

Tannehill, Robert C. *The Acts of the Apostles. Vol. 2 in The Narrative Unity of Luke-Acts: A Literary Appreciation*. 2 vols. Foundations and Facets. Minneapolis: Fortress, 1990.

Taylor, Justin. *Les Actes Deux Apôtres. Vol. 6. Commentaire Historique (Ac* 18,23–28,31*)*. Nouvell Serie 30. Paris: Librairie Lecoffre, 1996.

Theophylakti. *Expositio in Acta Apostolorum*. Patrologiae cursus completus, series graeca 125. Edited by J. P. Migne. Paris: Migne, n.d.

Wall, Robert W. "The Acts of the Apostles." In *The New Interpreter's Bible*. Vol. 10. Nashville: Abingdon, 2002.

Walaskay, Paul W. *Acts*. Westminster Bible Companion. Louisville: Westminster John Knox, 1998.

Weiser, Alfons. *Die Apostelgeschichte*. 2 vols. Ökumenischer Taschenbuchkommentar zum Neuen Testament 5.1–2. Gütersloh: Mohn, 1981, 1985.

Weiss, Johannes. *Die Apostelgeschichte*. Leipzig: Hinrichs, 1893.

Wendt, Hans Hinrich. *Die Apostelgeschichte*. Göttingen: Vandenhoeck & Ruprecht, 1913.

Wikenhauser, Alfred. *Die Apostelgeschichte*. 3rd rev. ed. Regensburg: Pustet, 1961.

Williams, David J. *Acts*. New International Biblical Commentary 5. Peabody, MA: Hendrickson, 1990.

Williams, R. R. *The Acts of the Apostles: Introduction and Commentary*. Torch Bible Commentaries. London: SCM, 1953.

Willimon, William H. *Acts*. Interpretion. Louisville: John Knox, 1988.

Witherington, Ben III. *The Acts of the Apostles: A Socio-Rhetorical Commentary.* Grand Rapids: Eerdmans, 1998.

Zahn, Theodor. *Die Apostelgeschichte des Lucas.* Kommentar zum Neuen Testament 5. Leipzig: Deichert, 1921.

Studies and Other Works

Alexander, Loveday C. A. *The Preface to Luke's Gospel: Literary Convention and Social Context in Luke 1.1–4 and Acts 1.1.* SNTSMS 78. Cambridge: Cambridge University Press, 1993.

———, editor. *Images of Empire.* JSOTSup 122. Sheffield: JSOT Press, 1991.

———. *Acts in Its Ancient Literary Context: A Classicist Looks at the Acts of the Apostles.* London: T. & T. Clark, 2005.

Alter, Robert. *The Art of Biblical Narrative.* New York: Basic Books, 1981.

———. *The World of Biblical Literature.* New York: Basic Books, 1992.

Ammonius Presbyter Alexandrinis. *Commentariorium in Vetus et Novum Testamentum Fragmenta.* Patrologiae cursus completus, series graeca 85. Edited by J. P. Migne. Paris: Migne, 1864.

Anderson, Hugh. "The Rejection of Nazareth Pericope of Luke 4:16–30 in Light of Recent Critical Trends." *Int* 18 (1964) 259–75.

Aune, David E. *The New Testament in Its Literary Environment.* Library of Early Christianity. Philadelphia: Westminster, 1987.

———. *Prophecy in Early Christianity and the Ancient Mediterranean.* 1983. Reprinted, Eugene, OR: Wipf & Stock, 2003.

Ball, Mieke. *Narratology: Introduction to The Theory of Narrative.* 2nd ed. Toronto: University of Toronto Press, 1997.

Babon, Octavian D. *On the Road Encounters in Luke–Acts: Hellenistic Mimesis and Luke's Theology of the Way.* Paternoster Biblical Monographs. Milton Keynes, UK: Paternoster, 2006.

Bakhtin, Mikhail M. *The Dialogic Imagination: Four Essays.* Edited by Michael Holquist and Translated by Caryl Emerson and M. Holquist. Austin: University of Texas Press, 1981.

Barrett, C. K. *The Epistle to the Romans.* Harper's New Testament Commentaries. New York: Harper & Row, 1957.

———. *Luke: The Historian in Recent Study.* Philadelphia: Fortress, 1970.

———. "What Minorities?" In *Mighty Minorities? Minorities in Early Christianity—Positions and Strategies*, edited by David Hellholm, Halvor Moxness, and Turid Karlsen Seim, 1–10. Oslo: Scandinavia University Press, 1995.

Bartholomew, Craig G., Joel B. Green, and Anthony C. Thistelton, editors. *Reading Luke: Interpretation, Reflection, Formation.* SHS 6. Grand Rapids: Zondervan, 2005.

Bauckham, Richard, editor. *The Book of Acts in Its Palestinian Setting.* Vol. 4 in *Book of Acts in Its First Century Setting.* Grand Rapids: Eerdmans, 1995.

Bauer, Bruno. *Die Apostelgeschichte: Eine Ausgleichung des Paulinismus und des Judenthums innerhalb der christlichen Kirche.* Berlin: Hempel, 1850.

Baur, Ferdinand Christian. *The Church History of the First Three Centuries*. 3rd ed. Translated by A. Menzies. Theological Fund Library. London: Williams & Norgate, 1878, 1879.

———. *Paul the Apostle of Jesus Christ: His Life and Works, His Epistles and Teaching*. Vol. l. Translated by A. Menzies. The Theological Fund Library. 2nd ed. London: Williams & Norgate, 1875.

Beardslee, William A. *Literary Criticism of the New Testament*. GBS. Philadelphia: Fortress, 1970.

Becker, E. M., editor. *Die antike Historiographie und die Anfänge der christlichen Geschichtsschreibung*. BZNW 129. Berlin: de Gruyter, 2005.

Bengel, Johann Albrecht. *Gnomon Novi Testament in quo ex nativa verborum vi simplicitas, profunditas, concinnitas, salubritas sensuum coelestium indicatur*. Tübingen, 1742. 8th ed. Stuttgart: Steinkopf, 1915. Eng. trans. ed. by A. R. Faussett. *Exegetical Annotations on the New Testament*. London: Williams & Norgate, 1859, 1862.

Benoit, Pierre. "Some Notes in the 'Summaries' in Acts 2, 4, 5." In *Jesus and the Gospels*, 1:95–103. Translated by B. Weatherhead. New York: Herder & Herder, 1973.

Berlin, Adele. *The Poetics and Interpretation of Biblical Narrative*. Bible and Literature Series 9. Sheffield: Almond, 1983.

Bieder, Werner. *Die Apostelgeschichte in der Historie*. Zurich: Evangelischer Verlag, 1960.

Bird, Michael F. "The Unity of Luke–Acts in Recent Discussion." *JSNT* 29 (2007) 425–48.

Bock, Darrell L. *Proclamation from Prophecy and Pattern: Lucan Old Testament Christology*. JSNTSup 12. Sheffield: JSOT Press, 1987.

Boismard, Marie-Émile and Arnaud Lamouille. *Le texte occidental des Actes des Apôtres: Reconstitution et rehabilitation*. Synthèse 17. 2 vols. Paris: Editions Recherche sur les civilizations, 1984.

Booth, Wayne C. *The Rhetoric of Fiction*. 2nd ed. Chicago: University of Chicago Press, 1983.

Borgman, Paul. *The Way according to Luke: Hearing the Whole Story of Luke–Acts*. Grand Rapids: Eerdmans, 2006.

Bovon, François. *Luke the Theologian (*1950–2005*)*. 2nd rev. ed. Waco, TX: Baylor University Press, 2006).

———. "'Schön hat der heilige Geist durch den Propheten Jesaja zu euren Vätern gesprochenen' (Acts 28:25)." *ZNW* 75 (1984) 226–32.

———. "Studies in Luke–Acts: Retrospect and Prospect." *HTR* 85 (1992) 175–96.

———. *Studies in Early Christianity*. WUNT 161. Tübingen: Mohr/Siebeck, 2003. First paperback ed. with Eng. trans. of chs. 3, 8–9. Grand Rapids: Baker Academic, 2005.

Brawley, Robert. *Centering on God: Method and Message in Luke–Acts*. Louisville: Westminster John Knox, 1990.

———. *Luke–Acts and the Jews: Conflict, Apology, and Conciliation*. SBLMS 33. Atlanta: Scholars, 1987.

———. *Text to Text Pours Forth Speech: Voices of Scripture in Luke–Acts*. Bloomington: Indiana University Press, 1995.

Breck, John. *The Shape of Biblical Language: Chiasmus in the Scriptures and Beyond.* Crestwood, NY: St. Vladimir's Seminary Press, 1994.

Brodie, Thomas L. "Luke as an Imitation and Emulation of the Elijah-Elisha Narrative." In *New Views on Luke and Acts*, edited by Earl Richard, 78–85. Collegeville, MN: Liturgical, 1990.

———. *The Crucial Bridge: The Elijah-Elisha Narrative as an Interpretative Synthesis of Genesis-Kings and a Literary Model for the Gospels.* Collegeville, MN: Liturgical, 2000.

———. "Greco-Roman Imitation of Texts as a Partial Guide to Luke's Use of Sources." In *New Perspectives from the Society of Biblical Literature*, edited by Charles H. Talbert, 17–26. New York, Crossroad, 1984.

Brosend, William F. II. "The Means of An Absent Ends." In *History, Literature and Society in the Book of Act*, edited by Ben Witherington III, 348–58. Cambridge: Cambridge University Press, 1996.

Brown, Raymond E. *The Gospel according to John.* AB 29, 29A. Garden City, NY: Doubleday, 1966, 1970.

Brown, Schuyler. *Apostasy and Perseverance in the Theology of Luke.* Rome: Biblical Institute Press, 1969.

———. "The Role of The Prologues in Determining the Purpose of Acts." In *Perspectives on Luke–Acts*, edited by Charles H. Talbert, 99–111. Danville, VA: Association of Baptist Professors of Religion, 1978.

Bruce, F. F. *The Speeches in the Acts of the Apostles.* London: Tyndale, 1942.

———. *The Spreading Flame: The Rise and Progress of Christianity.* Grand Rapids: Eerdmans, 1954.

———. "Is the Paul of Acts the Real Paul?" *Bulletin of the John Rylands Library* 58 (1976) 282–305.

Buckwalter, Douglas H. *The Character and Purpose of Luke's Christology*. SNTSMS 89. Cambridge: Cambridge University Press, 1996.

Bultmann, Rudolf. "Zur Frage nach den Quellen der Apostelgeschichte." In *New Testament Essays*, edited by A. J. B. Higgins, 68–80. Manchester: Manchester University Press, 1959.

Cadbury, Henry Joel. "Acts of the Apostles." In *Interpreter's Dictionary of the Bible*, edited by George A. Buttrick, 1:28–42. Nashville: Abingdon, 1962.

———. *The Book of Acts in History.* London: A. & C. Black, 1955.

———. "Commentary on the Preface of Luke." In *Beginnings of Christianity*, edited by F. J. Foakes-Jackson and Kirsopp Lake, 2:489–510. London: Macmillan, 1922.

———. "Four Features of Lucan Style." In *Studies in Luke–Acts*, edited by Leander E. Keck and J. Louis Martyn, 87–102.

———. "Luke's Interest in Lodging." *JBL* 45 (1926) 305–22.

———. *The Making of Luke-Acts.* 1927. Reprinted, London: SPCK, 1968.

———. "Roman Law and the Trial of Paul." In *Beginnings of Christianity*, edited by Kirsopp Lake and H. J. Cadbury, 5:297–338. London: Macmillan, 1933.

———. "The Speeches in Acts." In *Beginnings of Christianity*, edited by Kirsopp Lake and H. J. Cadbury, 5:402–27. London: Macmillan, 1933.

———. *The Style and Literary Method of Luke.* Harvard Theological Studies 6. Cambridge: Harvard University Press, 1920.

———. "The Summaries in Acts." In *Beginnings of Christianity*, edited by Kirsopp Lake and H. J. Cadbury, 5:392–402. London: Macmillan, 1933.

———. "The 'We' and 'I' Passages in Luke–Acts." *NTS* 3 (1957) 128–32.

Campbell, William Sanger. "Who are We? The First-Person Plural Character in The Acts of the Apostles." Ph.D. dissertation, Princeton Theological Seminary, 2000.

———. *The "We" Passages in the Acts of the Apostles: The Narrator as Narrative Character*. Studies in Biblical Literature 14. Atlanta: Society of Biblical Literature, 2007.

Carroll, John T. "Luke's Portrayal of the Pharisees." *CBQ* 50 (1988) 604–21.

Cassidy, Richard. *Jesus, Politics and Society: A Study of Luke's Gospel*. Maryknoll, NY: Orbis, 1978.

———. *Paul in Chains: Roman Imprisonment and the Letters of St. Paul*. New York: Crossroad, 2001.

———, editor. *Society and Politics in the Acts of the Apostles*. Maryknoll, NY: Orbis, 1987.

Cerfaux, Lucien. "Temoins du Christ d'apres le Livre des Actes." In *Recueil Lucien Cerfaux*, 2:157–74. Gembloux: Duculot, 1954.

Chadwick, Henry. *History and Thought of the Early Church*. London: Variorum Reprints, 1982.

Chatman, Seymour. *Story and Discourse: Narrative Structure in Fiction and Film*. Ithaca, NY: Cornell University Press, 1981.

Clark, Andrew C. *Parallel Lives: The Relation of the Paul to the Apostles in the Lucan Perspective*. Carlisle, UK: Paternoster, 2001.

Collins, Adela Yarbro. "Narrative, History, and Gospel." *Semeia* 43 (1988) 145–53.

Conybeare, Frederick Cornwallis. "The Commentary of Ephrem on Acts." In *Beginnings of Christianity*, edited by James Hardy Ropes, 3:373–453. London: Macmillan, 1926.

Conzelmann, Hans. "The First Christian Century: As Christian History." In *The Bible in Modern Scholarship*, edited by J. Philip Hyatt, 217–26. Nashville: Abingdon, 1965.

———. *An Outline of the Theology of the New Testament*. Translated by John Bowden. New York: Harper & Row, 1969.

———. *History of Primitive Christianity*. Translated by John E. Steely. Nashville: Abingdon, 1973.

———. "Luke's Place in the Development of Early Christianity." In *Studies in Luke–Acts*, edited by Leander E. Keck and J. Louis Martyn, 298–316.

———. *The Theology of St. Luke*. Translated by Geoffrey Buswell. 1960. Reprinted, Philadelphia: Fortress, 1982.

———. "Zur Lukanalyze." *Zeitschrift für Theologie und Kirche* 49 (1952) 16–33.

Cottle, Ronald Eastwood. "The Occasion and Purpose of the Final Drafting of Acts." Ph.D. dissertation, University of Southern California, 1967.

Crump, David Michael. *Jesus the Intercessor: Prayer and Christology in Luke–Acts*. WUNT 2/49. 1992. Reprinted, Grand Rapids: Baker Academic, 1999.

———. "Jesus, The Victorious Scribal-Intercessor in Luke's Gospel." *NTS* 38 (1992) 51–65.

Dahl, Nils Alstrup. *Jesus in the Memory of the Early Church*. Minneapolis: Augsburg, 1976.

———. "'A People for His Name' (Acts 15:14)." *NTS* 4 (1957–58) 319–27.

———. "The Purpose of Luke–Acts." In *Jesus in the Memory of the Early Church*, 319–27. Minneapolis: Augsburg, 1976.

———. "The Story of Abraham in Luke–Acts." In *Studies in Luke–Acts*, edited by Leander E. Keck and J. Lous Martyn, 139–58.

Danker, Frederick W. *Benefactor: Epigraphic Study of A Graeco-Roman and New Testament Semantic Field*. St. Louis: Clayton, 1982.

———. "Hardness of Heart: A Study in Biblical Thematic." *Concordia Theological Monthly* 44 (1972) 89–100.

Darr, John A. *On Character Building: The Reader and Rhetoric of Characterization in Luke–Acts*. Louisville: Westminster John Knox, 1992.

Davies, Philip R. "The Ending of Acts." *Expository Times* 94 (1983) 334–35.

Dawsey, James M. *The Lukan Voice: Confusion and Irony in the Gospel of Luke*. Macon, GA: Mercer University Press, 1988.

de Boer, Martinus C. "God-Fearers in Luke–Acts." In *Luke's Literary Achievement: Collected Essays*, edited by Christopher M. Tuckett, 50–71. JSNTSup 116. Sheffield: Sheffield Academic, 1995.

Delling, Gerhard. "Das Letzt Wort der Apostelgeschichte." *NovT* 15 (1973) 193–204.

Denova, Rebecca I. *The Things Accomplished Among Us: Prophetic Tradition in the Structural Pattern of Luke–Acts*. JSNTSup 141. Sheffield: Sheffield Academic, 1997.

Dibelius, Martin. *Studies in the Acts of the Apostles*. Translated by Mary Ling and edited by Heinrich Greeven. 1956. Reprinted, Mifflintown, PA: Sigler Press, 1999.

———. *The Book of Acts: Form, Style, and Theology*. Edited by K. C. Hanson. Fortress Classics in Biblical Studies. Minneapolis: Fortress, 2004.

Didymus v. Alexandrien. *De Trinitate*. Liber Primus 59. Patrologiae cursus completus, series Graeca 39. Edited by J. P. Migne. Paris: Migne, n.d.

Dillon, Richard J. *From Eyewitnesses to Ministers of the Word: Tradition and Composition in Luke 24*. Analecta Biblica 82. Rome: Biblical Institute Press, 1978.

Dodd, Charles Harold. *According to the Scriptures: The Sub-structure of New Testament Theology*. London: Nisbet, 1953.

———. *The Apostolic Preaching and Its Development*. New York: Harper & Row, 1963.

———. *The Epistle of Paul to the Romans*. Moffatt New Testament Commentary. New York: Harper, 1932.

Dupont, Jacques. "La Conclusion des Actes et son rapport a l'ensemble de l'ouvrage de Luc." In *Les Actes des Apôtres, Traditions, redaction, théologie*, edited by Jacob Kremer, 359–404. BETL 48. Leuven: Leuven University Press, 1979.

———. *Études sur les Actes des Apôtres*. Lectio Divina 45. Paris: Cerf, 1967.

———. "ΛΑΟΣ ΕΞ ΕΘΝΩΝ (Act XV. 14)." *NTS* 3 (1956) 47–50.

———. "La portee Christologique de l'evangelisation des nations d'apres Luc 24, 47." In *Neues Testament und Kirche*, edited by Joachim Gnilka, 125–43. Friedburg: Herder, 1974.

———. *The Salvation of the Gentiles: Essays on the Acts of the Apostles.* Translated by John R. Keating. New York: Paulist, 1979.

Easton, Burton S. *Early Christianity: The Purpose of Acts and Other Papers.* Edited by Frederick C. Grant. London: SPCK, 1955.

Eco, Umberto. *The Limits of Interpretation.* Advances in Semiotics. Bloomington: Indiana University Press, 1990.

———. *The Role of the Reader: Explorations in the Semiotics of Texts.* Advances in Semiotics. Bloomington: Indiana University Press, 1979.

Ehrhardt, Arnold. *The Acts of the Apostles.* Manchester: Manchester University Press, 1969.

Ellis, E. Earle. "'The End of the Earth' (Acts 1:8)." *Bulletin of Biblical Research* 1 (1991) 123–32.

———. *Eschatology in Luke.* Facet Books 30. Philadelphia: Fortress, 1972.

———. "The Role of the Christian Prophet in Acts." In *Apostolic History and the Gospel,* edited by W. W. Gasque and Ralph P. Martin, 55–67. Grand Rapids: Eerdmans, 1970.

Epp, Eldon J. *The Theological Tendency of Codex Bezae Cantabrigiensis in Acts.* SNTSMS 3. 1966. Reprinted, Eugene, OR: Wipf & Stock, 2007.

Esler, Philip Francis. *Community and Gospel in Luke–Acts. The Social and Political Motivations of Lucan Theology.* SNTSMS 57. Cambridge: Cambridge University Press, 1987.

Evans, Craig A. *To See and Not Perceive: Isaiah 6:9–10 in Early Jewish and Christian Interpretation.* JSOTSup 64. Sheffield: JSOT Press, 1989.

Evans, Craig A. and James A. Sanders, *Luke and Scripture: The Function of Sacred Tradition in Luke–Acts.* Minneapolis: Fortress, 1993.

Filson, Floyd V. "The Journey Motif in Acts." In *Apostolic History and the Gospel,* edited by W. W. Gasque and R. P. Martin, 68–77. Grand Rapids: Eerdmans, 1970.

———. "The Separation of Christianity from Judaism." *Anglican Theological Review* 21 (1939) 171–85.

———. *Three Crucial Decades: Studies in Acts.* Richmond: John Knox, 1963.

Fish, Stanley. *Is There a Text in This Class? The Authority of Interpretive Communities.* Cambridge: Harvard University Press, 1980.

Fitzmyer, Joseph A. *Luke the Theologian: Aspects of His Teaching.* New York: Paulist, 1989.

Flender, Helmut. *St. Luke: Theologian of Redemptive History.* Translated by Reginald H. Fuller and Inez Fuller. London: SPCK, 1967.

Foakes-Jackson, Frederick J. and Kirsopp Lake, editors. *The Beginnings of Christianity.* Part I: *The Acts of the Apostles.* 5 vols. 1922–33. Reprinted, Grand Rapids: Baker, 1979.

Franklin, Eric. *Christ the Lord: A Study in the Purpose and Theology of Luke–Acts.* Philadelphia: Westminster, 1975.

Friedman, Alan. *The Turn of the Novel.* New York: Oxford University Press, 1966.

Frye, Northrop. *Anatomy of Criticism: Four Essays.* With a new forward by Harold Bloom. Princeton: Princeton University Press, 2000.

———. *The Great Code: The Bible and Literature.* New York: Harcourt Brace Jovanovich, 1982.

Fuller, Daniel P. *Easter Faith and History.* Grand Rapids: Eerdmans, 1965.

Gasque, Ward W., and Martin, Ralph P., editors. *Apostolic History and the Gospel: Studies in Honor of F. F. Bruce.* Grand Rapids: Eerdmans, 1970.

Gasque, Ward W. "A Fruitful Field: Recent Study of the Acts of the Apostles." *Int* 42 (1988) 117–31. Reprinted in Ward W. Gasque, *A History of the Criticism of the Acts of the Apostles*, 345–59. 2nd ed. Peabody, MA: Hendrickson, 1989.

———. *A History of the Criticism of the Acts of the Apostles.* Grand Rapids: Eerdmans, 1975.

———. "The Speeches in Acts: Dibelius Reconsidered." In *New Dimensions in New Testament Study*, edited by Richard N. Longenecker and Merrill C. Tenney, 232–50. Grand Rapids: Eerdmans, 1974.

Gaventa, Beverly Roberts. "Acts of the Apostles." In *NIDB*, 1:33–47. Nashville: Abingdon, 2006.

———. "The Overthrown Enemy: Luke's Portrait of Paul." In *SBLSP* 1985, edited by Kent H. Richards, 439–49. Atlanta: Scholars, 1985.

———. "Toward a Theology of Acts: Reading and Rereading." *Int* 42 (1988) 149–53.

Gaventa Beverly R., and Patrick D. Miller, editors. *The Ending of Mark and the Ends of God: Essays in Memory of Donald Harrisville Juel.* Louisville: Westminster John Knox, 2005.

Geertz, Clifford. *The Interpretation of Cultures: Selected Essays.* New York: Basic Books, 1973.

Genette, Gérard. *Narrative Discourse: An Essay in Method.* Translated by Jane E. Lewin. Ithaca, NY: Cornell University Press, 1980.

———. *Narrative Discourse Revisited.* Translated by Jane E. Lewin. Ithaca, NY: Cornell University Press, 1988.

Gill, David W. J. and Conrad Gempf, eds. *Graeco-Roman Setting.* Vol. 2 in *The Book of Acts in Its First Century Setting.* Grand Rapids: Eerdmans, 1994.

Gnilka, Joachim. *Die Verstockung Israels: Isaias 6, 9–10 in der Theologie der Synoptiker.* Studien zum Alten und Neuen Testament 3. Munich: Kösel, 1961.

Goguel, Maurice. *The Birth of Christianity.* Translated by H. C. Snape. New York: Macmillan, 1954.

———. *Introduction au Nouveau Testament.* Vol. 3: *Le Livre des Actes.* Paris: Leroux, 1922.

Goppelt, Leonard. *Typos: The Typological Interpretation of the Old Testament in the New.* Translated by Donald H. Madvig. 1982. Reprinted, Eugene, OR: Wipf and Stock, 2002.

Goulder, Michael D. *Type and History in Acts.* London: SPCK, 1964.

Grässer, Erich. "Acta Forschung seit 1960." *Theologische Rundschau* 41 (1976) 141–94; 42 (1977) 1–68.

———. "Die Apostelgeschichte in der Forschung der Gegenwart." *Theologische Rundschau* 26 (1960) 93–167.

———. *Forschungen zur Apostelgeschichte.* Tübingen: Mohr/Siebeck, 2001.

Grant, Robert M. *Augustus to Constantine.* New York: Harper & Row, 1970.

Green, Barbara. *Mikhail Bakhtin and Biblical Scholarship: An Introduction.* SBL Semeia Studies 38. Atlanta: Society of Biblical Literature, 2000.

Green, Joel B. *The Theology of St. Luke.* New Testament Theology Cambridge: Cambridge University Press, 1995.

Green, Joel B., and Michael C. McKeever. *Luke–Acts and the New Testament: Historiography.* Institute for Biblical Research Bibliographies 8. Grand Rapids: Baker, 1994.

———, editor. *Hearing the New Testament: Strategies for Interpretation.* Grand Rapids: Eerdmans, 1995.

Gregory, Andrew. "The Reception of Luke and Acts and the Unity of Luke–Acts." *JSNT* 29 (2007) 459–72.

Haenchen, Ernst. "Acta 27." In *Zeit und Geschich: Dankesgabe an Rudolf Bultmann zum* 80. *Geburtstag*, edited by Erich Dinkler and Hartwig Thyen, 235–54. Tübingen: Mohr/Siebeck, 1964.

———. "Apostelgeschichte." In *Die Religion in Geschichte und Gegenwart.* Vol. 1. Tübingen: Mohr/Siebeck, 1957.

———. "The Book of Acts As Source-Material for the History of Early Christianity." In *Studies in Luke–Acts*, edited by Leander E. Keck and J. Louis Martyn, 258–78.

———. "Judentum und Christentum in der Apostelgeschichte." *ZNW* 54 (1963) 155–87.

———."Tradition und Komposition in der Apostelgeschichte." *ZNW* 52 (1955) 205–55.

Hahn, Ferdinand. *Mission in the New Testament.* SBT 1/47. London: SCM, 1965.

Hamm, M. Dennis. "This Sign of Healing, Acts 3:1–10: A Study in Lucan Theology." Ph.D. dissertation, Saint Louis University, 1975.

———. "Paul's Blindness and Its Healing: Clues to Symbolic Intent (Acts 9: 22 and 26)." *Biblica* 71 (1990) 63–72.

Harnack, Adolf. *The Date of Acts and the Synoptic Gospels.* Translated by J. R. Wilkinson. New Testament Studies 4. London: Williams & Norgate, 1911.

———. *Luke the Physician, the Author of the Third Gospel and Acts of the Apostles.* Translated by J. R. Wilkinson. New Testament Studies 1. London: Williams & Norgate, 1907.

———. *The Mission and Expansion of Christianity in the First Three Centuries.* Translated and edited by James Moffatt. 1906. Reprinted, Gloucester, MA: Peter Smith, 1972.

Hauser, Herman J. *Strukturen der Abschlusserzahlung der Apostelgeschichte (Apg 28:16–31).* Analecta Biblica 86. Rome: Biblical Institute Press, 1979.

Hays, Richard B. *Echoes of Scripture in the Letters of Paul.* New Haven: Yale University Press, 1989.

Hedrick, Charles W. "Paul's Conversion/Call: A Comparative Analysis of the Three Reports in Acts." *JBL* 100 (1981) 415–32.

Hellholm, David, Halvor Moxness, and Turid Karlsen Seim, editors. *Mighty Minorities? Minorities in Early Christianity—Positions and Strategies.* Oslo: Scandinavia University Press, 1995.

Hemer, Colin J. *The Book of Acts in the Setting of Hellenistic History.* Edited by Conrad H. Gempf. WUNT 49. Winona Lake, IN: Eisenbrauns, 1990.

———. "First Person Narrative in Acts 27–28." *TynBull* 36 (1985) 79–109.

Hengel, Martin. *Acts and the History of Earliest Christianity.* Translated by John Bowden. London: SCM, 1979.

———. *Between Jesus and Paul: Studies in the Earliest History of Christianity.* Translated by John Bowden. Philadelphia: Fortress, 1983.

Hickling, C. J. A. "The Portrait of Paul in Acts 26." In *Les Actes des Apôtres*, edited by Jacob Kremer, 499–503. Leuven: Leuven University Press, 1979.

Higgins, A. J. B. "The Preface to Luke and the Kerygma in Acts." In *Apostolic History and the Gospel*, edited by Ward W. Gasque and Ralph P. Martin, 78–91. Grand Rapids: Eerdmans, 1970.

Holmes, Michael W. "The Martyrdom of Polycarp and the New Testament Passion Narratives." In *Trajectories through the New Testament and the Apostolic Fathers*, edited by Andrew Gregory and Christopher Tuckett, 407–32. Oxford: Oxford University Press, 2005.

Holstein, W. "Judenmission und Heidenmission" *Judaica* 19 (1963) 113–26.

Hooker, Morna. *Endings: Invitation to Discipleship*. Peabody, MA: Hendrickson, 2003.

Hull, J. H. E. *The Holy Spirit in the Acts of the Apostles*. Cleveland: World, 1968.

Hur, Ju. *A Dynamic Reading of the Holy Spirit in Luke–Acts*. JSNTSup 211. Sheffield: Sheffield Academic, 2001.

Hurtado, Larry. *Lord Jesus Christ: Devotion to Jesus in Earliest Christianity*. Grand Rapids: Eerdmans, 2003.

Iser, Wolfgang. *The Implied Reader: Patterns of Communication in Prose Fiction from Bunyan to Beckett*. Baltimore: Johns Hopkins Press, 1974.

———. *The Act of Reading: A Theory of Aesthetic Response*. Baltimore: Johns Hopkins Press, 1978.

Jeremias, Joachim. *Jesus' Promise to the Nations*. Translated by S. H. Hooke. SBT 1/24. London: SCM, 1958.

Jervell, Jacob. *Die Apostelgeschichte*. KEK 3. Göttingen: Vandenhoeck & Ruprecht, 1998.

———. "God's Faithfulness to the Faithless People: Trends in Interpretation of Luke–Acts." *Word and World* 12 (1992) 29–37.

———. *Luke and the People of God: A New Look at Luke–Acts*. Minneapolis: Augsburg, 1972.

———. *The Theology of Acts of the Apostles*. New Testament Theology. Cambridge: Cambridge University Press, 1996.

———. *The Unknown Paul: Essays in Luke–Acts and Early Christianity*. Minneapolis: Augsburg, 1984.

Jewett, Robert. *A Chronology of Paul's Life*. Philadelphia: Fortress, 1979.

———. *Romans: A Commentary*. Hermeneia. Minneapolis: Fortress, 2007.

Johnson, Luke Timothy. *The Literary Function of Possessions in Luke–Acts*. SBL Dissertation Series 39. Missoula, MT: Scholars, 1977.

———. "Literary Criticism of Luke–Acts: Is Reception History Pertinent?" *JSNT* 28 (2005) 159–62.

———. "On Finding the Lukan Community: A Cautionary Essay." In 1979 *SBLSP*, edited by Paul J. Achtemeier, 67–100. Missoula, MT: Scholars, 1979.

———. *Septuagintal Midrash in the Speeches of Acts*. Milwaukee: Marquette University Press, 2002.

Juel, Donald H. *Luke–Acts: The Promise of History*. Atlanta: John Knox, 1983.

———. *A Master of Surprise: Mark Interpreted*. 1994. Reprinted, Mifflintown, PA: Sigler, 2002.

———. *Messianic Exegesis: Christological Interpretation of the Old Testament in Early Christianity*. Philadelphia: Fortress, 1988.

Karris, Robert J. "Poor and Rich: The Lucan *Sitz im Leben*." In *Perspectives on Luke-Acts*, edited by Charles H. Talbert, 112–25. Danville, VA: ABPR, 1978.

———. "Missionary Communities: A New Paradigm for the Study of Luke-Acts." *CBQ* 41 (1979) 80–97.

———. *What Are They Saying about Luke and Acts? A Theology of the Faithful God*. New York: Paulist, 1979.

Keck, Leander E., and J. Louis Martyn, editors. *Studies in Luke-Acts: Essays Presented in Honor of Paul Schubert*. 1966. Reprinted, Mifflintown. PA: Sigler, 1999.

Kennedy, George A. *Classical Rhetoric and Its Christian and Secular Tradition from Ancient to Modern Times*. Chapel Hill, NC: University of North Carolina Press, 1980.

———. *New Testament Interpretation through Rhetorical Criticism*. Chapel Hill, NC: University of North Carolina Press, 1984.

Kermode, Frank. *The Genesis of Secrecy*. Cambridge: Harvard University Press, 1979.

———. *The Sense of Ending: Studies in the Theory of Fiction with a New Epilogue*. Oxford: Oxford University Press, 1966, 2000.

Kiddle, Martin. "The Admission of the Gentiles in St. Luke's Gospel and Acts." *Journal of Theological Studies* 36:142 (1935) 160–72.

Klein, Gunther. "Lukas 1, 1–4 als theologische Programm." In *Zeit und Geschichte: Festschrift für Rudolf Bultmann*, edited by W. Eltester, 197–216. Tübingen: Mohr/Siebeck, 1964.

Klijn, A. F. J. "In Search of the Original Text of Acts." In *Studies in Luke-Acts*, edited by Leander E. Keck and J. Louis Martyn, 103–10.

———. *A Survey of the Researches into the Western Text of the Gospels and Acts*. Utrecht: Kemink en Zoon, 1949.

———. "The Western Text of the Gospels and Acts." *NovT* 3 (1959) 1–27.

Koester, Helmut. *Ancient Christian Gospels: Their History and Development*. Philadelphia: Trinity, 1990.

———. *Introduction to the New Testament*. 2 vols. New York: de Gruyter, 1995–2000.

Koet, Bart J. *Five Studies of Interpretation of Scripture in Luke-Acts*. Studiorum Novi Testamenti Auxilia 14. Leuven: Leuven University Press, 1989.

Kraabel, A. Thomas. "The Disappearance of the 'God-Fearers.'" *Numen* 28 (1981) 113–26.

———. "Immigrants, Exiles, Expatriates, and Missionaries." In *Religious Propaganda and Missionary Competition in the New Testament World: Essays Honoring Dieter Georgi*, edited by Lukas Borman, Kelly Del Tredici, and Angela Standhartinger, 71–88. Leiden: Brill, 1994.

Kristeva, Julia. *Revolution in Poetic Language*. Translated by Margaret Waller with introduction by Léon S. Roudiez. New York: Columbia University Press, 1984.

Kümmel, Werner Georg. "Current Theological Accusations against Luke." Translated by William C. Robinson. *Andover Newton Quarterly* 16 (1975) 131–45.

———. *Introduction to the New Testament*. Rev. ed. Translated by Howard Clark Kee. Nashville: Abingdon, 1975.

———. *The New Testament: The History of the Investigation of Its Problems.* Translated by S. M. Gilmour and Howard Clark Kee. Nashville: Abingdon, 1972.

Kurz, William S. "Narrative Approaches to Luke–Acts." *Biblica* 68 (1987) 195–220.

———. *Reading Luke-Acts: Dynamics of Biblical Narrative.* Louisville: Westminster John Knox, 1993.

Lake, Kirsopp, and Silva Lake. *Introduction to the New Testament.* London: Christophers, 1938.

Lambrecht, Jan. "Paul's Farewell-Address at Miletus (Acts 20:17–38)." In *Les Actes des Apôtres, Traditions, redaction, théologie*, edited by Jacob Kremer, 307–37. BETL 48. Leuven: Leuven University Press, 1979.

LaGrand, James. "Proliferation of the 'Gentile' in the NRSV." *Biblical Research* 41 (1996) 77–87.

Lampe, Peter. *From Paul to Valentinus: Christians at Rome in the First Two Centuries.* Translated by Michael Steinhauser. Edited by Marshall D. Johnson. Minneapolis: Fortress, 2003.

Lentz, John C., Jr. *Luke's Portrait of Paul.* SNTSMS 77. Cambridge: Cambridge University Press, 1993.

Levinskaya, Irina. *The Book of Acts in Its Diaspora Setting.* Vol. 5 in *Book of Acts in Its First Century Setting.* Grand Rapids: Eerdmans, 1996.

Lindars, Barnabas. *The New Testament Apologetic: The Doctrinal Significance of Old Testament Quotations.* Philadelphia: Westminster, 1961.

Litwak, Duncan Kenneth. *Echoes of Scripture in Luke-Acts: Telling the History of God's People Intertextually.* London: T. & T. Clark, 2005.

Lohfink, Gerhard. *The Conversion of St. Paul.* Chicago: Franciscan Herald, 1976.

Lohse, Eduard. "Lukas als Theologie der Heilsgeschichte." *Evangelische Theologie* 14 (1954) 256–75.

Loisy, Alfred. *The Origins of the New Testament.* Translated by Leonard P. Jacks. London: Allen and Unwin, 1950.

Longenecker, Richard N. *Biblical Exegesis in the Apostolic Period.* 2nd ed. Grand Rapids: Eerdmans, 1999.

———, and Merrill Chapin Tenney, eds. *New Dimensions in New Testament Study.* Grand Rapids: Zondervan, 1974.

Löning, Karl. *Die Saulustradition in die Apostelgeschichte.* Münster: Aschendorff, 1973.

Lund, Nils W. *Chiasmus in the New Testament: A Study in the Form and Function of Chiastic Structures.* 1942. Reprinted, Peabody, MA: Hendrickson, 1992.

Lundin, Roger, Clarence Walhout, and Anthony C. Thistelton. *The Promise of Hermeneutics.* Grand Rapids: Eerdmans, 1999.

MacDonald, Dennis R., ed. *Mimesis and Intertextuality in Antiquity and Christianity.* Harrisburg, PA: Trinity, 2001.

Mack, Burton L. *Rhetoric and the New Testament.* GBS. Minneapolis: Fortress, 1990.

MacRae, George W. "'Whom Heaven Must Receive until the Time': Reflections on the Christology of Acts." *Int* 27 (1973) 151–65.

Maddox, Robert. *The Purpose of Luke-Acts.* Studies of the New Testament and Its World. Edinburgh: T. & T. Clark, 1982.

Magness, J. Lee. *Marking the End: Sense and Absence in the Gospel of Mark.* 1986. Reprinted, Eugene, OR: Wipf & Stock, 2002.

Malina, Bruce J., and Jerome H. Neyrey. "Conflict in Luke–Acts: Labeling and Deviance Theory." In *The Social World of Luke–Acts: Models for Interpretation*, edited by Jerome H. Neyrey, 97–122. Peabody, MA: Hendrickson, 1991.

Malina, Bruce J., and Richard L. Rohrbaugh. *Social-Science Commentary on the Synoptic Gospels*. 2nd ed. Minneapolis: Fortress, 2003.

Marguerat, Daniel. "The Enigma of the Silent Closing of Acts (28:16–31)." In *Jesus and the Heritage of Israel: Luke's Narrative Claim upon Israel's Legacy*, edited by David P. Moessner, 284–304. Harrisburg, PA: Trinity, 1999.

———. *The First Christian Historian: Writing the "Acts of the Apostles."* Translated by K. McKinney, et al. SNTSMS 121. Cambridge: Cambridge University Press, 2002.

———. "Voyages et voyageurs dans le livre des Actes et la culture gréco-romaine." *Revue d'histoire et de philosophie religieuses* 78 (1998) 33–59.

Marshall, Ian Howard. "Luke's View of Paul." *Southwestern Journal of Theology* 33 (1990) 41–51.

———. "'Early Catholicism' in the New Testament." In *New Dimensions in New Testament Study*, edited by Richard N. Longenecker and Merrill C. Tenney, 217–31. Grand Rapids: Eerdmans, 1974.

———. "'Israel' and the Story of Salvation: One Theme in Two Parts." In *Jesus and the Heritage of Israel: Luke's Narrative Claim upon Israel's Legacy*, edited by David P. Moessner, 340–57. Harrisburg, PA: Trinity, 1999.

———. *Luke: Historian and Theologian*. Grand Rapids: Zondervan, 1971. Enlarged ed. Contemporary Evangelical Perspectives. Grand Rapids: Zondervan, 1989.

———. "Recent Study of the Acts of the Apostles." *ExpT* 80 (1968–69) 292–96.

———, and David Peterson, editors. *Witness to the Gospel: The Theology of Acts*. Grand Rapids: Eerdmans, 1998.

Marxsen, Willi. *Introduction to the New Testament*. Translated by Geoffrey Buswell. Philadelphia: Fortress, 1970.

Mason, Steve. *Josephus and the New Testament*. Peabody, MA: Hendrickson, 1992.

Mattill, A. J. Jr. "The Jesus-Paul Parallels and the Purpose of Luke-Acts: H. H. Evans Reconsidered." *NovT* 17 (1975) 15–46.

———. *Luke and the Last Things: A Perspective for the Understanding of Lucan Thought*. Dillsboro, NC: Western North Carolina Press, 1979.

———. "Luke as a Historian in Criticism since 1840." Ph.D. dissertation, Vanderbilt University, 1959.

———. "Naherwartung, Fernerwartung, and the Purpose of Luke-Acts: Weymouth Reconsidered." *CBQ* 34 (1972) 276–93.

———. "The Purpose of Acts: Schneckenburger Reconsidered." In *Apostolic History and the Gospel*, edited by Ward W. Gasque and Ralph P. Martin, 108–22. Grand Rapids: Eerdmans, 1970.

———. "The Value of Acts as a Source for the Study of Paul" *Perspectives on Luke-Acts*, edited by Charles H. Talbert, 76–98. Danville, Va.: National Association of Baptist Professors of Religion, 1978.

McComiskey, Douglas S. *Lukan Theology in the Light of the Gospel's Literary Structure*. Milton Keynes, UK: Paternoster, 2004.

McGiffert, Arthur C. "The Historical Criticism of Acts in Germany." Pages 363–95 in vol. 2. *Prolegomena 2: Criticism*. London: Macmillan, 1922. *The Beginnings of Christianity: Part One: The Acts of the Apostles*, edited by Frederick J. Foakes-Jackson and Kirsopp Lake.

McKnight, Scott. *A Light among the Gentiles: Jewish Missionary Activity in the Second Temple Period*. Minneapolis: Fortress, 1991.

Mealand, D. L. "The Close of Acts and Its Hellenistic Vocabulary." *NTS* 36 (1990) 583–97.

Menoud, Philippe H. "Le plan des Actes des Apôtres" *NTS* 1 (1954–55) 44–51.

Menzies, Robert P. *Empowered for Witness: The Spirit in Luke–Acts*. Journal of Pentecostal Theology Supplemental Series 6. Sheffield: Sheffield Academic, 1994.

Miesner, Donald R. "The Circumferential Speeches of Luke–Acts." In *SBLSP*, 223–37. Missoula, MT: Scholars, 1978.

Miles, Gary B. and Garry Trompf. "Luke and Antiphon: The Theology of Acts 27–28 in Light of Pagan Beliefs about Divine Retribution, Pollution, and Shipwreck." *Harvard Theological Review* 69 (1976) 259–67.

Mills, Watson E. *A Bibliography of the Periodical Literature on the Acts of the Apostles* 1962–1984. NovTSup 58. Leiden: Brill, 1986.

Minear, Paul S. *To Heal and to Reveal:The Prophetic Vocation according to Luke*. New York: Seabury, 1976.

Moessner, David P. "Christ Must Suffer: New Light on the Jesus-Peter, Stephen, Paul Parallels in Luke–Acts." *NovT* 28 (1986) 220–56.

———. " 'Completed End(s)ings' of Historiographical Narrative: Diodorus Siculus and the End of Acts." In *Die Apostelgeschichte und die Hellenistische Geschichtsschreibung*, edited by C. Breytenbach and J. Schröter 200–221. Leiden: Brill, 2004.

———. ed., *Jesus and the Heritage of Israel: Luke's Narrative Claim upon Israel's Legacy*. Harrisburg, PA: Trinity, 1999.

———. *Lord of the Banquet: The Literary and Theological Significance of the Lukan Travel Narrative*. Harrisburg, PA: Trinity, 1989.

———. "The Lukan Prologues in Light of Ancient Narrative Hermeneutics." In *The Unity of Luke–Acts*, edited by Joseph Verheyden, 399–413. Leuven: Leuven University Press, 1999.

———. "Paul in Acts: Preacher of Eschatological Repentance to Israel." *NTS* 32 (1988) 96–104.

———. "Paul and the Pattern of the Prophet like Moses in Acts." In *SBLSP* 22, edited by Kent H. Richards, 203–12. Chico, CA: Scholars, 1983.

Morgenthaler, Robert. *Die Lukanische Geschichtsschreibung als Zeugnis:Gestalt und Gehalt der Kunst des Lukas*, 2 vols. Abhandlungen zur Theologie des Alten und Neuen Testaments 15; Zürich: Zwingli-Verlag, 1949.

Moscato, Mary. "A Critique of Jervell's *Luke and the People of God*." In *SBLSP*, edited by George W. MacRae, 161–68. Missoula, MT: Scholars, 1975.

Munck, Johannes. "Israel and the Gentiles in the New Testament." *Journal of Theological Studies* 2 (1951) 3–16.

———. *Paul and the Salvation of Mankind*. Translated by F. Clarke. Richmond: John Knox, 1960.

Murphy-O'Connor, Jerome. *Jesus and Paul: Parallel Lives*. Collegeville, MN: Liturgical Press, 2007.

Neill, Stephen. *The Interpretation of the New Testament* 1861–1961. London: Oxford University Press, 1964.

Neirynck, Frans. "Luke 4:16–30 and the Unity of Luke–Acts." In *The Unity of Luke–Acts*, edited by Joseph Verheyden, 357–95. Leuven: Leuven University Press, 1999.

Neyrey, Jerome H., ed., *The Social World of Luke–Acts: Models for Interpretation*. Peabody, MA: Hendrickson, 1991.

———. "Luke's Social Location of Paul: Cultural Anthropology and the Status of Paul in Acts." In *History, Literature, and Society in the Book of Acts*, edited by Ben Witherington III, 251–79. Cambridge: Cambridge University Press, 1996.

Norden, Eduard. *Agnostos Theos: Untersuchungen zur Formgeschichte religiöser Rede*. 1912. Reprint. Stuttgart: Teubner, 1956.

Oliver, Harold H. "The Lukan Birth Stories and the Purpose of Luke–Acts." *NTS* 10 (1963) 202–26.

O'Neill, John C. *The Theology of Acts in Its Historical Setting*. 2d ed. London: SPCK, 1970.

Ong, Walter J. *Orality and Literacy*. New York: Methuen, 1988.

———. "The Writer's Audience is Always a Fiction." In *Interfaces of the Word: Studies in the Evolution of Consciousness and Culture*, 53–81. Ithaca: Cornell University Press, 1977.

O'Toole, Robert F. "Activity of the Risen Jesus in Luke-Acts." *Biblica* 62 (1981) 471–97.

———. *The Christological Climax of Paul's Defense (Acts 22:1—26:32)*. Analecta Biblica 78. Rome: Biblical Institute Press, 1978.

———. "Christ's Resurrection in Acts 13:13–52." *Biblica* 60 (1979) 361–72.

———. "How Does Luke Portray Jesus as Servant of YHWH?" *Biblica* 81 (2000) 328–46.

———. "Luke's Notion of 'Be Imitators of Me as I Am of Christ' in Acts 25–26." *Biblical Theology Bulletin* 8 (1978) 153–61.

———. *Luke's Presentation of Jesus: A Christology*. Subsidia Biblica 25. Rome: Pontifical Institute Press, 2004.

———. Luke's Understanding of Jesus' Resurrection-Ascension-Exaltation." *Biblical Theology Bulletin* 9 (1979) 106–14.

———. "Parallels between Jesus and His Disciples in Luke-Acts: A Further Study." *Biblische Zeitschrift* 27 (1983) 195–212.

———. "Reflections on Luke's Treatment of Jews in Luke–Acts." *Biblica* 74 (1993) 529–55.

———. *The Unity of Luke's Theology: An Analysis of Luke–Acts*. Good News Studies 9. Wilmington, DE: Glazier, 1984.

———. "Why Did Luke Write Acts (Luke–Acts)?" *Biblical Theology Bulletin* 7 (1977) 66–76.

Overbeck, Franz. "Introduction to W. M. L. de Wette's *Commentary on Acts*." 4th ed., 1870. In *The Contents and Origins of the Acts of the Apostles, Critically Investigated*. Edited by E. Zeller. Translated by J. Dare. London: Williams & Norgate, 1876.

Pao, David W. *Acts and the Isaianic New Exodus*. Grand Rapids: Baker, 2000.

Parsons, Mikeal C. *The Departure of Jesus in Luke–Acts: The Ascension Narratives in Context*. Sheffield: Sheffield Academic, 1988.

———. *Luke: Storyteller, Interpreter, Evangelist*. Peabody, MA: Hendrickson, 2007.

———. "Narrative Closure and Openness in the Plot of the Third Gospel: The Sense of Ending in Luke 24:50–53." In *SBL 1986 Seminar Papers*, edited by Kent H. Richards. Atlanta: Scholars, 1986.

———. and Richard I. Pervo. *Rethinking the Unity of Luke and Acts*. Minneapolis: Fortress, 1993.

———, and Joseph B. Tyson, editors. *Cadbury, Knox, and Talbert: American Contributions to the Study of Acts*. Atlanta: Scholars, 1992.

Pearson, Birger A., A. Thomas Kraabel, George W. E. Nickelsburg and Norman R. Peterson, editors. *The Future of Early Christianity: Essays in Honor of Helmut Koester*. Minneapolis: Fortress, 1991.

Penner, Todd C., Caroline Vander Stichele. *Contextualizing Acts: Lukan Narrative and Greco-Roman Discourse*. SBL Symposium series 20. Atlanta: Society of Biblical Literature, 2003.

Perrin, Norman. *The New Testament: An Introduction*. New York: Harcourt Brace Jovanovich, 1974. 2nd ed. by Dennis Duling, 1982.

———. *What Is Redaction Criticism?* GBS. Philadelphia: Fortress, 1969.

Pervo, Richard I. *Dating Acts: Between the Evangelists and the Apologists*. Santa Rosa, CA: Polebridge, 2006.

———. *Luke's Story of Paul*. Minneapolis: Fortress, 1990.

———. *Profit with Delight: The Literary Genre of the Acts of the Apostles*. Philadelphia: Fortress, 1987.

Peterson, Norman R. *Literary Criticism for New Testament Critics*. GBS. Philadelphia: Fortress, 1978.

———. "When is the End not the End? Literary Reflections on the Ending of Mark's Narrative." *Int* 34 (1980) 151–66.

Pherigo, Lindsey P. "Paul's Life after the Close of Acts." *JBL* 70 (1951) 277–84.

Plümacher, Eckard. *Lukas als Hellenistischer Schriftsteller: Studien zur Apostelgeschichte*. Göttingen: Vandenhoeck & Ruprecht, 1972.

Pokarny, Petr. "Die Romfahrt des Paulus und der Antik Roman." *ZNW* 64 (1973) 233–44.

Porter, Stanley E. *The Paul of Acts: Essays in Literary Criticism, Rhetoric and Theology*. WUNT 115. Tübingen: Mohr/Siebeck, 1999.

———. *Paul in Acts*. Peabody, MA: Hendrickson, 2001.

Powell, Mark A. *What Are They Saying about Acts?* New York: Paulist, 1991.

———. *What Are They Saying about Luke?* New York: Paulist, 1989.

———. *What is Narrative Criticism?* GBS; Minneapolis: Fortress, 1990.

Praeder, Susan Marie. "Acts 27:1—28:16: Sea Voyages in Ancient Literature and the Theology of Luke–Acts." *CBQ* 46 (1984) 683–706.

———. "The Problem of First Person Narrative in Acts." *NovT* 29:3 (1987) 193–218.

———. "Jesus-Paul, Peter-Paul, and Jesus-Peter Parallelisms in Luke–Acts: A History of Reader Response." In *SBLSP*, edited by Kent H. Richards, 23–39. Chico, CA: Scholars, 1984.

———. "The Narrative Voyage: An Analysis and Interpretation of Acts 27–28." Ph.D. diss., Graduate Theological Union, 1980.
Puskas, Charles B. *An Introduction to the New Testament*. Peabody, MA: Hendrickson, 1989, 2003.
———. *The Letters of Paul: An Introduction*. Good News Studies 25. Collegeville, MN: Liturgical, 1993.
———, and David Crump. *An Introduction to the Four Gospels and Acts*. Grand Rapids: Eerdmans, 2008.
Rajak, Tessa. *Josephus: The Historian and His Society*. Philadelphia: Fortress, 1984.
Radl, Walter. *Paulus und Jesus im Lukanische Doppelwerk*. Europäische Hochschulschriften, Series 23, vol. 49. Frankfurt: Lang, 1975.
Ravens, David. *Luke and the Restoration of Israel*. JSNTSup 119. Sheffield: Sheffield Academic Press, 1995.
Ramsay, William M. *The Church in the Roman Empire Before A.D. 170*. New York: Putnam, 1900.
———. *St. Paul the Traveller and the Roman Citizen*. 1897. Reprinted, Grand Rapids: Baker, 1962.
Rapske, Brian. "The Lukan Defense of the Missionary Prisoner Paul." *TynBull* 44 (1993) 193–96.
———. *Paul in Roman Custody*. The Book of Acts in Its First Century Setting. Grand Rapids: Eerdmans, 1994.
Ray, Lynn Jerry. *Narrative Irony in Luke–Acts. The Paradoxical Interaction of Prophetic Fulfillment and Jewish Projection*. Mellen Biblical Press Series 28. Lewiston, NY: Edwin Mellen Press, 1996.
Resseguie, James L. "Reader-response Criticism and the Synoptic Gospels." *Journal of the American Academy of Religion* 52 (1984) 302–24.
Richardson, Cyril C., editor. *Early Christian Fathers*. New York: Macmillan, 1970.
Richter, David. *Fable's End: Completeness and Closure in Rhetorical Fiction*. Chicago: University of Chicago Press, 1974.
Ricoeur, Paul. *Time and Narrative*. Vol. 2. Translated by Kathleen McLaughlin and David Pellauer. Chicago: University of Chicago Press, 1985.
Riley, Harold. *Preface to Luke*. Macon, GA: Mercer University Press, 1993.
Rimmon-Kenan, Shlomith. *Narrative Fiction: Contemporary Poetics*. London: Methuen, 1983.
Robbins, Vernon K. "By Land and By Sea: A Study of Acts 13–28." In *SBLSP*, edited by George W. MacRae. Missoula, MT: Scholars, 1976.
———. "By Land and By Sea: The We-Passages and Ancient Sea Voyages." In *Perspectives on Luke–Acts*, edited by Charles H. Talbert, 215–42. Danville, VA: National Association of Baptist Professors of Religion, 1978.
———. *Exploring the Texture of Texts: A Guide to Socio-Rhetorical Interpretation*. Valley Forge, PA: Trinity, 1996.
———. "The We-Passages in Acts and Ancient Sea Voyages." *Biblical Research* 20 (1975) 5–18.
———. "Luke-Acts: A Mixed Population Seeks a Home in the Roman Empire." In *Images of Empire*, edited by Loveday Alexander, 202–21. Sheffield: JSOT Press, 1991.

Robinson, William C. "Luke." In *Interpreter's Dictionary of the Bible, Supplementary Volume*, 55–60. Nashville: Abingdon, 1976.

———. "The Theological Context for Interpreting Luke's Travel Narrative (9:51ff)." *JBL* 79 (1960) 20–31.

———. *Der Weg des Herrn: Studien zur Geschichte und Eschatologie im Lukas Evangelium. Ein Geschspräch mit Hans Conzelmann*. Hamburg: Bergstedt, 1964.

Ropes, James Hardy. *The Text of Acts*. Vol. 3 in *The Beginnings of Christianity. Part One: The Acts of the Apostles*. Edited by Frederick J. Foakes-Jackson and Kirsopp Lake. London: Macmillan, 1926.

Rosner, Brian. "The Progress of the Word." In *Witness to the Gospel: The Theology of Acts*, edited by Ian Howard Marshall and David Peterson, 216–33. Grand Rapids: Eerdmans, 1998.

Rowe, C. Kavin. "Literary Unity and Reception History: Reading Luke–Acts as Luke and Acts." *JSNT* 29 (2007) 449–57.

Sanders, Jack T. *The Jews in Luke–Acts*. Philadelphia: Fortress, 1987.

———. "The Jewish People in Luke–Acts." In *SBLSP*, edited by Kent Harold Richards, 110–29. Atlanta: Scholars, 1986.

———. "Salvation of the Jews in Luke–Acts." In *Luke–Acts: New Perspectives*, edited by Charles H. Talbert, 104–28. New York: Crossroads, 1984.

———. "Who is a Jew and Who is a Gentile in Luke–Acts?" *NTS* 37 (1991): 434–55.

Schmeichel, Waldemar. "Christian Prophecy in Lucan Thought: Luke 4:16–30 as a Point of Departure." In *SBLSP*, edited by George MacRae, 293–304. Missoula, MT: Scholars, 1976.

Schneckenburger, Matthias. *Über den Zweck der Apostelgeschichte*. Bern: Fisher, 1841.

Scholer, David M., ed., *Social Distinctives of the Christians in the First Century: Pivotal Essays by E. A. Judge*. Peabody, MA: Hendrickson, 2007.

Scholes, Robert. *Semiotics and Interpretation*. New Haven: Yale University Press, 1982.

Scholes, Robert and Robert Kellogg, *The Nature of Narrative*. London: Oxford University Press, 1966.

Schubert, Paul. "The Final Cycle of Speeches in Acts." *JBL* 87 (1968) 1–16.

———. "The Place of the Areopagus Speech in the Composition of Acts." In *Transitions in Biblical Scholarship*, edited by John Coert Rylaardsdam, 235–61. Essays in Divinity 6. Chicago: University of Chicago Press, 1968.

———. "The Structure and Significance of Luke 24." In *Neutestamentliche Studien für Rudolf Bultmann*, edited by Walther Eltester, 165–86. Berlin: Töpelmann, 1954.

Scott, James M. "Luke's Geographical Horizen." In *The Book of Acts in Its Graeco-Roman Setting*, edited by David W. J. Gill and Conrad Gempf, 483–544. *The Book of Acts in Its First Century Setting*. Grand Rapids: Eerdmans, 1994.

Schweizer, Eduard. "Concerning the Speeches in Acts." In *Studies in Luke–Acts Essays Presented in Honor of Paul Schubert*, edited by Leander E. Keck and J. Louis Martyn, 208–16.

Sheeley, Stephen M. *Narrative Asides and in Luke–Acts*. JSNTSup 72. Sheffield: JSOT Press, 1992.

Shellard, Barbara. *New Light on Luke: Its Purpose, Sources, and Literary Context.* Sheffield: Sheffield Academic, 2002.

Sellin, Gerhard. "Komposition, Quellen, und Funktion des Lukanische Reiseberichtes: Lk. 9:51—19:28." *NovT* 20 (1978) 100–135.

Sherwin-White, Adrian Nicholas. *Roman Society and Roman Law in the New Testament.* Oxford: Oxford University Press, 1963. Grand Rapids: Baker, 1978.

Shillington, George V. *An Introduction to the Study of Luke–Acts.* Approaches to Biblical Studies. London: T. & T. Clark, 2007.

Shklovsky, Viktor. *Theory of Prose.* Translated by Benjamin Sher with an introduction by Gerald L. Bruns. Russian Literature Series. Normal, IL: Dalkey Archive Press, 1990.

Skinner, Matthew L. *Locating Paul: Places of Custody as Narrative Settings in Acts 21–28.* SBL Academia Biblica 13. Atlanta: Society of Biblical Literature, 2003.

Smith, Robert H. "The Theology of Acts." *Concordia Theological Monthly* 42 (1971) 527–35.

Soards, Marion L. *The Speeches in Acts: Their Context, Content, and Concerns.* Louisville: Westminster John Knox, 1994.

Songer, Harold S. "Paul's Mission to Jerusalem, Acts 20–28." *Review and Expositor* 71 (1974) 499–510.

Spencer, F. Scott. *The Gospel of Luke and Acts of the Apostles.* Interpreting Biblical Texts. Nashville: Abingdon Press, 2008.

Spencer, Patrick E. "The Unity of Luke–Acts: A Four-Bolted Hermeneutical Hinge." *Currents in Biblical Research* 5:3 (2007) 341–46

Squires, John T. *The Plan of God in Luke–Acts.* SNTSMS 76. Cambridge: Cambridge University Press, 1993.

Stagg, Frank. "The Unhindered Gospel." *Review and Expositor* 71 (1974) 451–62.

Steiner, George. *Grammars of Creation.* 1990 Gifford Lectures. New Haven: Yale University Press, 2001.

Stendahl, Krister. *The School of St. Matthew and Its Use of the Old Testament.* Philadelphia: Fortress, 1968.

Stenschke, Christoph W. *Luke's Portrait of Gentiles Prior to Their Coming to Faith.* WUNT 108. Tübingen: Mohr/Siebeck, 1999.

Sterling, Gregory E. *Historiography and Self-Definition. Josephus, Luke–Acts and Apologetic Historiography.* NovTSup 64. Leiden: Brill, 1992.

Sternberg, Meir. The *Poetics of Biblical Narrative: Ideological Literature and the Drama of Reading.* Bloomington: Indiana University Press, 1987.

Stolle, Volker. *Der Zeuge als Angeklagter: Untersuchungen zum Paulusbild des Lukas.* Beiträge zur Wissenschaft vom Alten und Neuen Testaments 102. Stuttgart: Kohlhammer, 1975.

Strauss, Mark. *The Davidic Messiah in Luke–Acts: The Promise and Its Fulfillment in Lukan Christology.* JSNTSup 110. Sheffield: Sheffield Academic, 1995.

Tajra, Harry W. *The Trial of St. Paul: A Juridical Exegesis of the Second Half of Acts of the Apostles.* WUNT 2/35 Tübingen: Mohr/Siebeck, 1989.

Talbert, Charles H. "An Introduction to Acts." *Review and Expositor* 71 (1974) 437–50.

———. *Literary Patterns, Theological Themes and the Genre of Luke–Acts.* SBLMS 20. Missoula, MT: Scholars, 1974.

———. *Luke and the Gnostics. An Examination of the Lucan Purpose.* Nashville: Abingdon, 1966.

———, editor. *Perspectives on Luke–Acts.* Danville, VA: Association of Baptist Professors of Religion, 1978.

———, with John H. Hayes. "A Theology of Sea Storms in Luke–Acts." In *SBLSP* 1995, edited by Eugene H. Lovering Jr., Atlanta, 1995.

Tannehill, Robert C. *The Shape of Luke's Story: Essays on Luke–Acts*. Eugene, OR: Cascade Books, 2005.

Tate, W. Randolph. *Interpreting the Bible: A Handbook of Terms and Methods.* Peabody, MA: Hendrickson, 2006.

Tiede, David L. *Prophecy and History in Luke–Acts.* Philadelphia: Fortress, 1980.

Tompkins, Jane P., editor. *Reader-Response Criticism: from Formalism to Post-Structuralism.* Baltimore: Johns Hopkins University Press, 1980.

Torgovnick, Marianna. *Narrative Closure.* Princeton: Princeton University Press, 1981.

Trocmé, Etienne. *Le Livre Des Actes et l'Historie.* Paris: Presses Universitaires de France, 1957.

Trompf, Garry W. "On Why Luke Declined to Recount the Death of Paul: Acts 27–28 and Beyond." In *Luke–Acts: New Perspectives*, edited by Charles H. Talbert, 225–39. New York: Crossroads, 1984.

Tuckett, Christopher M., ed. *Luke's Literary Achievement: Collected Essays.* JSNTSup 116. Sheffield: Sheffield Academic, 1995.

———. *Reading the New Testament: Methods of Interpretation*. London: SPCK, 1987.

———, editor. *The Scriptures in the Gospels*. Leuven: Leuven University Press, 1997.

Turner, Cuthbert Hamilton. "Chronology of the New Testament." In *A Dictionary of the Bible*, edited by James Hastings, 1:421–22. New York: Scribners, 1905.

Turner, Max. *Power from on High: The Spirit in Israel's Restoration and Witness in Luke–Acts.* Journal of Pentecostal Theology Supplement Series 9. Sheffield: Sheffield Academic, 1996.

Tyson, Joseph B., editor. *Luke–Acts and the Jewish People: Eight Critical Perspectives.* Minneapolis: Augsburg, 1988.

———. *Luke, Judaism, and the Scholars: Critical Approaches to Luke–Acts*. Columbia: University of South Carolina Press, 1999.

Van de Sandt, H. "Acts 28:28: No Salvation for the People of Israel? An Answer in the Perspective of the LXX." *ETL* 70 (1994) 341–58.

Van Unnik, Willem Cornelis. "Der Ansdruck *hōes eschatou tēs gēs* (Apg 1, 8) und sein altestamentliche Hintergrund." In *Studia biblica et semitica Th. C. Vriezen qui munere profesori theologiae per 25 annos functus est, a amicis, collegis, discipulis dedicata*, edited by Willem C. Van Unnik and Adam C. van der Woude, 335–49. Wageningen: Veenan & Zonen, 1966.

———. "The 'Book of Acts' the Confirmation of the Gospels." *NovT* 4 (1960) 26–59.

———. "Luke–Acts: A Storm Center in Contemporary Scholarship." In *Studies in Luke–Acts*, edited by Leander E. Keck and J. Louis Martyn, 15–32.

Verheyden, Joseph. "The Unity of Luke–Acts: What Are We Up To?" In *The Unity of Luke–Acts*, edited by J. Verheyden, 11–21. Leuven: Leuven University Press, 1999.

Via, E. Jane. "Moses and Meaning in Luke–Acts: A Redaction-Critical Analysis of Acts 7:35–37." Ph.D. dissertation, Marquette University, 1976.

Wagner, Günter. *An Exegetical Bibliography of the New Testament. Vol. 2: Luke and Acts*. Macon, GA: Mercer University Press, 1985.

Walaskay, Paul W. *"And so we came to Rome": The Political Perspective of St. Luke*. Cambridge: Cambridge University Press, 1983.

Walker, William O. Jr. "Acts and the Pauline Corpus Reconsidered." *JSNT* 24 (1985) 3–23.

Walworth, Allen James. "The Narrator of Acts." Ph.D. diss., Southern Baptist Theological Seminary, 1984.

Wasserberg, Gunter. *Aus Israels Mitte—Heil für die Welt: Eine narrative-exegetische Studie zur Theologie des Lukas*. Berlin: de Gruyter, 1998.

Wehnert, Jürgen. *Die Wir-Passagen der Apostelgeschichte: Ein lukanisches Stilmittel aus Jüdischer Tradition*. Göttingen: Vandenhoeck & Ruprecht, 1989.

Weiss, Bernard. *A Commentary on the New Testament*, vol. 2. Translated by Gerhard H. Schodde and Ernest Wilson. New York: Funk & Wagnalls, 1906.

Weiss, Johannes. *Earliest Christianity: A History of the Period A.D.* 30–150. Books 1 and 2 in one volume. Translated by Frederick C. Grant et al. 1937. Reprint, Gloucester, MA: Peter Smith, 1970.

———. *Über die Absicht und die literarischen Character der Apostelgeschichte*. Göttingen: Vandenhoeck & Ruprecht, 1897.

Wengst, Klaus. *Pax Romana and the Peace of Jesus Christ*. London: SCM, 1987.

Wikenhauser, Alfred. *Die Apostelgeschichte und ihr Geschichtswert*. Münster: Aschendorff, 1921.

———. *New Testament Introduction*. Translated by J. Cunningham. New York: Herder & Herder, 1960.

Wilder, Amos. *Early Christian Rhetoric: The Language of the Gospel*. 1964. Reprinted, Peabody, MA: Hendrickson, 1999.

———. "Story and Story-World." *Int* 37 (1983) 353–64.

Wilkens, Ulrich. "Die Bekehrung des Paulus als religionsgeschichtliche Problem." *ZTK* 56 (1959) 273–93.

———. *Die Missionsrede der Apostelgeschichte*. Neukirchen-Vluyn: Neukirchener, 1961.

———. "Interpreting Luke–Acts in A Period of Existentialist Theology." In *Studies in Luke–Acts*, edited by Leander E. Keck and J. Louis Martyn, 60–83.

Wilson, Stephen G. *The Gentiles and the Gentile Mission in Luke–Acts*. SNTSMS 23. Cambridge: Cambridge University Press, 1973.

———. *Luke and the Law*. SNTSMS 50. Cambridge: Cambridge University Press, 1983.

Windisch, Hans. "The Case Against Tradition." In *Beginnings of Christianity*, vol. 2: *Prolegomena, 2: Criticism*, edited by F. J. Foakes-Jackson and K. Lake, 298–348. London: Macmillan, 1922.

Winter, Bruce W., and Andrew D. Clarke, eds. *The Book of Acts in Its First Century Setting*, vol. 1: *The Book of Acts in its Ancient Literary Setting*, edited by Bruce W. Winter. 5 vols. Grand Rapids: Eerdmans, 1993.

Witherington, Ben III, ed. *History, Literature, and Society in the Book of Acts*. Cambridge: Cambridge University Press, 1996.

Woodman, Andrew J. *Rhetoric in Classical Historiography.* London: Croom Helm, 1988.

Wright, Nicholas Thomas. *Jesus and the Victory of God.* Vol. 2 in *Christian Origins and the Question of God.* Minneapolis: Fortress, 1996.

Wuellner, Wilhelm. "Where is Rhetorical Criticism Taking Us?" *CBQ* 49 (1987) 448–63.

Zahn, Theodor. "Das dritte Buch des Lukas." *Neue Kirchliche Zeitschrift* 28 (1917) 373–95.

———. *Introduction to the New Testament.* Translated by J. M. Trout et al. 3 vols. 1909. Reprinted, Grand Rapids: Kregal, 1953.

Zeller, Eduard. *The Contents and Origins of the Acts of the Apostles.* 2 vols. Translated by J. Dare. London: Williams & Norgate, 1876.

Zwiep, Arie W. *The Ascension of the Messiah in Lukan Christology.* NovTSup 87. Leiden: Brill, 1997.

Scripture Index

OLD TESTAMENT

OLD TESTAMENT APOCRYPHA AND PSEUDEPIGRAPHA

NEW TESTAMENT

Luke (*continued*)

Acts (*continued*)

Acts (*continued*)

Index of Ancient and Early Medieval Authors

Index of Modern Authors

www.ingramcontent.com/pod-product-compliance
Lightning Source LLC
LaVergne TN
LVHW050634100826
845148LV00011B/1867
* 9 7 8 1 5 5 6 3 5 2 3 5 5 *